For ███,
hopefully,
even though he does not believe in the
determinist evolution of style.

Rkip Carpentier

GREEK ART

GREEK ART

A STUDY OF THE FORMAL EVOLUTION OF STYLE

BY RHYS CARPENTER

PHILADELPHIA

UNIVERSITY OF PENNSYLVANIA PRESS

7275

Printed in the United States of America

TO DAVID M. ROBB,
TEACHER AND DISCIPLE OF ART THROUGH THE AGES,
TO WHOSE INSISTENT INTEREST
THIS BOOK OWES ITS ORIGIN

FOREWORD

It may be objected that this book does not wholly conform to its title. But if so, fault should rather be found with the title than with the book. Every printed work must have a title, much as every person must have a name. However, "A Study of the Formative Evolution of Artistic Style in the Three Major Arts of Painting, Sculpture, and Architecture from their Inception in Greek Classical Times until the Mid-Hellenistic Period" (which might claim to be an adequate description of the volume's scope and content) could hardly find place on a title-page nor yet in a publishers' trade-list. The briefer title was therefore chosen, at risk of displeasing those who feel that they are entitled to find within the covers whatever has been promised them on the exterior jacket of a book.

A glance at any compendious account of the Greek achievement in art, such as Miss Richter supplies in her recent *Handbook of Greek Art*, will make clear how much of it the present study has failed to consider. Although most of the cast and repoussé design appearing on Greek ornamental metal-work adheres closely to the tenets of sculptural low relief, and although Greek gems mediate in miniature between the Greek pictorial and sculptural repertory of themes, the Greek terracotta figurines, despite their intimate reliance on the major sculptural traditions from the fourth century onward, must still be appreciated critically as a realm to themselves apart; and except for their dependence on lifesize bronze portrait heads during the second century, Greek coins go their own sufficient way, while Greek jewelry throughout the centuries strives for effects unrelated to those attainable by the other arts. Because of such variety in their aims and methods, the inclusion of these branches of so-called "minor" (but not always lesser) industry would have obscured the main issue to which this book is devoted and for which the three "major" (and in general greater) arts offer so clearly delimited and so intelligibly formed a field for enquiry.

It may be objected further that this study concentrates its attention too narrowly on Attic vase-painting and Attic sculpture to the neglect of work from other centers, and that a distorted picture necessarily results from this restriction of interest. To this it may be replied that not only did the mainstream of all the arts move through Athens until the widening currents of the Hellenistic Age set in, but that even where Attic accomplishment did not wholly coincide with what was being produced elsewhere in Greece, a study such as the present, which concerns itself with the evolu-

8

tionary phases of stylistic form without attempting to recount the historic course of events, can safely be confined to a single local strain, provided this strain exhibits the successive phases of the three great arts fully and clearly in their incidence and development, in abundant examples of high technical quality. These conditions are met by Attic art, which has as it were distilled for us the quintessence of Hellenism.

It should be pointed out that the chapters dealing with sculpture follow closely, and in part do little better than summarize, my lengthier exposition which has recently appeared under the title *Greek Sculpture: A Critical Survey* under the imprint of the University of Chicago Press. Where I have already covered so much of the same ground it would be pretentious to imagine that I could make any very different contribution to a topic on which my views have so long been formed and so lately expressed. But mere repetition has been avoided by bringing sculptural style into relation with the evolution of graphic form under the general perspective of the physiology of vision.

Originally delivered as a course of lectures at the University of Pennsylvania (where I held the post of Visiting Professor of the History of Art in the School of Fine Arts for the spring term of 1959), the present text is in no sense a reprinting of verbal or extempore material, having been presented in much its present form as a manuscript intended for careful reading rather than for casual classroom audition.

I have to thank Professor David Robb for his suggestion that I should bring a previous work of mine into altered form by recasting my *Esthetic Basis of Greek Art* (since then reprinted by the Indiana University Press) as well as for his cordial concurrence in my decision to do nothing of the sort, but to write down afresh, as I view them at present, my opinions on the formal evolution of style in painting, sculpture, and architecture.

R.C.

"Jerry Run"
May, 1960

CONTENTS

ILLUSTRATIONS

FIGURES IN TEXT

10

PLATES AT END OF VOLUME

GREEK ART

"For Sight, even when it fails to discern Wisdom, is still the keenest of our senses." Plato.

"Whoever approaches the threshold of Art without madness of the Muses, convinced that he will be artist enough through technical skill alone, will be without accomplishment for himself or his work." Plato.

"Vision at any moment is instantaneous and entire; and so it seems is Pleasure also .... It completes an activity not as though it were an inherent state or condition but as something over and above, like the bloom of beauty upon youth." Aristotle.

I

GENERALITIES

It may seem unprofitable to inquire why it is that certain races or cultural groups are set apart from the rest of mankind by unusual artistic sensibility and creative power. No matter how penetrating it strives to be, any critique of ancient Greek art—as of Greek literature, philosphy, or science—must reconcile itself to accepting rather than explaining the "Greek miracle." Investigation and analysis may succeed in establishing the What, the When, and the How, but scarcely the Whence and the Why, since final causes remain obscure to the point of seeming to be beyond the reach of reason. Yet enough examples of Greek art are still extant after more than two thousand years of loss and disintegration to make its characteristic qualities accessible to our inspection, our comment, and our criticism. And in so far as every product must betray something of the process through which it has passed in the making, it would seem to be a reasonable expectation that a rational review of Greek art in its entirety may achieve some sort of understanding of the formative forces that made Greek art what it was.

Perhaps the most sweeping generalization that can be made about the peculiar nature of the Greek genius stems from the observation that, by and large, the Greek-speaking communities, as they emerged from the inbred biological and cultural isolation of the early centuries of the first millennium,* were possessed of an extremely acute and highly active *visual sensibility*.

There are individuals among us today who differ from their fellows in that they think (and even reach rational conclusions) in terms of mental pictures rather than through conceptual verbal processes, who remember past events by direct visual recall in lieu of factual formulation and verbal description, who gloss with some sort of pictorial visualization their own speech and others', who even see arithmetical relations kinetically and kaleidoscopically rather than as a formal manipulation of static symbols. I have no explanation why certain persons should be thus endowed; nor have I

*Throughout this book, unless the contrary is expressly stated, whenever millennia or centuries are mentioned, the reference is to those *before* the Christian era. The ubiquitous "B.C." has been omitted, since the reader will not be misled by its absence.

15

any statistics to show that the artists have in general been recruited from their ranks. Nor can I conceive any persuasive reason for asserting that entire racial or linguistic groups, rather than occasional and sporadic individuals, might be thus endowed with heightened visual sensibility. Yet something of the sort must be postulated for the Greeks of the classic age, since so much of their behavior seems to depend on just such an innate capacity and be inexplicable on any other ground.

A heightened visual sense, such as I have described, would have its most obvious occasion to reveal itself in representational art, since this, by virtue of its mimetic character, necessarily concerns itself with visual subject matter. But in other activities, where its intrusion would scarcely be anticipated, the dominance of visual awareness is equally conspicuous in ancient Greek cultural occupations. For example, we do not class philosophic speculation (in spite of the visual metaphor in the phrase) as a visual activity; yet it seems to have been so for most of the Greek thinkers, who betray its controlling presence by their unquestioning acceptance of the reality of the world of sense in an incurable materialistic bias which allies their metaphysics to our modern science. Again, literature may be contemplative, intellectualized, didactic, and even provocative of strong emotional response, without greatly appealing to pictorial suggestion or visual imagination. Thus, *Samson Agonistes* (as is perhaps appropriate to a poem about a blind man by one who himself had long been without eyesight) is singularly devoid of visual appeal, being content to make its tremendous impact through starkly verbal meaning and connotation. But this is not true of Greek poetry and drama or prose narrative such as Herodotus could write for history and Plato for philosophic dialogue. The glitteringly vivid quality of Homeric epic has been universally recognized. On closer scrutiny this property will be seen to derive from the focal sharpness and immediacy of the induced mental images, combined with an avoidance of purely conceptual discourse. That the Homeric vocabulary is in truth visually suggestive and the epic selection of incident essentially pictorial may be tested by anyone familiar with *Iliad* or *Odyssey* through the simple experiment of recalling at random some notable passage from either poem. It will be found impossible to do so without an accompanying mental picture of extremely sharp definition and minute accuracy. Of all the world's literary masterpieces the Homeric epics (together with Dante's *Divine Comedy*) least tolerate pictorial illustration to accompany the text, because that text itself supplies better imagery than any artist can create for it.

Again, it would be a thoroughly plausible observation that fifth-century Athens elected to develop drama as its foremost literary type because drama, among all verbal devices, is the most completely visual form in which human behavior can be delineated. It has more than once been remarked (by others than Aristotle) that there is a close kinship between Attic tragedy and Ionic epic; but it has not always been noticed that this kinship resides chiefly in the vividness of their visual presentations. Although the characters in epic are invisible except to the inward eye there is little more than a metrical distinction between Attic theatrical dialogue and the Homeric declamation of heroes; and the familiar device of the Messenger's recounting of offstage happenings is a purely metrical variant of epic narrative.

In mathematics, geometry is presumably the most visual (as algebra and trigonometry are the least visual) discipline of quantitative calculation. It can hardly be a coincidence that algebra was unknown to the Greeks or that (judging by the not infrequent errors in their recorded computations) Greek arithmetic tended to be rather inadequate—presumably because it depended on the visible behavior of the abacus instead of the abstract device of ciphers and symbols. *Per contra,* geometry, where reasoning was cast in visible shapes, was intensely congenial to the Greeks—so much so that they ascribed to their high God its everlasting exercise even as they made of themselves its first great practitioners. For, without discounting Egyptian and Babylonian initiative, it is no exaggeration to assert that mankind attained its first insight into the labyrinth of mathematical truth through the Greek invention of geometric method. Where Euclid's propositions are startlingly ingenious, the further elaborations by Apollonios of Perga strain the unmathematical critic's vocabulary of wonder. Yet algebra had no root in the classical Greek mind, but derives from Indian and Arabic nonvisual thinking. It was the Arabs and not the Greeks who gave us the abstract symbols of our numerical notation and a method for manipulating them by purely mechanical rule.

In medicine, the remarkable advances epitomized in the Hippocratic School seem largely ascribable to great acuteness in making visual observation and accurate retention thereof in visual remembrance. To say that Greek medicine was purely empiric is tantamount to characterizing it as accumulated visual experience.

The identification of the visual world with reality, as though only that which could by sight be made accessible to the senses had actual existence, could not fail to reflect itself linguistically in Greek verbal idiom. Thus, by virtue of that peculiar continuative or "perfective" aspect which hardly has a counterpart in English usage, the normal Greek word for "knowing" may be paraphrased as "having seen, still to be seeing" (*oida* being the continuative perfective of *idein*), thereby indicating that, for a Greek, knowledge was taken to be a recall of visual experience. The metaphysical repercussion is eloquently clear in Plato, for whom the ultimate formative cause of all discrete existents was their generic *visual* shape (*idea*), and *a priori* knowledge was somehow recollection of past experience. Metaphysicians deplore the unbreakable tie with sensuous appearances which Plato's theory of ideated forms implies, and have challenged Socrates' famous intimation of immortality as nothing more than unconscious psychological reflex; but such strictures again bring out the Greek inability to transcend the immediate visual world. It is symptomatic of an intervening lapse in visual awareness that we still employ Plato's word, *idea*, but have stripped it of all reference to sight.

The tacit acceptance of the complete reality of the world of visible appearances had as necessary corollary the denial of reality to any other mode of existence. It was this which made the Greek conception of life after death so unattractively wan, sunless, and void. But it was in the Greek theogony that the unavoidable consequences of an innate visual prejudice have seemed —at least to Christian minds—most disastrous. Since men can with difficulty conceive divinity in other than their own likeness, a heightened visual imagination can only intensify the human appearance and material guise of the Divine Presence. Demonstrably, the Greek concept of divinity extended to such visualized detail as clothes and jewelry to wear, chairs to sit upon, beds to sleep in, food and drink for banqueting, and horses and cars for transportation. To a mind enmeshed in such a net of visual images derived from everyday custom and behavior, spiritual sublimation becomes self-contradictory and hence incredible. So actual and factual are Homer's Olympians that one wonders what title they have to true deity in any strict theologic hierarchy, since they differ in no way from ordinary mortals except that they are immune to sickness, serious physical injury, and death, and have no need to toil. Without responsibilities or worry, they lead a life of idleness, intent on themselves and, unless importuned by prayer and stirred by sacrifice or festival, heedless of others. Stripped of the divine prerogative of mystery beyond the range of sense, they have for us this all-important quality: that they raise no barrier in art between the human and divine. The Greek gods, like all the Greek heroic company of myth and legend, were as immediately accessible to artistic representation as anything in the world of sight.

Just as there could be no distinction between Greek secular and religious art, so too there could be no diversion of art to magical or mystical purposes, as in Egypt and elsewhere. The archaic statues of nude standing youths, once called Apollos and now more appropriately known as *kouroi* ("youths"), afford an admirable illustration of this unmagical—or if you choose, materially commonplace and unimaginative—prejudice of the Greek artistic understanding. The theme of the *kouros* had been derived from Egypt, being the specific type-form for monumental sculpture which Ionian settlers in the Delta had learned from Egyptian artisans to cut and polish in quarried piers of stone. Egyptians made such figures to be placed in tomb chambers, where they were imagined to serve as enduring refuge for the souls of the deceased, helping to facilitate their unextinguished spiritual existence. In Attica, judging from the locations in which they have been unearthed, often in or near burial ground remote from any temple site or sanctuary, it has been very generally concluded that the early Attic *kouroi* were similarly intended as funereal statues to be set over graves. Yet to a Greek mind such memorial images could not have possessed any of the magical properties of their Egyptian prototype, since there was no comparable Greek superstition to give them such significance. In consequence, the Greeks soon divorced them from their original function by converting them into images, not of the dead, but of the living: the *kouros* became an athlete, a deity, a human votary, or anything else that he might be seen to be, provided that he was understood to represent a materially actual and physically living body, not a symbol of superstitious belief or an act of magic ritual.

The instinctive acceptance of the visual world as the primary real is seemingly responsible for Plato's insistence that so many human activities are imitative duplications of the visual world, being reproduction of it through mimicry or, to use his favorite word, *mimēsis*. Thus, one can reproduce visual appearances physically by imitative deed and act, and thereby initiate political conduct, social behavior, and right custom; or one can reproduce it verbally by descriptive speech, to produce poetry of varying sorts and, by combining speech with imitative action, the dramatic spectacle of the theater; or finally, one can reproduce visual appearances directly as visual appearance—and this is art.

Such, at any rate, was Plato's view; and though it may strike us as a strange approach to ethics and poetry, it may be accepted as a correct formulation of the general Greek conception of art as the imitative reproduction of visible objects in the world of sense. Not otherwise should we understand Plato's memorable assertion in the *Philebus:* "This is the privilege of beauty, that being the loveliest, she is also the most accessible to sight."

To summarize, it is our suggestion that a people who considered all human experience as visually occasioned and optically transmitted must be greatly inclined—perhaps one might say mentally conditioned—to produce mimetic art. With the exterior physical and even the interior mental world thought of as optical appearance, the reproduction of appearances—whether materially as statuary, or optically as drawing and painting, or verbally as drama—could not fail to have the support and approval of every Greek community endowed with this national heritage of keen visual apprehension and visually conditioned judgment. Herein we may find a reason why Greek philosophy turned from cosmologic myth and eyeless theologic speculation to material science and visual mathematics, why Greek ethical judgment identified physical beauty with moral value, why Greek practical thinking never questioned that the material world supplied the only practical sanction for political and social action, and lastly why, in the realm of the arts mimicry of the visual world almost wholly displaced all other possible forms of artistic expression.

Under compulsion of such a prejudice, art could not be a symbol of some-

thing unseen or otherwise transcending ordinary sense. With no other significance than its own visual content could supply, art must be a self-contained
activity. And since a highly active visual sensitivity implies a keenly observant
critical eye, mimetic representation would be appraised according to its
fidelity to its prototype, so that any departure from accurate visual reproduction could not long escape detection and censure. For this reason, Greek representational art in all its aspects is subject to unremitting pressure toward
realism, if by realism we understand visually exact imitation of the material
world of sight.

Such a conception of the nature of art must necessarily operate to make
it earthbound to sensuous appearances and hence unimaginative and spirit-
ually uninventive. Specifically, any monstrous or unreal subject, precisely because it contradicts the actuality of visual experience, must be abhorrent. This
is well illustrated by one of the early experiences of Greek artistry. In the
course of the eighth century, commercial contact with the eastern border-
lands of the Mediterranean brought the hitherto severely isolated Greeks into
contact with the long-established and highly evolved art of Syria, eastern An-
atolia, Mesopotamia, and Egypt, bringing to their inspection, along with
other matters, a veritable phantasmagoria of hybrid creatures of eastern im-
agining,—sphinxes, sirens, bird-men, griffins, and other imaginary confla-
tions and deformations of living forms. All these the Greek eyed with curiosity and—since these monsters were already cast in artistically assimilable
form—incorporated in his own repertory of designs for painted vases of clay,
carved plaques of bone and ivory, and beaten and incised sheets of metal. It
is common knowledge that few of these exotic creatures long survived their
transplantation to Hellenic soil. Only the addition of wings to creatures normally unequipped with them appealed to the Greek mind (for some reason
which I cannot elucidate) as a rational and engaging suggestion. What
Daedalus could not do for Icarus, the Greek artisan did for the image of man
and horse; but in giving these an unnatural power of flight, he carefully observed and followed natural truth by closely regarding the race of birds to
see how wings were shaped and put together from gristle, quill, and feather-
plume, how attached to their bodily supports of bone and muscle. In fine,
though the professional zoologist may rightly have his qualms, the generations of mankind have for more than two thousand years accepted the Greek
winged man and woman as more than a distraught artistic fantasy or an
abstract noetic symbol, and given credence to these celestial creatures as
though Nikes and Angels were physically actual beings. The winged horse,
or *pegasus*—presumably because he lacked Christian sanction—did not endure so long.

It was a comparable phenomenon that the desert lion, which reached
Greek art in company with sundry other beasts of the orientalizing period,

was not evolved into an imaginary creature compounded of animal strength and human fear (as might have been anticipated for something so exotically unfamiliar to Greek experience) but, instead, was made zoologically real and factually convincing by attaching to it the unchallengeable genuiness of canine anatomy. The so-called lion which still (or more strictly, once again) sits on its pedestal above the massed Theban dead from the Chaeronean battlefield, is little other than an overgrown Molossian hound.

It is not quite so simple to derive from a heightening of visual perceptiveness a further fundamental quality of Greek art which was as basically determinative of its distinctive type and its characteristic career as this insistence on visual realism which I have so strongly underscored. I am referring to that remarkable sense of structural form which rescued Greek submission to mimetic accuracy from triviality of detail and the banality of everyday actuality and interposed itself to prevent graphic representation from lapsing into mere illustration and restrained sculpture from degenerating into mere physical factualism.

It must not be overlooked that there is in all visual apprehension a psychic contribution, an interposed mental activity that converts the act of intelligent seeing into something wholly other than the camera film's passive acceptance of a lens-transmitted picture. Pragmatically, every act of conscious seeing involves a dismemberment of the visual field into an aggregate of heeded objects within an unheeded environment. This is merely to say that when we look about us we behold *things* which, by capturing our attention, become segregated from the remainder of the field. It would be a pertinent enquiry to ask *how* we know what it is that we are looking at when we view our surrounding world. Whatever we decide in such a difficult matter, where physiology, psychology, and epistemological metaphysics may all have their say, it should be clear that objects exist for us and are adequately identified by us because they appear to us as characteristically colored and illuminated areas of characteristically defined shapes in characteristic setting of rest or motion. I do not wish—or intend—to be academically tedious, but only to draw attention to the vital part played by our recognition of distinctive areal shapes in making any presented field of vision interpretable. From which it should follow that the more intensively our power of visual discrimination is exercised on the external world of sight, the more extensively accurate and detailed must be our apprehension of objective form. In other words, a heightened visual sense must induce a heightened consciousness of structural configuration.

The philosophic formulation of such an outlook on the world is supplied by Plato and Aristotle, for whom all existent objects, whether animate or inanimate, came into being through the imprint of generic form upon undifferentiated matter. Such a dogma, if we consider it critically, will be seen to offer no physical explanation for the objective variety of the exterior world, but is merely the projection of the mental process by which the human mind attains to knowledge of that variety. It is another version of the thesis of "the One and the Many" that so enthralled Greek metaphysical speculation, wherein the mentally supplied form is the One and the objective world harbors the Many. Such a theory of Being ascribes to geometric form a vitalizing potency over inert matter. If it appealed to the Greek philosopher as plausible, it should reflect an attitude toward the visual world sufficiently deep-seated to determine (beyond reach of mere logical theorizing) the instinctive behavior of the artist. For the artist, like Nature, was confronted with inert material substance, such as wood or stone or metal or clay or wax; and on these, as in the natural world, it was the shaping and organizing form which converted meaningless matter into art. Even as words in human speech were artistically unactual, being mere discourse of conversation, patter, gossip, or debate until their purposeful coercion by structural form re-created them into lyric ode or tragic chorus or forensic oration, so it was with visual art. So, in architecture, block and beam could be raised on beam and block to make a building within which men could be sheltered; but only with the imposition of a formally articulated order could useful masonry become architectural art. This involved a realization that artistic forms were not one and the same with natural forms, but implied a further reshaping to humanly devised norms; and it was this comprehension that made it impossible for Greek art ever to be merely the mimetic image of the visible world. The painter, the sculptor, the ornamental metal worker, the engraver of intaglio gems and of coin dies, all perceived that upon the appearances of the natural world, from which they drew their subject matter, there must always be imposed that structure of formal devices which pertained to art and were not manifest in the physical world. There is consequently a paradox, amounting almost to self-contradiction, in Greek art which has caused it, again and again, to be misunderstood and misinterpreted in later times, because it is the inborn and innermost nature of that art to be a punctiliously accurate imitation of the visual world and yet to be scrupulously heedful never to confine itself to imitating. It is *mimesis* truly enough, even as Plato said; but it is *mimesis* metamorphosed by formalization.

My insistence on the primacy of a visual element in all Greek thinking and artistic making is not an idle prelude to a critical study of the various Greek arts; for, as we shall see, the entire morphological evolution of these arts in ancient Greece was directly conditioned by the mechanism of human vision.

At what point, or from what period, should a survey of Greek art begin? The engagingly simple answer is that it should begin at the beginning. But this seemingly self-evident reply tacitly involves the remarkable assumption that Greek art had a beginning, and misleadingly (inasmuch as there is excellent reason for believing that a Greek-speaking population had already established itself in present-day Greek territory by the opening of the second millennium) seems to imply that the investigation of Greek art must range far before the classical period. But this is not the case. If by Greek art we mean—as the present study throughout intends—the arts in vogue in the classical civilization of Greece, these were all of wholly new inception and without appreciable connection with earlier times. Thus, classical Greek graphic art—in vase decoration and *repoussé* metalwork as well as in the painting of panel pictures—is not older than the eighth century; gem-cutting starts afresh with this acquisition of a graphic repertory; the architectural orders (without which no Greek building can be considered to be an artistic product) cannot be traced farther back than, at the earliest, this same period; Greek monumental sculpture in stone is still younger, not having come into vogue until the final quarter of the seventh century; monumental sculpture cast in bronze is a still later invention; and the most distinctive of the minor arts, the cutting of metal dies for coins, is at earliest a late-seventh-century innovation.

This is a very surprising situation; and its inevitable corollary, that there was no genetic continuity between the arts of classical Greece and those (however "Greek") of Mycenaean times, is thoroughly unwelcome to the general classical scholar, who very naturally inclines to derive the classical civilization from its demonstrably Greek predecessor.

It is a scarcely explicable and yet incontrovertible fact that the classical civilization of Greece emerged from a stage of culture very much lower than the eastern Mediterranean had known for a thousand years. After the splendid flowering of Minoan Crete and its mainland Greek afterbloom, after the luxury and elegance of the court at Knossos, the hardy strength and material prosperity of Tiryns, Mycenae, Pylos, Athens, Thebes, and Orchomenos, Greece had sunk into an economic and cultural depression of the most extreme severity and of prolonged duration. A synchronous retrogression toward the close of the twelfth century overtook the entire Near East. It was marked by the extinction of the Hittite empire, with the disappearance of its ruling people from the Anatolian plateau, and by the collapse of the great Egyptian power of the New Kingdom.

There is as yet no generally accepted or even remotely plausible explanation for this, the most severe retrogression in Western civilization within historic record, appreciably greater than the otherwise comparable lapse in the seventh century of our era after the disintegration of the dismembered Roman empire. The event was too widespread to be due to local or episodic catastrophe of a political or commercial nature, since it was not confined to any one or two kingdoms or cultures, but embraced the entire civilized world of the time, affecting regions as remote as Italy and southern Spain. Migrations and movements of people were symptomatic of it, but rather as results than as causes. Thus, the Doric "Invasion" (a tendentious term of modern invention) seems to have been an imbellic infiltration into a countryside already largely deserted by its previous occupants: if Mycenae and Tiryns and Pylos were burned—as they demonstrably were—it still remains to prove who or what set fire to them. Similarly, in Asia Minor the Phrygians do not seem to have destroyed the Hittites, but rather to have replaced them after a considerable interval of time. Throughout mainland Greece, towns and territories which had been highly prosperous were abandoned or reduced to near-desolation: Gabriel Welter, in his monograph on Aegina, asserts that at some period between Helladic and Hellenic times the island was deserted *("menschenleer")*; Desborough, in his study of *Protogeometric Pottery*, having noted that Mycenaean pottery "disappears completely" from Rhodes and the Dodecanese by the early eleventh century without trace of any continuity of tradition in later times, speculates on the possibility of "complete depopulation" in the area, a possibility which he also considers for other islands such as the southern Cyclades; and a present-day Anatolian scholar has become convinced that after the collapse of Hittite power the interior plateau of Turkey was for a time without human inhabitants.

Since all these events lie far behind the range of Greek written chronicles, there is little that resembles specific statement to be found in the Greek historians bearing on this period of wretchedness. However, Herodotus *(vii.171)* records that the people of Praisos in the extreme eastern end of Crete preserved a tradition that after the Trojan War such famine and pestilence descended on men and their herds that the island was all but emptied of inhabitants; and Thucydides in the memorable passage of the opening chapter of his *History* ascribes extreme cultural poverty and depression to a period which, because of his reference to migration and change of domicile, must be intended for the age intervening between the Siege of Troy (which marked for classical tradition the disintegration and dispersal of Mycenaean power) and the rise of classic civilization. In Crawley's translation the Thucydidean passage reads:

Without commerce, without freedom of communication either by land or sea, cultivating no more of their territory than the exigencies of life required, destitute of capital, never planting their land (for they could not tell when an invader might not come and take it all away, and when he did come they had no walls to stop him), thinking that the necessities of daily sustenance could be supplied at one place as well as another, they cared little for shifting their habitation, and consequently neither built large cities nor attained to any other form of greatness.

We may challenge the validity of Thucydides' appraisal of times so remote from his own, concerning which he could have learned only by oral tradition unsupported by written record. But the archaeological evidence bears him out. Most emphatic testimony to a profound cultural degeneration in these times of trouble is the lapse into illiteracy which overtook the entire Greek-speaking world, with the possible exception of geographically remote Cyprus.

In 1953, after several years of unrewarding effort, a youthful English architect named Michael Ventris rather abruptly succeeded in constructing a consistent scheme of phonetic values for the hitherto wholly incomprehensible Mycenaean system of writing, for which the archaeologists had resigned themselves to the linguistically noncommittal designation, "Linear B." Ventris lived barely long enough thereafter to receive the world's congratulations on his exploit; but his discovery lived on. In the almost universal judgment of scholars, "Linear B" in accord with Ventris' code of decipherment records *Greek* speech.

In itself, this was not really a surprising revelation. Long before Ventris, the majority of classical scholars had postulated some form of Greek as a widespread linguistic stratum in "Helladic" territory because it was otherwise impossible to suggest how Greek had come to be the established tongue of the Aegean and its adjoining shores. But an unconfirmed assumption, however plausible, must remain an unproved hypothesis. Ventris once for all put an end to uncertainty. As a consequence of his brilliant contribution, every classicist must, from now on, extend his range of interest by half a thousand years.

Clay tablets from Pylos and much less extensive documents from other Mycenaean sites testify to a Greek use of the "Linear B" syllabic script to record ownership or disposition of a great variety of materials—in short, as a device for keeping tallies and accounts. Whether there was any more extensive application of this method of writing to perpetuate decrees, laws, political and priestly annals, or literary compositions is at present very generally viewed as highly doubtful. In any case, at some time before the close of the second millennium all evidence for the continued use of this (or any other) script in the Mycenaean homelands fails us. There are scholars today (perhaps only a small minority) who choose to believe that such a lack of evidence is merely an accident of nonsurvival of the documents (because writings were normally inscribed on unbaked clay tablets such as would have been preserved into modern times only through the chance accident of their conversion into terracotta by conflagration). They hypothesize, accordingly, that the Linear B syllabary continued in use among the Greeks until the greater simplicity and phonetic clarity of the Semitic alphabet caused its supersession by the classic letter-forms. On this view, the Greek world never lapsed into illiteracy, but merely changed its script. Such a thesis cannot possibly be sound.

Whenever a change of script occurs among a literate people—as for example when in the present century the Turks exchanged the Arabic for the Latin alphabet—there is no perceptible diminution in the bulk and scope of literary output or any other discoverable change in the uses to which writing is put. But when knowledge of the use of writing has been lost and only reacquired after a period of illiteracy, whether by revival of the same or another system of symbols (as when the Norse settlers of Iceland, having neglected to perpetuate rune-masters in their company, learned to use the Latin alphabet after an intervening period of total illiteracy), the outcome is entirely different. If poetry and other literary forms have persisted, they will exhibit traits of an oral composition and a mnemonic transmission. When writing is resumed, past national and personal happenings may be recorded; but their character and content will reveal that they are not excerpted from recorded annals or written chronicle. As the new acquirement of writing is introduced and spreads, there will be an initial restriction to inscribing owners' or dedicants' names on objects, names and titles of self and forebears on tombstones or other memorials, registers of the succession of priests or magistrates or other notables, followed only after an interval by more ambitious efforts at preserving and rendering accessible the more important material of oral memory. These last will be, primarily, community customary ordinances and laws; secondly, brief annalistic statement of outstanding events; finally, longer texts of cherished poets' verse or storytellers' prose.

Whoever is familiar with the epigraphic corpus of early classical inscriptions and graffiti will appreciate how exactly this description of protoliterate behavior applies to prove a classical Greek emergence out of entire illiteracy. From the tenth, ninth, and early eighth centuries there is nothing. At some not yet precisely dated decade of the eighth century, a use of the Phoenician alphabetic symbols for spelling out Greek words makes its appearance in Late Geometric context. Most of these earliest texts are extremely brief, being little more than proper names of human beings or deities in laconic formulas of ownership, authorship, or dedication. Occasional exceptions, in which longer and less usual words occur, are metrical excerpts or imitations from the copious flow of oral verse; but that these are scribal *tours-de-force* is suggested by the famous pot inscribed for a dancers' prize, which breaks down ignominiously after a single triumphant hexameter. During the seventh century, literacy makes only slow headway until, with its close, commercial contact with the Nile delta brought papyrus to stimulate more copious recording. By the middle of the sixth century, matter as voluminous as the Homeric epics and the gathered utterance of the oracles could be rescued by scriptural enterprise from the Lethe of mnemonic disintegration. So extensive an application of letters to literature indicates, unquestionably, complete mastery of the medium; but it should be noted that the use of writing was not yet in any sense universal, either geographically throughout all Greek-speaking territory or socially through all strata of the community. Even in the fifth and fourth centuries, when Athens was as literate as mankind need ever be, there were districts in the northwest hill country where writing was still a highly restricted accomplishment.

To recapitulate: the archaeological attestation that none but the latest Geometric objects are ever inscribed with written legend, the epigraphic contestation that the earliest inscriptions announce only possession or authorship or dedication in briefest terms, and the fact that there is no example or record of, or reference to, any more protracted text such as a set of laws or a legal contract, will, or deed until the seventh century was well advanced, and no extensive literary texts until the sixth century (as is evidenced also by the oral cast of the poetry preserved from an earlier date) —all this constitutes circumstantially sufficient proof that nothing written in the Mycenaean script of "Linear B" has been recovered from post-Mycenaean times because nothing of the sort ever existed.

The art (if art it may be called) which has survived from this troubled period attests the profound depth of cultural decline by its lapse from representational into nonrepresentational design. Mycenaean art, inheriting and assimilating Minoan Cretan, was markedly pictorial with a repertory of human, animal, and botanic motives; whereas Geometric design preserved none of these. Nor did it invent equivalent substitutes for these themes beyond a very few abstract formulas for bird or beast. Instead, as though it had sunk to the level of neolithic accomplishment, it built up the nonmimetic linear patterns which have given it its modern title of "Geometric." Characteristic decorative motives are zigzags, triangles, checkerboards, battlement meanders, and, most frequent of all, mere parallel lines, now running horizontally to the axis of the wheel-turned pots, now with vertical strokes framing rectangular panels. Curvilinear motives, such as concentric circles, spirals, and undulant waves, occur on very early geometric vases as moribund echoes of the freer movement of the older pictorial stage; but the compact rigidity of rectilinear design soon chokes them off in the profusion of the fully developed Geometric surface-cover. Compared with Minoan virtuosity, late Mycenaean draughtsmanship is weak and inaccurate; but its intent continued to be pictorial. The surprising denouement is not that pictures thereafter became more and more lifeless, but that they ceased altogether!

The cultural regression symptomatized by the lapse into scriptural illiteracy thus finds an exact parallel in art in the lapse into nonrepresentational design, an artistic state which might justly be termed pictorial or graphic illiteracy. Just as Greece must learn entirely anew how to read and write, so Greece must begin all over again in order to learn how to draw. Greek classical art is no more a continuation of Mycenaean art than the Greek alphabet is a continuation of the "Linear B" syllabary.

Such a diagnosis is in apparent disagreement with the perfectly clear and entirely certain fact that a major part of the classical Greek population was directly descended from Mycenaean ancestors and had inherited from these its speech and social customs together with many of its religious beliefs, heroic legends, and historic traditions. Continuity must further be presumed in order to explain the perseverance of traditional skills and practical knowledge in such crafts as metallurgy; carpentry; and spinning, dyeing, and weaving; and for procedures such as plowing, sowing, and reaping; the care of vines and olive trees; and the management of flocks and herds. But to these objections against our thesis of a profound economic and cultural collapse it should be replied that all such cultural continuants were too deeply rooted in the day-to-day struggle for existence to share the fate of the more superficially engrafted attainment of the knowledge of writing and the pursuance of art. Only the complete eradication of the Greek stock would have extinguished these millennium-old traditions in the Aegean. Life had been broken back to a neolithic and early metal-using economy, with the cultural luxuries of more advanced civilization cut away by dour adversity.

Admittedly, if the Geometric vases are examined for their fabric and firing and glaze, for their variety and self-assurance of wheelthrown shapes, they must be rated as the product of mature skill and developed taste. And equally beyond doubt is the direct descent of these shapes from Mycenaean forms. But technical proficiency and processes, however intimately allied with artistic activity, are not in themselves indices of artistic accomplishment, because art and technology do not run identical or parallel courses. Cultural retrogression and collapse are not uniform all-embracing occurrences comparable to the ebbing tide which everywhere withdraws its waters. Rather they may be likened to the blight and canker which destroys fruit and flower yet leaves the main trunk and boughs and buried roots alive.

As for oral epic poetry, whose high level of attainment is attested by our written versions of its two chief masterpieces, the *Iliad* and the *Odyssey*, Mycenaean descent is not proved by heroic reference to Mycenaean times; and it is not known what artistic level epic verse had reached in the earlier centuries of the Geometric period. On internal evidence, the *Iliad* was composed toward the close of the Geometric Age, while the *Odyssey* is redolent of the resurgence of maritime enterprise which marked the incipient rise of classical Hellenism. Thanks to the decipherment of the Mycenaean script, we are now assured that, however much the poetic dialect of epic verse may have owed to older usage, the speech of Homer differs far more from the speech of Mycenaean Greece than from the literary language of the classical period.

The discontinuity between heroic and historic times (which is to say, between the Mycenaean and the classic Greek civilization) is even more apparent in an art other than pottery, where, as already noted, many of the shapes and functional uses had been transmitted, cultural interruption being restricted to the painted decoration with its lapse into "graphic illiteracy." But in a different activity, the cutting of designs on seal-stones, the entire practice seems to have dropped so completely into disuse that not even a technical tradition survived. Not only the repertory of designs, but the very knowledge and use of the gem-cutter's craft was forgotten. Thus, the Homeric poems contain no reference to rings or carved gems or seals; and no such objects attributable to the tenth or ninth centuries have ever been turned up in Greek soil. Their manufacture was not resumed until renewed contact with the older cultures surviving in the Mediterranean's easternmost lands brought them once more to Greek attention.

It is not permissible to claim that it is the accident of nonsurvival which has deprived us of all Early-Geometric seals. Mycenaean and the earliest classical gems are so different in shape, material, and technique of execution that it is obvious that every connecting tie has been broken. The Mycenaean period favored extremely hard, semitransparent, semiprecious stones which could be cut only with help of special tools such as drills and the engraver's wheel, while Late-Geometric stones are opaque and so soft that they could be hand-carved with a metal blade or an obsidian splinter. In their shape, Mycenaean gems tend to be flat lentoid disks, while the Late-Geometric gems take the form of squat seal-stamps or slender cones or cushion-shaped scaraboids. As for their use, Mycenaean gems were bored horizontally to be strung and suspended as amulets or talismans, whereas the Late-Geometric gems seem to be properly seals intended for making imprints of their intaglio emblems. Finally, in the designs which adorn them, there is much the same difference between the vivacious but photographically heedless pictorial Mycenaean and the childishly crude but naively earnest Late Geometric as there is between a Tiryns fresco and a Dipylon jar.

It is true that primitive Greek gem designs do not necessarily resemble Phoenician, Syrian, Mesopotamian, or Egyptian products; so that they might be considered to be of independent Greek invention and therefore of scarcely determinable date. But it does not seem likely that the idea of using ring-stones or block-stamps with distinctive designs as personal tokens would occur spontaneously to the Greek mind; and the eastern influence is apparent in so many of the shapes to which the stones have been cut, and the drawing of the crudely scratched men and beasts of the designs is so reminiscent of the earliest picture-making on the Late-Geometric vases, that a late eighth-century date is archaeologically imposed as the earliest reconcilable with the evidence. Finally, the purely abstract angular linear pattern-work of the earlier Geometric vases before the advent of picture-making is so rarely found on seals that this too argues against any extensive production before the end of the eighth century. For (as we shall see) the occurrence of pictorial representation marks the end of the Geometric phase and, however painful, the birth-throes of classic Greek.

Our final verdict on the position which a critical appraisal of Greek classical art must assume toward Mycenaean art and its Minoan precursor is, accordingly, a categorical refusal to take it into account. Admittedly, the general historian of art must give his attention to Minoan and Mycenaean as to every other significant manifestation of art's compelling power over mankind; but the examiner of Greek classical art need admit no such obligation because, where art is in question, an unbridged gulf intervenes between Mycenaean Greek and classical Greek, a gulf not profound enough to have swallowed up the race or its speech or its rememberable traditions, yet deep enough to have put an end to any written literature that may have formed and to every vital tradition of artistic expression.

This is an important conclusion to reach, and a very welcome one, because it means that in surveying classical Greek art we enjoy the extremely rare opportunity of examining the graphic, the glyptic, the plastic, and the structural arts of a peculiarly gifted people from their all but totally independent beginnings, and of studying their undiverted morphological development through those evolutionary phases to which, by the physiological and psychological exigencies of human vision, mimetic art is naturally impelled.

This, then, will determine the program for our study.

II

THE GENESIS OF GRAPHIC FORM

In his well known essay on *Primitive Art* Franz Boas convincingly maintained that representational art does not grow out of abstract art by natural evolution, but that the two species are materially and psychologically distinct. Even more certain would be the converse proposition that abstract art does not grow naturally out of representational art, so that Geometric design cannot be an outgrowth of Mycenaean pictorial decoration. With the disintegration of Mycenaean civilization in the course of the eleventh century, representational art became extinct in Hellas; and Geometric design is a new birth, an entirely unrelated phenomenon, marking a new beginning and not a mere resumption of suspended activity. The problem remains, why Greek art did not once again devote itself to representational picture-making but turned instead to abstract linear patterns without pictorial significance. And for further corollary the question arises, why representational graphic art was not even attempted in Greece until two hundred years of abstract geometric tradition had elapsed.

If we page through the illustrations in Boas' essay we shall find an answer to these queries. Abstract linear design there shows itself to be a decorative device applicable to utilitarian products and employed by the artisan to make these attractive. All such products—whether they be loom-woven fabrics, basketry, clay vessels, or carved wooden implements—have each their appropriate shape and structure already imposed upon them by their material use or function. They are not freely formed works of art. But where by chance their utilitarian shape recalls in any way the look of some other more animate creature (as the shaft and knobbed end of a spoon might suggest the neck and head of a bird, or the leg of a couch or table suggest, even as common speech bears witness in many tongues, an actual leg of a four-footed animal) the conversion of the meaningless inanimate shape into an animate representation determines the direction which ornamental decoration may take. Otherwise, when no such inherent suggestion exists, as when a basket seems only a basket and a jug is merely a pot, the craftsman must draw on his own undirected interest for arbitrary design. In this event he inclines to cover the surface of his product with whatever ornamental strokes and scratches the simplest movement of his hand can make and his sense for symmetry can organize into pattern. On this score, Greek geometric design should be considered the potters' own immediate contribution to their craft, specifically invented for decorating clay vessels and devoid of any other intent. From this it follows that Geometric graphic art did not have its origin in any major school of painting but existed in and for itself—unless perhaps there were related linear designs in use in weaving cloth, from which the potters may have drawn for their repertory.

There are other compelling reasons for attributing the invention of Geometric vase-design to the potters themselves, inasmuch as the restriction of Geometric ceramic ornament to narrow zones of superposed horizontal courses was the outcome of a particular technical practice. If the kiln-dried pot were returned to the table of the potter's wheel and made to revolve while a brush dipped in pigment was brought into contact with it, a horizontal girdling band of constant width and accurate alignment would automatically result. The natural temptation to repeat so easy a means of faultless linear embellishment would have led to the division of the body of the vase into a series of parallel rings with intervening blank zones. Into these zones, after the wheel was stopped, additional decoration could be added freehand. Such mechanical division into panel strips induced the painter to search for motives which might be indefinitely repeated within a narrow frame. As he was engaged in an abstract shuffling of strokes and dashes for otherwise meaningless ornament, he facilely hit upon such uncomplicated combinations as the running meander, the chevron formed of alternately erect and inverted triangles, checkerboard diaperwork, lattices of interlaced lozenges or dotted diamonds—all of which will be seen to recur on the two-handled jar herewith illustrated (Fig. 1).

Geometric linear design in horizontal bands is thus explicable; but it is not immediately clear why such design should so strongly favor sharp angles and straight rather than curved or flowing lines. On the weaver's loom, however, where warp and woof are set at right angles to each other and the thread is drawn through on an even level, designs woven into fabric naturally tend toward rectangularity and the rigidity of vertical and horizontal lines; so that it is entirely possible that such patterns as the meander were loom-distortions of curvilinear loops and spirals, which the potters borrowed. For it will be discovered on inspection that there is almost nothing in Geometric vase ornament which could not be admirably and easily woven on the loom. The only striking exceptions to this observation are the concentric circles and compass-drawn wheels which occasionally occur. These belong to a different order of geometry; and it is significant that theirs seems to have been a losing struggle for survival. On most vases, at the level

Fig. 1 Geometric Vase with Abstract Linear Ornament

where handles protruded, the wheel-made girdling lines could not well be added because the handles would have interfered as the pot revolved. For this reason, horizontal panels between handles were very generally left as fields for freehand designs; and it is here that the compass-drawn circles found an appropriate place. They occurred rather frequently in this location on Protogeometric ware, but became increasingly rare as the rectangular and other straight-edged patterns were more liberally introduced, until finally it seems to be only in the Cyclades that they survived. But here, in final refuge, they added a distinctive and elegant note to late linear decoration before the advent of picture-making swept abstract motives into the discard. It is difficult to account for this discrimination against curvilinear design in Geometric vase-painting; but presumably it was due to the potters' awakened sense for linear harmony, which could not condone two geometrically incompatible systems in a single patterned field.

If Geometric vase-designs may be ascribed to a conflation of themes from the weaver's repertory with abstract linear motives of the potters' own invention, it follows that we are not entitled to infer for this period any major art of painting to which the decoration of vases was subordinate or from which it drew its inspiration. Whatever may have been in later periods the relation between the major and the minor graphic art, in its initial phase painting seems to have been exclusively the humble art of decorating pots with banded lines and freehand strokes to form continuously repeated linear designs that were not pictures.

There is, however, a rather surprising amplification to this straightforward theorem. It might be expected that geometric decorative design should have sprung up wherever pots were being turned in early Hellas: like the hydra of Lerna it might have thrust up many heads at once. But if Desborough's conclusions from his study of *Protogeometric Pottery* are substantiated by other students, we must believe that not merely was Greek geometric design a new invention, marking a new artistic impulse at the beginning of the millennium, but this invention was made in a single limited area, in only one community of the inhabited Greek world of islands and towns—at Athens. Thence, during the second half of the tenth century, the tradition spread ("as though almost the whole of Greece had come to life overnight") as communication was once more established among the moribund tiny settlements of Greeks in and around the Aegean.

This is a curious, perhaps an incredible, discovery; for, *if true,* it would mean that Athens kindled a spark from which all later Greek pictorial art was to derive its fire, and that after the fall of Mycenae the artistic flame had sunk so low that nothing but this single spark rescued it from extinction.

A second inference, of importance for the racial contribution to Greek art, concerns the native character of the Geometric tradition. Since Attica was immune to the Doric infiltration into Greece, it follows that Geometric design was not an importation, not a South-European intrusion, but was as strictly Ionic Greek as the Attic dialect. Linear Geometric—we are forced to conclude—was a spontaneous generation, and not an importation of "peasant art" from more backward regions. In Protogeometric we see it originate out of nothing more substantial or meaningful than the craftsman's urge to use his glaze not merely to waterproof, but also to adorn, his wares. From Protogeometric to Late Geometric the morphological development is self-contained and analytically explicable.

The possible combinations of linear pattern being mathematically infinite, the specific character of Greek geometric design demands our critical attention. Because it is thrown on a wheel revolving horizontally, every wheel-turned vase is accurately symmetrical to its central vertical axis but unlikely to be symmetrical in any other sense. As we have already remarked, when the glaze was applied to the dry clay fabric, the wheel was again put into use, since it was convenient and simple to hold a loaded brush against the spinning vase and allow the revolving movement to spread the paint. In this way, quite mechanically, horizontal black bands were produced, whose thickness could be controlled from the finest hairline to the broadest girdle. If freehand ornaments were added, it was inevitable that these should be placed within the empty zones between adjacent girdle-lines, so that the decorative devices acquired a strictly horizontal rhythm, developed, like everything else about the vase, symmetrically to the vertical structural axis. So, by a technical accident, the Geometric vase-painters were forced to think in terms of superimposed horizontal registers.

Once established, linear surface decoration employing motifs that have no significance in themselves and bear no specific relation to the object they adorn can progress only toward more and more elaborated complexity. This process causes the individual elements to shrink in scale, in order to make room for their profusion. Protogeometric decoration is so sparse as to be almost niggardly: a zone or two of running meanders or a series of shields made of concentric circles stands out from the rest of the body which has been evenly submerged under a covering layer of black glaze. Early-Geometric slightly increases the number of patterned zones and inclines to distinguish a static panel-design between handles. Mid-Geometric continues the process of elaboration, which by Late-Geometric times has reached such proportions that the entire vase is often covered with tier upon tier of ornamented zones. This final state is so floridly intricate as to be virtually without compositional structure or coherence, since the profusion of repetitious small-scale pattern overwhelms the over-all design. Many of the later Dipylon jars (on which, incidentally, men and horses have now been intro-

duced into some of the zones) are rankly repulsive in their uncontrolled
splashing of dark and light. Craftsmanship is always thus prone to destroy
itself artistically by succumbing to the temptations of virtuosity. The entire phase from restrained beginning to tempestuous conclusion occupied
three whole centuries, thereby demonstrating how slowly artistic formal
evolution may move through its initial stages.

With such a trend toward micropattern once firmly initiated, there was
no possibility of escape from linear over-elaboration into any different phase
or manner unless and until an interest supervened for drawing *pictures* of
things from the outside visual world. But such an interest, as it gathered
strength, was certain to prove disastrous to abstract linear design. Both gen-
era could not flourish long together; and it was foreordained which must
destroy which. *"Ceci tuera cela!"* It was picture-making—the delight in
drawing recognizable objects—which put an end to the Geometric phase
and ushered in the evolutionary processes of classic painting.

But for a time the two manners, the long-tried old and the excitingly untried new, existed side by side. Where they both appear on the same vase,
with a zone or two of pictures substituted for the abstract linear motifs, as
on the great Dipylon jars, we may speak of a *Geometric Transitional* phase.
In other instances, where the older fashion lingered on intact with little or
no concession to the new vogue of picture-making, the term *Subgeometric*
is current. How long the overlapping of the two contrary manners endured
is difficult to determine. In Athens, Geometric was moribund after the turn
of the century at the year 700; whereas in the Italian and Sicilian West, it
may have persisted through two or even three more generations, playing
mischief with the modern excavator's scheme of chronology, since the belated and outdated survivals are with difficulty distinguishable from the
original earlier forms.

This novel interest in drawing pictures on the vases, which at first supplemented and then gradually replaced the older abstract linear patterns,
seems to have originated spontaneously in the Attic workshops; but because
the date of its inception coincides rather closely with the resumption of
Greek contact with the outside world, it is quite possible that there was an
added stimulus from outside example. At least, in Corinthian vase painting
it is clear that the impulse for drawing animate representations was derived
from contact with Oriental decorative art imported from Syria, producing
a bestiary phase in which lions, sphinxes, griffons, bird sirens, ibexes, and
other less exotic animals only slowly and with seeming regret yielded place
to the innately Greek predilection for human beings as art's proper theme.

Since Geometric decorative design is an abstract linear exercise without
further graphic intent, it would be a critical inquiry of considerable interest
to determine why representational art was ever introduced into this nonrep-

resentational environment. At first glance there may not seem to be any problem here: since picture-making is a common human resource, why would not the potters have become interested in drawing pictures on their vases? But it is not altogether obvious why pictures should be drawn on the surface of vases at all, inasmuch as pictured scenes or subjects have no categorical relevance to the turning, firing, and ornamenting of clay vessels — particularly where custom has established a tradition of unpictorial decoration. It would be interesting to know whether the intrusion of water bird, goat, and stag on Attic Geometric vases was not somewhat of a random happening, something that might be termed a material accident of artistic behavior. For these earliest pictorial themes (cf. Plate I) were not copied from life, but are generic visual symbols for the recumbent animal (the "goat"), the grazing or moving animal (the "stag"), and the walking bird (the "wading wildfowl"). Archaeologists have debated what precise species from the Greek fauna the Geometric painters were here attempting to depict; but it is a gratuitous assumption that they were intending anything so specific as an actual kind of beast or bird. And it would be untrue to say that these themes are treated as though they were actually pictures, because they are decorative linear patterns that differ from meanders, lozenges, triangles, and other patterns for geometrically exact repetition only in this single respect: that they have the additional property of visual reference to the world of living things. But it is precisely this seemingly superfluous and novel reference to the visual world that demands critical attention.

It might be suggested that mere idle experimentation with ornamental strokes and dashes in linear combination might have produced an accidental resemblance to some living form, which struck the craftsman's eye. The eye having detected this resemblance, the geometrically informed hand could have seized upon and made more apparent its mimetic suggestion. But it is much more probable that, amid a people with no knowledge of representational drawing, crude graphic mimicry, based on habitual recall of visual experience, came spontaneously into being, producing such primitive linear formulas as children use when, with a few crayon strokes, they repeat an acquired accomplishment of drawing a cat, or a dog, or a pig, or a man, or a house. Being linear formulas rather than correct visual record, such inventions belong to the category of geometric abstractions and for that reason are fit companions to the vase-painter's nonmimetic motives. They were introduced into vase decoration not so much because they were pictures as because they were new and diverting patterns with a novel reference to the visible world.

Nonetheless, once such themes had found their way into the repertory of ornamental design they had broken the great barrier between abstract and representational art. A new impulse to pictorial mimicry of the real world, intervening on the century-old tradition of nonmimetic design, was destined to drive this latter into oblivion.

Under any explanation, Attic draughtsmanship remains a self-taught accomplishment. As such, it is an enthralling process to observe as it advances from helplessness to self-assurance.

There is a Protogeometric amphora from a grave in the Athenian Kerameikos (Fig. 2A) on which the area between the handles has been decorated with a sprawling three-lined wave drawn freehand with no great accuracy. Under one of the crests of this wave there stands, lone and forlorn, a tiny horse so crudely depicted that he might almost equally well be taken for a croquet hoop with a saucepan handle, were it not that the artist's intention is manifest: a horse it is. Yet there is neither logic nor meaning in his irrelevant location on the pot. Seemingly, the potter had learned how to draw such a horse and could not resist the temptation to do so here. What

Fig. 2 (A) Protogeometric Amphora from the Kerameikos

he is doing under the huge wave, his maker could hardly explain; but it may be significant that he put the horse upon a level band to serve him for ground to stand on. Here, then, is a gratuitous intrusion of picture-making into unpictorial abstraction. The occurrence of compass-drawn semicircles and other curvilinear motives shows that the date must be extremely early —earlier, as far as we know, than any such drawing of an animal on any other Greek ware.

In the Metropolitan Museum in New York there is a Geometric *kantharos* (Fig. 2B) of considerably later date than the amphora from the Keramei-

Fig. 2 (B) Geometric Kantharos in New York

kos. On it the zone between the handles has been, as often, reserved for picture-making; and here again a horse appears, or rather, a pair of horses. They are not strikingly better drawn than the tiny lone horse on the amphora; but they are no longer a merely decorative adjunct without further meaning. For a man stands between them, and a vague rambling cobweb of a line connects each of the horses with his hands. These must be reins. And the man faces and moves toward one of the horses as though he were encountering unruly resistance, while the other horse stands docilely by. Perhaps this is interpreting more than the artist intended to show; but none the less he has produced a *scene* of three characters, a *pictorial situation*.

So, Greek graphic art arises under our very eyes, with mimetic drawing emerging from nonmimetic abstractness. But the process was slow; and we should examine it more at leisure.

The slender twin-handled jar now in Munich (Plate I) was revolved on the spinning table of the potter's wheel while a brush dipped in pigment was firmly but lightly held against it to produce the numerous lines which divide the surface into horizontal zones. Then the wheel was stopped and the decoration added freehand. Inevitably the long narrow strips of blank ground induced the painter to repeat his motifs in lateral sequence; and within each zone the consequent uniform repetition built up pattern. The themes are limited: a unilinear meander in two forms, a dogtooth, erect or inverted, a checkerboard diaper, and a lattice of diamonds comprise the list of abstract linear motifs. But in addition, three of the zones are filled with motifs shaped to convey a pictured meaning: in the topmost zone, a stag grazing; at the bottom of the handles, a goat recumbent; and in the lowest decorated tier, a long-necked fowl feeding. If there are positions of honor in such an array of parallel registers, they have been reserved for the animate motifs; but in no other respect have these been treated differently from the abstract pattern-forms. Each of the three animals is repeated in its particular zone as nearly identical in its size, spacing, and silhouetted outline as freehand draughtsmanship can attain, with no more individual variation than the keyed meanders or the dogtooth triangles. The animate patterns are more complex than the abstract geometrical ones because they are derived from a more highly organized realm of meaning; but they are equally stereotyped, rigid, and decoratively repetitious in spite of their reference to the visual world wherein stags, goats, and fowl live and move. It is only right to use the rather roundabout expression "reference to the visual world" because there are no such animals as these in real life, but only in the geometric world of abstract linear form. The bivalence of such graphic decorative schemes, as linear patternizations and as pictured presentations, is as interesting as it is remarkable.

This primitive bestiary was soon supplemented with themes from the human realm. In the Athens museum there stands a huge five-foot jar (Fig. 3) adorned from the same repertory of designs as those on the Munich amphora—meanders in single and multiple stories, diamond latticework, dogtooth, the identical grazing deer and recumbent goats—but in the place of honor between the handles there is (Fig. 4) a frieze of spidery men with their hands clasped above their heads, facing a central bedstead upon which a man lies prone while underneath there are two men kneeling and two seated on stools. Repetition (though not quite so rigidly enforced) has expanded the thematic unit to a patterned band interrupted by this central interlude, which is not merely an axis of composition but deliberately aspires

Fig. 3 Late-Geometric Dipylon Vase

to pictorial rank as a visual scene with narrative content. Purely decorative design with motifs abstracted from the animate world has begun to evolve into picture-making: a man who has died is laid out for burial with mourners attendant.

And because the panel does not run continuously around the vase without beginning or end, being checked by the handles, the picture does not run like a stream in uniform direction (as the deer graze or the goats turn their heads in their endless round), but the two sets of mannikins face in opposite directions toward the center of the panel; and that center is marked and held by a single and strikingly different theme, which in turn is so constructed that its pattern and its parts are symmetrical to its own center: the two kneeling figures face the two seated ones, and the bedstead and quilt

Fig. 4 Detail from the Dipylon Vase in Fig. 3

are deployed in balance. (And here a strange query suggests itself: did the artist not notice until it was too late that, whereas he had drawn seven men on the left, he had managed to get only six into the corresponding area on the right, and in order to make amends crowded in the little boy by the bed? or —less probably—had he been worried by the unescapable asymmetry of the dead man's body and tried to weight the scales with the larger forms of the kneeling men at the lesser end and lighten them with the smaller boy at the other? The question would not deserve to be asked did it not exemplify an embarrassment which forever plagues the close observer of Greek art, who finds himself faced with the. choice between indifferent carelessness and suble sophistication as the correct explanation for deviations from exact perfection of form.)

Despite its utter crudeness of draughtsmanship, the panel is intelligently composed as a triptych in terms of bilateral axial symmetry. For half a thousand years this compositional formula will dominate the Greek mind. And the simple logical distinction between the framed panel (whose fixed boundaries demand a static composition) and the continuous field (which has directional flow without structural pause) will reappear as a fundamental principle governing the compositional diversity that distinguishes the Doric metope from the Ionic frieze. It is by esthetic awareness such as this that the childish art of the Dipylon reveals that it was not the work of children.

Even so, the representation of the human figure on such a vase gives no hint of the supreme classical achievement in centuries to come, being almost as geometrically stereotyped as the goat, the deer, and the waterfowl of the accepted repertory. Torsos are carefully exact triangles whose blunted points serve for waists while they are extended above into still larger triangles by straight strokes intended for arms bent at the elbows. Heads are only blobs accented with what may be taken for either nose or chin or mistaken for beard; a few radiate tiny bristle-strokes for hair. Realistically evaluated, it would be difficult to draw worse. To be sure, there is greater concession to visual reality in the curving of hips and the bulging of calves and the proportioning of parts in the lower limbs; so that, geometrically transfigured above but mimetically suggestive below, these creatures seem to belong to two mutually exclusive graphic styles—much as the entire panel exists simultaneously as abstract pattern and concrete representation.

As already remarked, where handles had been attached to the wheel-thrown body, these interfered with the mechanical process of glazing and girdling at their level, leaving blank panel strips at handle-height to attract freehand decoration. It was here that the new art of picture-making had its opportunity. Yet the opportunity was not seized immediately; for the panels were felt to be out of scale with the rest of the decoration and for this reason were subdivided into smaller fields separated by simple vertical strokes, as on the vase in Figure 5. Because such an arrangement of vertical lines and rectangular panels suggested to the modern eye the succession of triglyphs and metopes in the Doric Order of architecture, these framed panels on Geometric vases have been nicknamed "metopes," without any intention of implying that they have an architectural source or connection. But though they drastically reduced the area for pictures, such "metope" panels, by bruskly interrupting the continuous flow of ornament, enforced statically balanced compositions; and it was here that his latent desire for drawing mimetic pictures induced the vase painter, desirous of something more than monotonously reproducing the standard linear patterns, to try his hand at pictorial imagery.

On the great Dipylon jar already described, the funeral scene is framed as a panel between the attached handles. On a slightly later (or at any rate, more ambitious) example now in New York (Fig. 6) the funeral scene between the handles is supplemented by a girdling frieze below it, showing a procession of driven carts and armed warriors. Here the pictures have crowded out the abstract linear ornament to such an extent that the latter is now little more than a decorative frame for closing off the pictorial scenes. But although the new fashion of picture-making has supplanted the abstract linear themes, the pictures still conform to the areal restriction of the narrow girdle zones. As far as compositional style is involved, the final upshot for Geometric vase design was the continued preservation of horizontal movement around the vase, with a restriction of the scale of ornamentation

Fig. 5 Geometric Vase from the Cyclades

Fig. 6 Dipylon Vase in New York

to the limits of narrow friezes and small quadrangular panels. Bold flourishes, splashed hardily across the entire belly of a jug or jar, are seen occasionally on Proto-Attic ware and a few other subgeometric fabrics; but their
promise of a wholly different conception of ceramic design was never ful-
filled. Ornament in Greek art is not permitted thus to run wild and dominate the design, but is held in strict subordination to the representational
theme.

By comparison with the secure self-assurance of the older abstract linear
style, the new efforts at pictorial presentation may seem to be an artistic
retrogression. But the exact contrary is true. Abstract linear art leads nowhere beyond itself, while pictorial representation (however crude, primitive, and unpromising) initiates a process capable of occupying the energies
of many generations of artists. It marks the emergence of a new mentality:
on the artistic side it marks the naissance of the classic civilization of Greece,
germane to our own.

The thematic repertory of these earliest picture-makers was remarkably
limited. It seems to be a common notion that artists always draw from living or natural models, putting directly on paper or canvas something which
they see before them. But children do not do so, nor do primitive artists.
These, instead of mimetically reproducing in the flat the spatial world
around them, repeat over and over the limited graphic themes which they
have learned to use. The repertory of the Dipylon painters is quickly and
briefly listed. There are standing men and women in a few simple attitudes
and with a few descriptive accessories such as shields and weapons. Such
figures, by lateral repetition, can be combined into processions of walking
or dancing files. Horses in full profile become particular favorites and can
be drawn with a rider on them or shown harnessed and attached to a car.
As for animals other than the long familiar stalking water birds, grazing
deer, and recumbent goats (which are not really part of the pictorial repertory, but are animate themes diverted to decorative abstractions), there is
little attempt in Attic early-seventh-century art to master zoologic form.
Natural objects of geologic or botanic nature are equally neglected. Toward the close of the period, as a spectacular addition to an otherwise mo-
notonous list, ships suddenly come into vogue, and especially an extraordinary craft, long and low, propelled by as many as twenty rowers seated in
line. The device of continuous repetition of an identical theme is the same
for these oarsmen as for the files of dancers or the strings of cars, though the
unifying hull of the ship on which they perch gives a specious suggestion of
a more complex spatial setting. But the real interest in this galley pertains
to history rather than to art; and the particular bowl here reproduced in
Figure 7B is an historic document of such importance that I venture to digress
from my general topic long enough to call attention to it.

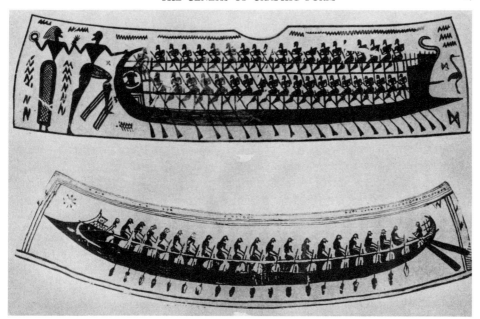

Fig. 7 (A) From a Geometric Bowl in the British Museum
    (B) From the Toronto Bowl

Long classed as of Boeotian origin, this Toronto bowl has been more recently claimed for the Corinthian workshops and assigned to the belated Geometric manner which there survived contemporaneously with the more elegant and more advanced Proto-Corinthian style. As such, it should belong to the end of the eighth century or the opening of the seventh. As far as our evidence goes, it marks the first occurrence of a nautical theme in Corinthian drawing (in general a rare subject on the vases from one of the most actively seafaring of Greek towns). Its historic interest derives from association with a passage in the introductory section of Thucydides' *History,* which reads;

It is said that ... Corinth was the first place in Greece where triremes were built; and it appears that a Corinthian shipwright, Ameinokles, constructed four ships for the Samians close on three hundred years before the ending of the present war. (I. 13) .

The "present war" was the Peloponnesian War, and its ending occurred in the year 404. Ameinokles of Corinth and our Corinthian bowl were therefore contemporaries. Misled by Homer, who attributes fifty-oared ships to the Greek armada in the *Iliad* and to Odysseus in the *Odyssey*, Thucydides imagined that the many-oared longboats which (according to Herodotus) revolutionized Greek commerce and colonization and actually extended Greek seafaring to the Gibraltar Straits in the West and to Crimea and the Caucasus in the East, had been in use since remote heroic times. Hence, since these could not have been invented by Ameinokles, Thucydides inferred that it was the much later three-banked war-vessel, or trireme, for which he was responsible. But our bowl instructs us what kind of ship was actually being made at Corinth at that time. That it shows only twenty instead of twenty-five rowers to a side is probably not due to any carelessness of artist or the accident of available panel-space on the bowl, but indicates that the original longboats were manned by forty oarsmen, a number subsequently raised to the maximum practical limit of fifty. Although all this is a matter of indifference to the history of art, it has a certain significance in the hint which it offers that the period in which the change from abstract to pictorial design was effected was a time of new stirring of energy and new interest in the surrounding world.

To revert to the Dipylon drawings with their limited repertory of themes and schematic repetitiousness, it is apparent at a glance that they too, like the old linear patterns that still accompany them, are mental abstractions with little more than semantic value as visual forms. Like the words combined to make a spoken phrase, a pictured object is here assembled by enumeration of its distinguishable elements. Thus, for the favorite theme of the horse-drawn car with driver (Fig. 8) a wheel is put in place by drawing

Fig. 8 From a Dipylon Vase

a circle for the felloe with a cross inside it for the spokes. Atop of this a rectangle represents the platform for the driver, often drawn in the draped-standing-woman schema. Forked tines are added to indicate rails for the car; and after a profile horse has been drawn adjoining it, pole or yoke-beam, and reins are added to consolidate the whole. Horse and driver, first fixed by tracing a characteristic outline, are substantialized by filling in with solid color. There is usually no axle shown because the full-front wheel is conceived as concealing it from view; and except by counting the number of reins in the driver's hands it is often impossible to tell whether more than one horse is supposed to be in harness to pull the car.

It may seem pointless and pedantic to enquire why the Dipylon draughtsman drew the wheels for his cars as perfect circles. Who is not aware that wheels have this shape? Yet the inquiry is not inapposite. As wheels present themselves to us in everyday vision they seldom show true circles to our eyes. Why, then, does every primitive artist insist on so representing them? The reply must be that however wheels may be *seen,* they are *known* to be circular (and not only because we reason that they would not otherwise function). Among all the projected deformations which a circular object displays as it is viewed from various angles, the viewer accepts the pure circle as alone "real," as reproducing the physical actuality, all other manifestations being mere appearance. It is this "reality" which primitive artists insist on. It may not be quite so evident that the silhouette of a horse similarly is more "real" than its other visual aspects; yet it is always the unforeshortened shape which is recognized as the primary form from which all other appearances derive. Presumably this recognition is due to our ability to apprehend foreshortening as extension *in depth,* whereas the unforeshortened areal shape is accepted as unmodified extension in the visual field and therefore complete and entire.

There is thus in primitive drawing a potent mental intrusion into visual experience which sharply differentiates it from the mindless record of the camera or the mirror, a *noetic* correction and organization which signally alters the phenomena of everyday visual experience. It is through this noetic reorganization that pictorial art originates in an abstract esthetic creation incorporating nonmimetic elements. The primitive artist does not reproduce the picture on his retina (which he has no means of contemplating as a reproducible pictorial projection), but constructs mentally an equivalent noetic image.

Significant art need not necessarily result from this procedure. In Pesaro on the Adriatic shore of northeastern Italy there is exhibited a stone slab from the early burial site of nearby Novilara with a crudely engraved scene of boats and fishermen (Fig. 9A). An accompanying uninterpretable inscription in letters of Greek derivation suggests that the artist was not a

Fig. 9 (A) Gravestone from Novilara
(B) Detail from the Vase by Aristonothos

speaker of Greek. His picture is equally eloquent that he was not a Hellene. Although the pictorial intent can be read by us more clearly than the alphabetic legend, because it has *noetic* organization to make its sense communicable, yet it has no *esthetic* organization. It is picture-writing rather than art. The Dipylon drawings belong to a different category; and to these we may profitably return.

In the drawing by a Greek artist, reproduced in Figure 9B, the areas which have not been covered by the pictured objects have not been left blank but have been decorated with ornamental scrawls. We may best explain these as due to the painter's interest in adorning his vase with decorative design and not exclusively in constituting a pictorial scene. Such irrelevant additions are traditionally explained as manifestations of a psychological indisposition passing under the clinical phrase *horror vacui*. The term is apt enough; but fails to draw attention to the simple distinction between decorating a surface and drawing a picture. It is the intrusion of the former interest upon the latter which accounts for the phenomenon.

For, of course, every picture has a twofold existence, once as an areal shape of patterned surface, and once as a visual evocation of an external material world. And as long as every object is drawn in profile silhouette exhibiting extension without depth, the panel-space of the decorated surface and the suggested visual-space of the pictured objects will not be in serious conflict. This spacelessness of primitive and archaic pictures is one of their most striking characteristics, of which everyone is aware, though few seem to have ventured an explanation of its cause.

If we look attentively at the Dipylon horse in Figure 8, we must conclude that first an outline was traced and then the area thus delimited was filled in with solid color. There is in consequence no interior detail of any sort, the entire impression being due to the areal shape as it is made precise and intelligible by its contour. Since the contour came first, the areal shape is derivative and secondary and as an over-all structure may be surprisingly inaccurate. But the contour is extremely sensitive and informative, breaking direction to define hoof, fetlock, hock, and pastern. By its linear career, chest and flank are distinguished from loin and body; a long pendant tail is attached; short bristle-strokes add a mane; two ears and possibly *two* eyes articulate the narrow-muzzled head. The resulting animal is long-legged, small-headed, lean-waisted, and somehow suggests a brisk-stepping and nervously active gait. Incontrovertibly, horse, car, and driver in such a picture have been constructed by the same genetic method that a child would use; yet there is an over-all pattern which is more balanced and deliberate than a child would have produced, and a communication—even though by completely unrealistic shapes—of an impression of living energy and movement. Though confined within the same technical phase as a child would be, the mental maturity and outlook of the adult has been able to exploit the resources of such a crude manner of representation to better purpose than any child could do. The graphic phase is infantile, but the artist's grasp and use of it is not mentally childish. However, it would be overstraining all sound judgment to claim that the Dipylon painters had any creatively significant control of their medium, since he who speaks the language of children must be content to say childish things. To say that we are here looking at the childhood of Greek art is to indulge in metaphor. Yet the metaphor has meaning, in the sense that the technical problems which confronted the Dipylon painters and the manner of their solution at that time were of the same nature as those which children encounter.

More pertinent information on the early development of Greek graphic art comes from an unexpected source—the metal coverplates which served as clasp-protectors or ornamental shields for the huge metal safety pins then in vogue. Such pins were often as much as four or five times as large as their modern counterparts. Their guards were irregularly square plates of thinly beaten bronze or silver, frequently as much as three inches across. On these plates rude drawings were engraved with a sharp-pointed tool. These seldom formed coherent pictures, being usually mere space-filling with a scattered miscellany made out of ducks, swans and other birds, horses, grazing deer, devouring lions, fish, snakes, ships, and of course men. The frequent sailing ships show that the historical Geometric Age is ending; and the lions reflect renewed contact with the un-Hellenic East. The engravings are later than the Dipylon vases; but the art of picture-making has not advanced much. In particular, the throwing together of unrelated objects merely to fill the square surface means that for the artist only panel-space exists and pictorial-space has not yet been discovered.

By *panel-space* I mean—and shall continue to mean throughout this study—the continuous but strictly limited surface upon which a picture is located. For the child, panel-space is the sheet of paper on which he scrawls; for the painter, it is the stretch of canvas or of plastered wall on which he works. Such panel-space is part of the ordinary material world in which paper, canvas, and wall exist. It is the physical support and carrier of pictures, comparable to the piece of ground glass which serves as finder on a camera. By *pictorial-space* I mean the depth and distance which accrue to a pictured representation by virtue of its transmission to us of tri-dimensional visual experience. Quite simply, it is the deeper space in which we see pictured objects deployed. When we look into a mirror we behold a type of visual-space very closely comparable to pictorial-space. In the sense that everything in the mirror is lodged on the metallic surface of reflection, the mirror presents panel-space; while, in the sense that Looking-glass Land is spatially actual with its own depth and distance, it displays pictorial-space.

It is a common supposition that pictorial-space is an illusion and that only the material panel-space is real. But such a distinction is a mere matter of verbal terminology; and "illusion" is not a happily chosen term where no deception is either intended or occasioned. The perennial (and usually badly confused) topic of pictorial "composition" hinges on the simultaneous apprehension of these two spatial appearances, since every represented object in a painted scene belongs as a colored area to panel-space and at the same time as a visible extension in depth and distance to pictorial-space.

The interplay of these two spatial forms is an extremely important factor in painting's esthetic appeal.

Mais revenons à nos fibules!

In the Athens National Museum there is a guardplate (Fig. 10) from a

Fig. 10 Geometric Fibula-plate with engraved designs

Late-Geometric safety pin which has been engraved on both sides. On one, the square field is decoratively filled with a walking horse beneath whose belly is a four-petalled star while a duck fills the void above his croup. Bird, star, and steed are related only in panel-space: if the duck seems to be riding the horse, that can hardly be the artist's intent. But on the other face, though the panel has been filled in much the same fashion with a sailing ship, two birds, and a large fish, the occurrence and location of the fish is not casual, since he swims beneath the ship to show that this is afloat on the sea; and the birds perched atop of the bow and stern belong to the air because they grasp their supports as though they had in truth alighted. There is neither depth nor distance to this scene since there is no attempt at landscape setting and all the objects are only isolated profile silhouettes; but the *scenic theme* is there. Ship, fish, and birds may be nowhere, but at least they belong together in significant relation. But how little freedom of invention yet exists is proven by the striking fact that three such pins have survived—to be scattered as far apart as Athens, London, and Berlin—with exactly the same horse and duck on all three, and the same ship, fish and birds on two of them! The artists still do not draw what they see, but what they have *learned to draw.*

By the first quarter of the seventh century the repertory has been extended to include themes of single combat. On one example (which like the previous specimen is now in Athens), a man rides a horse and seemingly swings a weapon, while an adversary lies prone beneath his steed, yet manages to thrust a long sword upward at its belly (Fig. 11). The rider is rather

Fig. 11 Geometric Fibula-plate engraved with combat scenes

too literally astride; and if we turn the picture sideways we shall discover that the man lying on the ground is actually a standing warrior brandishing his sword, who has stepped out of the artist's limited repertory and been upset to do duty for a still unmastered pose. Shades and phantoms of the future—the gravestone of Dexileos, and the Borghese Fighter! Here in this childish scratching is the embryonic conception of one of the finest of Greek sculptural themes. Before we leave it, let us note as a minor point of some importance that the artist has availed himself of the looped border with which he has framed the panel in order to make of it the ground on which the fallen warrior rests his arm. In sophisticated painting, pictorial space always begins where the ground is cut by the picture-frame, and depends primarily on the existence of both a near ground and a far horizon. In the previous design (Fig. 10) the horse and the ship float in empty air; but as time goes on, beasts and men will become firmly attached to the panel bottom, from which only the discovery of a graded foreground will ultimately allow them to remove themselves.

Compared with the rigidly angular Dipylon men, the human contours have undergone great change. Although the torsos are still triangular wedges, most of the straight lines outlining the limbs have now given place to curves. It would not be very convincing to suggest that the Dipylon artists had never noticed that living men thus bulged at hip and thigh and calf. In primitive drawing it is not a question of visual observation, but of graphic record. But that this record should now be changing to conform more closely with everyday appearances, that is, with the actual areal shapes of the visual field of the retina, is a matter of real moment. For if this is to be the trend and if fidelity to visual appearances of the objective world is to be accounted essential, then a technical goal has been sighted and a course set for generations still unborn.

The discovery that the artist by judicious arrangement of the stock material of his established repertory could set a scene and illustrate an event was of great import for the development of graphic art. Though it might seem to demean imaginative art to mere illustration, nothing more stimulating could have befallen the early artists; for what they lacked was subject matter. How true this is may be divined by considering the East-Greek vase-painters, who preferred to perfect themselves in the repetition of their repertory themes, their lions and panthers, wild goats, deer, pigs, and swans, till these had taken on a liveliness of pattern, a delicacy of line, a tremulousness of movement and pose such as rarely has been attained in decorative design. But theirs was an attainable objective which opened up no new vistas of slow-maturing possibilities because they remained devoted to decorative design and did not take the crucial step to pictorial art with its presentation of a fully articulated visual world beyond itself. Elsewhere— in Athens, Corinth, Chalkis, Melos, Caere—the conjuring up of a spatial world with all its interest and variety upon a flat visual field spread over a panel surface proved to be task enough to test the mettle of many successive generations of craftsmen. That Greeks were the first people in mankind's history to set their feet determinedly and consciously upon this far-stretching path is an event that should not be lightly dismissed or unintelligently ignored.

Yet, at the outset, when we contemplate the graphic achievements of the Geometric period, we scarcely foresee how long and how intricate a career has here been begun. Nor do we derive the impression of having here encountered an especially talented race of artists. Comparison of the Novilara stone (Fig. 9A) with the vase signed by Aristonothos (Fig. 9B), where ships and sea fighters are also depicted, may betray some portentous difference between Greek and barbarian genius to the deeply discerning eye; but it would not be easy to make this clear nor to be certain in what it consists. Perhaps the greatest distinction between Greek and barbarian art in this early phase is not one of accomplishment, but of potential development. Certainly there is nothing preternaturally gifted or precocious in

Greek Geometric drawing. Nor, as we shall see, was the plastic art of the period at any more promising level. In other artistic enterprise the prospect is equally unencouraging. In building, whether by the mason or the carpenter, there was as yet no architecture worthy of the title; monumental sculpture did not yet exist; and none of the minor arts had been notably developed. Yet, for all that, Greek Geometric art has often (though only in comparatively recent days) been rated as of very high quality and of deeply serious significance.

The representation of men, animals, and inanimate objects on the vases of the Dipylon phase so precisely parallels untutored children's graphic productions under our own cognizance, that it can hardly be rated as anything but inexpert (because inexperienced) and primitive (because technically undeveloped). Yet it has its modern admirers, who deny that the practice of nonpictorial linear design necessarily betokens a rude or crude artistic state of mind (they are strongly affected here by their interest in modern abstractionism), or that unrealistic drawing is in itself evidence of immaturity of artistic ability (in view of certain present-day demonstrations it would be disloyal to admit otherwise). Under this orientation of taste and emotional apprehension, Greek Geometric art is not something less than Greek Classic art, but something generically other. Absorbed in its own unrealistic world of noetic form, it attains to a greatness peculiarly its own, with its own esthetic validity. To appraise it for photographic fidelity to the everyday world of visual experience is to demean it unjustly and to measure it by an entirely irrelevant rule. I recall (from several years back) a professional colleague who was so deeply and so genuinely enamored of Greek Geometric metallurgic art—its hammered shields and repoussé veneering strips of bronze, its solid-cast bronze figurines—that (as he confided to me) classic art or, for that matter, any Hellenic production after the seventh century made no appeal to him. He regarded classic perfection of form as a deplorable lapse from an earlier, more unaffectedly expressive state of unspoiled artistry.

It is largely an accident of contemporary outlook that a rudimentary phase of artistic development can be thus overrated. Two different but interacting causes are responsible. In the first instance, the classical archaeologists have been "'overplaying'" Greek Geometric because it is almost the only phase of classical antiquity which has not already been extensively explored and exploited: it is still *dernier cri,* and the modern world owes its revelation almost exclusively to the archaeologists, who have dug it up, photographed, published it, and made much of it. Secondly, the art historians and the art critics, abetted by the discriminating collectors and dealers, attach a disproportionate value to Geometric objects, not only because they are a novel field which can be profitably exploited, but because the contemporary revolt against representational fidelity in art especially commends to modern taste everything abstract and primitive. During the last hundred years there has been a continuous temporal regression in interest and appreciation, from the timid backward gaze of the pre-Raphaelite mannerists to the cult of the archaic, thence to the primitive, and finally to the savage and infantile.

The attraction, verging on fascination, that primitive art exerts upon a portion of the modern public is not difficult to explain. The primitive draughtsman's inability to construct graphically a correct visual field with appropriate gradients and other optical conversions, which results in the omission of all visual setting and environment, gives an impression of emotional concentration, of utter absorption in an artistically isolated theme. It is easy to mistake this for deliberate creative volition—for *Kunstwollen* when it is actually unevolved *Kunstkönnen*. The primitive rigidity of line, which substitutes the straight stroke or the geometrically simple curve for the complex fluctuations of contour and inner structure in the living appearance, is accepted as a conscious reinterpretation of material accident in terms of inner artistic vision. It is quite true that, by this procedure of abstract reduction into geometric form, the primitive artist has created a noetic symbol; and this the modern sophisticate can interpret to fit his own esthetic outlook. But for the Geometric artisan himself there was no such esoteric intent. What would be an act of willful discrimination in a modern artist electing to work in terms of a primitive style is nothing of the sort when it proceeds from the hand and brain of a genuinely primitive master. An authentic work of primitive origin may indeed possess the admirable qualities which the modern critic, collector, or connoisseur detects in it; but these qualities are not produced through conscious choice by rejection of a more naturalistic manner in favor of abstraction. The stylistic phases through which a mimetic art evolves toward realistic maturity are not deliberately created modes of individual invention, expressing the tastes and talents of the artificer: in a word, they are not arbitrarily chosen "fashions," but conditioned behavior. And that which thus conditions these styles and determines their succession is the universal physical and mental mechanism on which all human vision depends. Our modern elevation of the earnest, but innocently helpless, primitive draughtsman or modeler to the rank and dignity of consummate artist is reminiscent of Schopenhauer's tragic characterization of religion as *"jene phantastische Unterhaltung mit einer erträumten Geisterwelt."*

In passing, it may be of interest to note that Egyptian art—which intentionally created a conventional style of noetic abstraction in order to serve (like Early Christian art) a transcendent world inaccessible to ordinary sight—has enjoyed comparatively little modern popular vogue or deliberate imitation. Is this because Egyptian abstractions convey their magic intent too unequivocally to permit of esthetic reinterpretation?

The modern appreciation of primitive art as self-conscious artistry of deep spiritual significance has seemingly sensed no logical difficulty in the ability of children to produce drawings which observe the same conventions and indeed bear a truly remarkable likeness to many of the Dipylon vases. With admirable courage and consistency, albeit with extreme tactical indiscretion, the modern cult of primitivism has been generously extended to include the "art" of children as well as of savages, on the claim that their productions, having never been corrupted by realistic technical traditions, display "the glory and the freshness of a dream," inasmuch as (if we may credit Wordsworth's intuition) "Heaven lies about us in our infancy" before the trailing clouds fade in the prosaic light of adult academic day. This is all part and parcel of the modernist contention that art should not be (despite Plato and classic example) a mimicry of the physically actual world. This may be a valid thesis for those who have reached the end of the long road of stylistic evolution in the visual arts. But it cannot hold good for those who, like the Greeks of the Geometric phase, have only just set their feet upon that path.

Even if children's inchoate efforts may be commended as uninhibited esthetic self-expression, it is not for comparable "infantilism" in its graphic inventions and conventions that we should extol Greek Geometric art, but for its inherent qualities of strongly accentuated stylization, structural coherence, purposeful directness, and unperturbed simplicity. For on examination we must see that these qualities belong to it in no stinted measure. And because these are not characteristic of children's accomplishment, we are entitled to rate their possessors not as children, but as intelligent and gifted artists turning to effective use the elementary means at their disposal.

And there, for the time being, we shall have to leave them.

III

EARLY FIGURINES

Out of the same inexpensive and plentiful material from which the Geometric pots were fashioned, diminutive shapes of men and animals were modelled in a rude freehand style and, like the pots, made perdurable by baking in an oven. The chances of survival were not so great for these clay figurines as for the painted pottery because superstition did not so strongly insist on their inclusion in graves as offerings for the dead and casual domestic calamity did not so often cause their broken pieces to be thrown (like the painted vases) into dry wells or dumped into refuse heaps to await the modern excavator's exploratory zeal. Nonetheless, religious habit caused many to be preserved because vast numbers of such figurines were dedicated to the gods and heroes at shrines and sacred precincts, mainly perhaps by the poor and humble among the donors, though the selection of such inexpensive offerings may also have been determined by the slightness of the occasion as much as by the indigence of the dedicant. In consequence, Geometric figurines have been in fairly abundant supply in modern times, even though until rather recently they have been prized more for their archaeological interest than for their esthetic virtue. Considerably greater value has attached to those that were solid-cast in bronze, although between the two categories of fired clay and poured metal (because the latter were usually made in moulds taken from the former) there is little significant artistic difference other than the obvious one of material. Whether the product was in one or the other medium, the art (if something so undeveloped and innocent may be so called) was one of freehand plastic modelling.

Plastic, glyptic, toreutic are well-established terms, apt for frequent use in any discussion of Greek art and susceptible to precise definition. Taken strictly, they refer to technical procedures: *plastic* pertains to modeling, and implies a pliant and amorphous medium such as clay or wax; *glyptic* involves carving, cutting, or hewing, and demands a firmly compact but not intractable material such as stone or wood; *toreutic* (though strictly it should mean "lathe-turned") is applied to chasing, engraving, boring, and beating in any metallic medium. The three terms are mutually exclusive, but not

59

Fig. 12 Two Geometric Bronze Groups

restricted to distinct artistic forms. Statuary, for example, may be produced plastically, as in Etruscan terracotta figures; glyptically, as in Greek marbles; or toreutically, as in Greek bronzes, except that these last also involve a pre-casting phase which, as we shall see, was glyptic in earlier and plastic in later periods. During and since the Renaissance, marble statuary has normally been a glyptic translation of a plastic preliminary; while bronzes, being more definitively cast in the mould, have involved considerably less toreutic "cold-work" than their ancient classical counterparts.

Geometric clay figurines were purely *plastic* creations; and Geometric bronzes (Fig. 12) were little more than solidified bronze pourings from clay moulds taken directly from clay or wax plastic models. Since Greek marble statuary was glyptic, produced by cutting away and abrading solid stone, the early Greek clay figurines should not be termed statuettes, indeed, were not statuary art at all. So different is the plastic from the glyptic process that, until and unless mutual contamination sets in, the two artistic forms have little in common. This explains how it was possible for figurines to have been made by Greek artisans for many hundred years without ever suggesting to them the possibility of monumental statuary.

We cannot doubt that figurines of baked clay and their poured replicas in solid bronze were being made in considerable quantity throughout the eighth and seventh centuries; but there is no reliable indication that any monumental statues were carved in any Greek land prior to the end of this span, after the Geometric phase had already ended. There can thus be no question but that in ancient Greece plastic art preceded monumental glyptic art by a very considerable margin of years. This was due not only to the inherent character of the figurine as a more instinctive form of artistic expression, but also to the apparent accident that the culturally highly evolved earlier civilization in the Aegean basin had never been attracted to attempt monumental sculpture. For there does not seem to be any likelihood that Minoan Crete or Mycenean Hellas ever produced lifesize human statues in the round. In any event no such statuary tradition was transmitted from the earlier civilization to classical times. A generic disparity between monumental sculpture (by which is meant sculpture in-the-round on a lifesize or larger scale) and figurines derived from freehand modeling is thus manifest from the earliest times.

The bulk of artifact material surviving from the Late Geometric period is very considerable; but it is all made up of objects of inconsiderable dimensions, such as clay vases (with the great Dipylon jars the outstanding achievement for size), figurines, ivories, cast or hammered metal-work, and seal-stones, but with no traces of any major architectural effort—whether temple in stone, or public buildings, or palaces, or extensive fortification walls with gates and towers—and no monumental statuary. And there is nothing compelling us to suppose that these missing items ever existed.

It is true that various scholars have assumed that throughout this early period large images of anthropomorphized deities were carved from round tree trunks and flat adze-hewn timbers and that these were the *xoana* and *bretea* to which classical writers allude. But whenever any hint is vouchsafed of the size of these primitive wooden idols we seem to discern portable figurines, very much like the *lares* and *penates* of the Latins, which were kept in rude shrines or set up beside outdoor altars. Some of the oldest *xoana* appear to have been little better than aniconic pillars or poles on which garments and jewels could be hung. The famous presentation of a new *peplos* for the "old image" of Athena-of-the-City, which was the ritual pretext for the splendid Panathenaic festival immortalized in the frieze of the Parthenon, tacitly admitted the need of a covering of drapery to make the time-honored idol worshipful. The legendary image of the same goddess, the Palladion of Troy stolen by Diomede and Odysseus, must have been small enough to carry; later illustration always pictured it as extremely minute. And although the *Iliad* contains a reference to a seemingly lifesize image of Athena within a temple on the acropolis of Troy, to which fine raiment is brought, the unprimitive character of such a seated statue, large enough to have women's gowns spread upon its knees and to be housed in a temple, has been one of the centers of controversy on the date and manner of composition of the poem. Since the orally transmitted *Iliad* was reputedly reduced to written form in Athens around the middle of the sixth century, it is entirely possible that this particular passage was due to some reciter who introduced it with sixth-century conditions and even with contemporary Athenian ritual in mind. There were, indeed, *xoana* of statuary size, but these seem to be explicable as a modification of the older tradition in post-Geometric times. Thus, the Hera of Samos made by Smilis and the colossal Amyklaean Apollo on the throne adorned by Bathykles of Magnesia may have perpetuated earlier types whereas their scale would have been novel. The extremely rare indications of *xoana* on sub-Geometric vases depend too much on modern interpretation to be acceptable evidence. And technically, the tradition of monumental sculpture cannot be derived from *xoana* or any other form of woodcarving, so that the burden of proof is decidedly laid on those who maintain the existence of any monumental sculpture more than a decade or two earlier than our earliest surviving examples from the final years of the seventh century.

In any case, the clay and bronze Geometric figurines are not the ancestors of Greek statuary art and to assert that by mere change of scale, however gradual, an art of monumental sculpture could have evolved out of the practice and tradition of making figurines has nothing to recommend it except a specious plausibility. The suggestion that, as time passed, figurines were made larger and larger until at length they reached lifesize proportions disregards the generic and genetic differences which raise an impassable barrier between the two arts.

The Geometric clay and bronze figurines were created by an entirely different method from that by which Greek statues were produced. Whether intended to be directly oven-baked into terracotta or used as the matrix for a mold for forming clay or for casting molten metal, the models were produced by puddling and rolling lumps of moist clay, adding to or removing from the pliant mass at will until this assumed a satisfactory shape, whereas statues were made to emerge from the interior of a rigid block of stone by continuous removal through chipping or abrading of superfluous obstructive matter. Where the modeler feels his way by trial and correction toward an overall shape which actualizes itself in and through this formative process, the stonecutter must pre-envisage the latent shape within the sculpturally amorphous and rigid mass and assign sufficient profiles and perfectable proportions to it before proceeding to unveil it. The maker of figurines, like his public, accepts the miniature reduction as a visual equivalent for the object which it represents, showing no hesitation in making a man or a horse a few Lilliputian inches in height. If this does not disturb him, it is difficult to see why he should sense any advantage in the Brobdignagian exaggeration in labor and material necessary to convert his miniature symbol into a fullsize physical replica. On the other hand, it is eminently characteristic of true sculpture that from the very start it aims at approximating actual dimensions in its representations, reproducing spatially and measurably the creature of the outside world which it seeks to recreate in enduring substantiality. Among all the differences between modeled figurines and carved statues, the most decisive and significant is that which might be mistaken for a purely casual accident, the distinction in *scale*.

It is difficult to suggest any adequate explanation for the disregard of absolute size and the preference for diminutive scale which attach to modeled figurines, the world over, unless these are due to the same simple principle which determines size and scale in painting. Since a painting is an artificial visual field (its essential structure being that of an enlarged and externally stabilized retinal image), the measurable magnitude of its visible objects stands in no fixed ratio to the physical size of the originals of those objects. Mathematically expressed, pictorial scale is a function of objective size compounded with apparent distance. This may be made clear by appeal to a familiar example from the cinema screen. There, when a person appears to move away from us, he will seem to us to maintain his normal physical size even while, considered merely as an areal shape on the screen, he shrinks and dwindles. In our *visual world* (which is the realm of objective appearances) size must remain constant, whereas in the *visual field* of our eyes (as on the cinema screen) it is just as constantly variable (though always consistently, in direct ratio to the linear distance from us to the externalized object).

The craftsman who is modeling a clay figurine maintains, while he is engaged in his task, a uniform distance from his eyes to the work in hand, a distance which may be termed "a working-arm's-length." This would normally amount to a few inches more than a linear foot. It is at this interval of some fourteen or fifteen inches from his eye that he beholds the clay creature which he is shaping. If we inquire at what distance an actual physical specimen of the object which he is modeling would have to be situated in order to appear at the same magnitude on his retinal screen (which is to say, be projected so as to occupy the same area on the field of his vision), simple geometrical calculation will supply an exact answer. Thus, a figurine of a standing man measuring six inches high and located at fourteen inches from the eye, corresponds in retinal magnitude to an actual man of average height at a distance of slightly more than thirteen feet. Now, thirteen feet is roughly the critical distance at which we begin to see an erect human figure completely, intelligibly, distinctly, and without focal strain. It is consequently a feasible suggestion that the craftsman visualizes the object which he is reproducing in clay as though it were located at this convenient and manageable distance from him. Its resultant diminutive size is its *pictorial magnitude* for him.

It is not relevant to inquire whether a craftsman engaged in working from a living model stationed before him would pose his model at this same critical distance (though obviously he would have to do so if he wished to hold his scale). The primitive artist does not work from a model. He is not directly reproducing an object in the external world, but recreating a visual experience, just as in the graphic domain the primitive draftsman does not copy his visual world of external appearances but constructs a noetic (or mentally evoked) equivalent.

On this theory, then, a primitive figurine is the tactile reconstruction of a pictorial image.

Further it should be noted that in modeling a figurine the craftsman's hand supplies more than his eye could have seen or his visual imagination could picture, because he is forming a solid shape where vision provides him only with areas and silhouettes. Nothing more recondite is intended by this assertion than the obvious statement that while the eye cannot at any given moment see more than the exposed surface of a solid object, the modeling hand must reach around behind the visible appearance and must therefore work by manual touch within an invisible domain. In this sense and to this extent, plastic construction is a groping-out into tactile space, subject to visual control and correction, but momentarily independent of direct visual information.

A plastic vase from the Kerameikos (Fig. 13) affords an excellent illustration of this tactual groping outward into solid form which, at this early period, distinguishes the modeler's art from the art of the sculptor. Each component element—the central stand, the supporting "ears" (as the Greeks would have called the protruding ribbon handles), the assisting "caryatids," the snakes coiling out of the interior of the bowl—has been manufactured separately, and out of these, by assembly to a preconceived plan (or perhaps to a plan which only emerged as the work proceeded), the final structure has been put together. The result is a tridimensional complex of very considerable intricacy. But just as Geometric graphic complexes—such as the wheeled cars with their drivers and horses on the Dipylon vases—were constructed by a kind of enumerative assembly, with the draftsman adding part to part as its turn came, so Geometric plastic complexes such as the vase under examination were spatial creations due to serial assembly of part to part in accord with a determining idea. The spatial symmetry of the result was implicit in this idea, but its spatial complexity had not been mentally envisaged or foreseen, but owes to an accident of accretion whatever spatial elaboration it possesses.

Fig. 13 Plastic Vase from the Kerameikos

It would, of course, be entirely practicable to construct such an object out of glyptic material. Indeed, the *perirranterion,* or holy-water basin, of which fragments sufficient for a restoration were recently discovered in excavating Poseidon's sanctuary on the Corinthian isthmus, is precisely such a construction. Instead of being modeled out of clay, equivalent pieces were cut out of marble, and these were assembled exactly as were their clay prototypes. But such a creation is a borrowing from the potter's domain of fictile form and (except incidentally) is not sculpture as I am defining it.

It may have been because of this intrusion of a non-visual factor that purely plastic art did not greatly attract the ultra-visualist Greek technician. We may fairly call the creation and enjoyment of sculpture an obsession of classical Greek mentality, since no other people in human history have given that art more devotion or greater acclaim. But sculpture, as the Greek understood it, was a completely visual, and not at all a tactual, creation. For it should be clear that lifesize statues, released from unformed blocks of stone, could not be produced by such a tactile technique as plastic

figurines required for their shaping, nor did their scale of magnitude have
any connection with *pictorial* size such as controlled the miniature dimensions of the figurines. Monumental glyptic sculpture and freehand modeling
in clay must therefore belong to generically distinct categories. And since
figurines could not be much increased in size without contravening the optical and psychological restrictions controlling their kind, monumental sculpture could not be an outgrowth of a prior tradition of plastically modeled
figurines.

Valentine Mueller made a well-documented contribution to the study of
early Greek statuary form by assembling and classifying according to shape
and subject the earliest figurines from Greece and the neighboring lands
to the East. He had no difficulty in showing that Syrian and Anatolian themes
had strongly influenced the Late Geometric and Orientalizing Greek output; but this evidence had no apparant relevance to monumental sculpture and threw no light on its origin. Inspection of Mueller's 452 illustrated
examples indicates that the Oriental influence affected only figurines, since
the Syrian and Anatolian types that are shown bear not the slightest resemblance to Greek monumental sculptural themes. Further, the comparatively
rare examples of Greek figurines which approximate or suggest Greek monumental statuary cannot be dated with sufficient precision to establish whether any of them are earlier than the statues which they recall. And lastly, the
predominating male sculptural type of ancient Greece, the nude standing
youth or *kouros,* does not appear at all among the types of the Geometric
Greek or foreign figurines, so that it is out of the question that it could have
been derived from them.

A very striking distinction in pose and structure was brought out by Mueller, who made of it the two fundamental categories for his system of classification. In one category of human beings (Mueller did not extend his study
to animal figures) arms and legs coalesce with the rest of the body to form
a single mass or block; in the other category the legs are spread, the arms
reach out, and these projecting elements are given exaggerated length, so
that the overall shape is the very antithesis of a self-contained and simple
solid. The earliest figurines belong to this second class, while the "block-
style" seems to appear in Greece rather suddenly and comparatively late.
The further inference that both categories were introduced into Greece
from the non-Greek world may be correct, but it should be observed that the
two categories depend primarily on a simple technical difference of method,
applicable to the two contrasting themes of a figure in motion and a figure
motionless. Any visual memory of the former recalls the posture of legs and
arms, which most effectively modify the contour relative to the static interior
shape of the body. (Centuries later, in trying to introduce movement into
monumental sculpture, Myron in his Discus-thrower was to illustrate this

principle by spreading and bending arms and legs outward from a comparatively unmodified central torso.) In contrast, an unmoving figure, whether
seated or standing erect, is envisaged as an undisturbed continuum within
which all features, including arms and legs, are enclosed. In consequence
of these differences in visual recall, a primitive modeler will construct a moving figure by rolling clay between the palms of his hands into long narrow
round strips which he will attach to the larger mass of the central torso to
make active arms and legs and then bend to show the joints. A figure at rest,
on the other hand, will be formed by pressure out of a single lump of clay
and only later, by internal differentiation, will have its parts and divisions
articulated. If a less pliantly responsive medium is attempted, such as
ivory or bone, it is obvious that the figure at rest could be more easily carved
out of the solid piece, while a figure in motion might involve the troublesome attachment of separately carved splinters of foreign pieces. Probably
it is for this simple technical reason that Geometric ivories favor compact
poses. And quite possibly the comparative simplicity of the requisite mold
would occasion a like preference where a figurine was to be solid-cast in
bronze, were it not that here, where arms and legs were mere rolled and
bent clay strips in the model, these would exist as simple hollow tubes in the
casting-mold and not act as an effective technical deterrent if the total size
were inconsiderable.

The emergence of monumental sculpture in late seventh century Greece
as an art of accurately carved detail was to have a powerful repercussion on
the already established and thematically (but not technically) related art
of figurines. Nevertheless the precisely cut and minutely detailed definition
of marble could not be adequately reproduced in clay nor effectively rendered in miniature. In consequence, the free-hand modeling of tiny men and
animals remained a stagnant art in a perpetually primitive state. It did not
for that reason cease to exist. On the contrary, it continued to be practised
for centuries. But it had to content itself with an humble and economically
depressed status.

At Corinth a potters' quarter was discovered and excavated several
decades ago. The chronology of the various layers and levels could be as-
certained with sufficient accuracy to prove that rude hand-modeled figurines
of men and animals were being made contemporaneously with painted pottery which was not in the least primitive or early in style. It might be imagined that these artless productions were made by the potters' apprentices in
idle moments for their own amusement. But it is much more probable that
they were made for the market, to be sold, however cheaply, and that they
met some sort of popular demand as token dedications at temple shrines or
as children's playthings, like the tin soldiers of yesteryear. On any explanation, their date remains the same and serves to prove that *primitive* is not

necessarily synonymous with *early*. Museum cases are full of technically primitive Greek terracottas, and almost without exception the museum labels assign them to the late Geometric or archaic period. Much more probably, they derive from every and any classical period, as we should discover could we but know how and where they were unearthed before they came into dealers' hands. The highly sophisticated and deliberately amusing terracotta group in the Boston Museum of Fine Arts, in which a barber cuts the hair of a seated customer, bespeaks a sense for spatial composition which would put the authenticity of the piece under serious suspicion were it obligatory to ascribe it to a sixth-century artisan. There are innumerable similar examples.

If it be asked why this branch of art failed to develop stylistically, remaining immune to the realistic trend which dominated Greek representational form, the proper reply would be that the question evades the answer because, in certain respects, the art of modeled figurines *did* develop by enlarging its thematic repertory to include a miscellany of genre subjects and by introducing greater complexity of plastic composition, but in other respects lack of progress was due to the inadequacy of the material medium. What may be termed the standard of focal definition in Greek art is amazingly sharp. Greek workmanship assumes good eyesight and challenges the closest scrutiny. Even in architecture, despite its monumental scale, the precision of cutting and fitting is phenomenal, with the definition of detail in the moldings and other ornament greatly surpassing the norm of Gothic and modern work, while in arts where the scale was necessarily minute, as in the intaglio cuttings in semiprecious stone, the accuracy of draftsmanship is so spectacular that the designs can be photographically enlarged five or six diameters without revealing any awkwardness or error. The same observation applies to Greek coins of the best periods. But puddled clay, rolled between the palms of the hands or pressed into shape with the fingers, admitted no remotely comparable precision. To Greek esthetic judgment such a medium, so handled, was by nature insusceptible to the basic requirements of serious art. Hence it was relegated to the casual and offhand, to token dedications and children's toys, to caricature and amusing trifles. By its own intrinsic fault it failed to attain artistic status.

This is not to say that there was no classic art of terracotta figurines. On the contrary, as everyone is aware, such an art flourished exceedingly, particularly in the later classic and Hellenistic periods. But this was, technically, a different craft, and one so violently deflected into the orbit of the major art of monumental sculpture as almost to require classification as a sculptural satellite. And because monumental sculpture did not grow out of Geometric figurines, the later mold-cast terracotta statuettes, being small-scale derivatives of monumental art, had no Geometric ancestry. We should accordingly have to consider them elsewhere in our survey.

The coroplast, or maker of clay figurines of both the hand-modeled and the mold-formed variety, was colleague to the potter, with whom he was allied by his material medium and comparable workshop equipment of trough, bench, and oven. On the other hand, true *statuary,* lifesize or nearly so, fashioned hollow like hollowcast bronze, existed also in terracotta; but this was an accomplishment of a wholly different technical order and seemingly did not often venture into competition with major productions in bronze and marble. (There is no Greek parallel to Della Robbia ware.) Because terracotta is destructible only in the limited sense that it is reducible to fragments but cannot be totally obliterated as bronze may be in the foundry crucible and marble in the limekiln, we should have recovered much more terracotta statuary from ancient sites if there had ever been any considerable output of it. What output there was, it would seem, was mainly due to Corinth or to Corinthian inspiration—primarily, perhaps, because Corinthian territory contained abundant clay but no good marble, while Sicily (where Corinth had her greatest colony, Syracuse) and central Italy (where on Etruscan soil she had her most eager pupil) were likewise destitute of stone of sculptural quality. In conformity with this observation, terracotta statuary has been found in appreciable quantity only in Sicily, Magna Graecia, and Etruria, and not in the central homeland of the sculptor's art, and our finest examples, being Etruscan with one notable exception, are on that account beyond the purview of this survey. The "notable exception" is the *Rape of Ganymede* discovered in the resumed German excavations of Olympia. But this, too, having—like the considerably later "Tanagrettes"—no direct descent from Geometric fictile art, cannot concern us at this point in our study.

Our examination of the distinctive natures of plastic form and glyptic form, whether in sculptural or fictile art, will have suggested that plastic production is the less mechanically restricted activity because it is able to evade the visual barrier to spatial perception. But even with this advantage —and presumably because in plastic modeling the critical guidance and control remain visual, with the artisan's eye dictating to his hands what is to be done and approving or disapproving what has been accomplished—primitive plastic form is far less successsful in mimicking the objective world than might be anticipated. Actually, though modeling may seem to be a purely tactile accomplishment in which solid shapes are created by manual exploration, it remains a visual art. And it is visual not only in the sense that its productions are intended to be seen, quite as fully as those of glyptic and graphic art, but also in the sense that it is created visually by visual control and appraisal. Indeed, a truly tactile art, produced only by tactile sense and intended only for tactile perception, does not exist, even though such an art is theoretically an entirely possible one (and among the blind might perhaps be welcome).

How much the plastic creation of solid form tends to grope and feel its way without achieving any notable mimetic accuracy in its exploration of spatial depth, becomes convincingly apparent on close inspection of Geometric figurines. The angle of visual control—by which is meant the artisan's position relative to the work in hand—is immediately evident. It is responsible for an intelligible silhouette and an attractive composition (on which the modern photographer and the appreciative commentator are quick to seize) while other aspects oblique to this working-angle pay the penalty of neglect in the making and of chance effect in the outcome. Arms and legs tend to be tubular (which shows that they are inadequately apprehended as solid forms); chests are flat or evenly cylindrical (which similarly signifies inadequate apprehension of the dimension of depth); and the entire body remains rigidly confined to the plane of its expressive silhouette (which proves that it has been visually projected and has therewith surrendered its spatial complexity). Where more than a single figure has been combined to make a group, although the mere fact that such a spatial complex has been attempted indicates an advance in plastic sensibility, we are nonetheless given an impression that arms and legs and whatever else may be detachably movable have been pushed and pulled together without any awareness of solid symmetry or peripheral pattern. The novel complexity of overlapping shapes which such a group displays is still only a visual projection, achieved by tactual experimentation.

That this is an adequate description of certain fundamental characteristics of early plastic enterprise is best proven by appeal to other than Greek productions in this genre. Notably, there are the bronze figurines from Sardinia, (Fig. 14) created in great quantity during that island's preclassical period and now, thanks to the modern interest in primitive art, treasured in abundance in Cagliari's National Archaeological Museum.* These exhibit primitive plastic form uncontaminated by any contemporaneous knowledge of glyptic or graphic technique, and afford an instructive insight into the untutored artisan's tactile response to mimetic themes. They reveal to us what Greek Geometric figurines might have been like if Greece had known no other form of art at the time and the Greeks had been rather less spectacularly endowed with acuity of visual perception.

There is, however, a quality present in many early Greek bronzes which their Sardinian counterparts rather conspicuously lack—a quality which, wherever it is detectable, rescues technically immature productions from being merely amusing essays, childishly naive and artistically vapid. The

---

*Cf. *Bronzetti Nuragici*, published by Alfieri, Venice, as an illustrated catalog for the exhibition of Sardinian art held in Venice in 1949.

Fig. 14 Bronze Figurines from Sardinia, pre-Roman period

only available critical term in today's professional parlance to distinguish this rather elusive property is "tectonic form," though how tectonic form should be defined, or what its proper province and function may be, is far from clear. Apparently, its presence is easier to sense than to analyze, and its emotional impact more accessible to feeling than to rational definition. "Tectonic power," "tectonic force," "tectonic sensitiveness," "tectonic structure" are all favorite phrases (especially among German scholars) which give some clue to its nature, but they are left otherwise unelucidated. Perhaps one should condone imprecision in defining a term which may be so loosely applied and seems so troublesome to ensnare in the net of logical analysis. Etymologically, "tectonic" must derive from *tecton* (the Greek word for a worker in wood such as a carpenter or joiner) as applied in extended meaning to the mason and builder. This is a sense abundantly familiar to us in the word "archi*tect,*" which signifies literally "*builder*-in-chief." "Tectonic" should accordingly apply to matters structural, but since it is also applied to such unarchitectural creations as vases and figurines and graphic representations as well as to buildings, the structural quality to which it refers might be either a secondary derivative or a purely metaphorical property.

Tectonic form is clearly not identical with symmetry or pattern, even though tectonic form may be highly symmetrical and involve an appreciably distinctive pattern. Its force lies elsewhere. And since it seems to reside most conspicuously in the builder's domain, it should be easiest to isolate and identify in its architectural setting. We are accordingly tempted into deserting chronological sequence and, because architecture as a self-conscious art had not yet been developed in the period to which our attention so far has been confined, digress into a later age for a new chapter.

IV

TECTONIC FORM

Both of the canonically established Orders of Greek architecture, whether "Doric" (Plate VIII) or "Ionic" (Plate IX), exhibit continuous symmetry of *horizontal* disposition. Structural elements recur in consistent repetition of constant sizes and (except for the Doric corner columns) at identical intervals. At the same time, their *vertical* superposition displays complete *a*symmetry, inasmuch as every component—fluted column shaft, capital, epistyle, triglyph-and-metope in Doric or continuous frieze in Ionic, overhanging cornice, and ornamented gutter—differs from all the rest in height, profile, and decoration. Yet there is an appreciable balance between the superstructure (or "entablature") and the columns which support it—a balance which results not so much from any measurable relation of column height to entablature height, nor yet from any areal balance between open and solid support, but from some scarcely demonstrable compounding of these with something yet more elusive and subtle.

This rather surprising combination of strict horizontal symmetry with complete vertical asymmetry corresponds to the strange (but easily verifiable) fact that we are much more acutely aware of symmetrical patterns when these are arranged horizontally than when they are superposed in vertical sequence. This is persuasively exemplified in Figure 15. Here, the photograph of a calm sheet of water reflecting the further shore of a lake has been turned on its side. The bilaterally symmetrical pattern, of which the viewer is relatively unconscious while the picture is disposed in normal alignment, suddenly becomes intrusively obvious when it is thus viewed sideways. Of course, the discrepant effect is partly due to the presence or absence of pragmatic vision: in viewing the correctly oriented picture we behold pictorial-space with an objective content deployed in depth and distance (that is, we are aware of the scene with its water, rocks, trees, and sky stretching away from us); whereas in the uptilted version, which corresponds to no intelligible visual experience, we apprehend only the flat panel-space. Since pattern exists only in the latter, we are naturally quicker to detect pattern where no pictorial-space supervenes. But this is not the en-

73

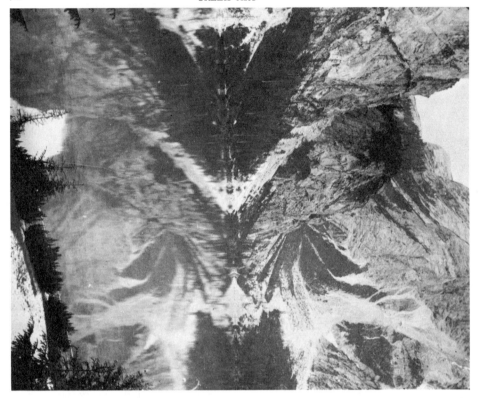

Fig. 15 Illustrating Awareness of Bilateral Symmetry Displayed Horizontally

tire explanation, because the experiment can be repeated with non-repre-
sentational patterns such as American North Pacific carvings (Fig. 16),
which are meaningless to us and admit of no spatial comprehension in depth.
Where there is symmetry of pattern on both vertical and horizontal axes, in
turning the page about we shall discover that we are instantly sensitive to
the symmetry presented horizontally and relatively unresponsive to that
which confronts us vertically.

I find it difficult to suggest any convincing explanation for this phenomenon. It can scarcely be that we have encountered horizontally symmetrical pattern so much more frequently in our visual experience of the world
that we expect, and therefore see, no other. Perhaps, because we ourselves in
our bodily structure are strikingly bilaterally symmetrical in a horizontal
sense and at the same time entirely unsymmetrical in our vertical ordering,
it might be argued that we instinctively apprehend right-left mirror-images,
but are insensitive to their vertical occurrence. But I doubt that such a
projection of the inner man as a symmetrical measuring-stick for his visual
environment is a sound notion. In a different explanation, our sense of grav-

Fig. 16 American North Pacific Carvings

itational equilibrium, continuously operative within us, can inform us of balance and imbalance (which are matters of horizontal equivalence) in the content of our visual field, whereas when confronted with vertical superpositions in that same field it informs us of such wholly different matters as weight, with its earthward pressure, and resistance to compression. This seems an even more fanciful supposition; and yet it would admirably fit the architectural situation. For here successful resistance to the destructive gravitational force is the chief determining factor in the vertical alignment, to which an enduring equilibrium, most vividly suggested by horizontal balancing of a pattern, is the counterpart in horizontal alignment (cf. the Doric Order on Plate VIII).

Without venturing a verdict on an issue so delicate, debatable, and obscure, I am inclined to urge that, whatever may be the physiological or psychological cause, architecture makes some such appeal to our gravitational sensibilities by availing itself of this imparity in our awareness of symmetrical disposition within our visual field. In all his activities, the architect must cope with the gravitational obstacle; and wherever his art has reached a mature phase of esthetic as well as technological attainment, his success in conquering this unrelenting adversary, by establishing an unmoving equilibrium of gravitational stresses and strains, very naturally and commendably is given some sort of visual embodiment—as in the magnificent Gothic visualization thereof in terms of protruding ribs and groins and clustered piers within, and buttresses, both free-flying and massively attached, without; or again, as in the scarcely less eloquent contours and proportional dispositions of patternized structural elements devised for the classic Orders.

And yet tectonic form (which was the original matter for inquiry) cannot be defined solely in terms of our gravitational sensibilities. Nor, for that matter, could the articulated orderliness of a classical Greek façade have been intended merely as a visible balance-scale of gravitational forces, any more than a Gothic cathedral can be rightly characterised as only a stark skeletonizing of gravitational pressure downward and lateral thrust outward. We must re-examine classic architecture for something more than its assertion of enduring triumph over gravity (enduring, to be sure, only until earth-shaking Poseidon intervenes to throw the structure headlong).

In the Greek Orders, gravitational equilibrium and horizontal symmetry are very openly expressed; and it is through the formal detail of the component elements that this expression is made articulate. If the surfaces were left blank and the various structural elements were not distinguishably set off from one another, or if irrelevant ornament and decorative design were allowed to intrude on them, the afore-mentioned effect would no longer be visually communicable. Much of the detail of the Orders is structurally inactual and hence materially unnecessary. It exists for its esthetic function, and pertains not to engineering but to art.

It should be apparent to every critical spectator that the Greek Orders are an assembly of abstract formal elements of pre-established shape and proportionally calculated size, that each of these elements is sharply differentiated and separated from its fellows, and that each is superficially adorned in carved and colored design with intent of suggesting some structural function contributory to the total constructional scheme. It is significant that this structural function is far more frequently only *suggested* and seldom literally performed. Thus, in the complex assembly of squared and closely fitted blocks of marble or limestone which a Greek Order presents, a column base between platform and column shaft is not structurally required (as the Doric norm concedes); the capital (though perhaps not its abacus) could be omitted without weakening the column-support; the Doric triglyph is not the protruding end of a ceiling beam (as it seems to pretend), nor does the metope close any intervening empty gap; no rafter carrying the roof ever beds in the overhang of the mutule, nor would a rafter be trimmed and nailed in the way which a mutule depicts; the Ionic dentils correspond to nothing behind them; and the Ionic epistyle, though functioning as a master beam for supporting the remaining entablature precisely as it appears to do, has not been assembled as its three-banded articulation pretends; and only the column shafts below and the upturned gutter along the roof above are entirely what they seem to be and in physical actuality perform the offices in which they are seen to be engaged.

The current explanation for these anomalies asserts that these structurally inactual aspects of the two Orders have resulted from transferring to stone, unmodified by any further thought, all the detail of timberwork, precisely as beam and plank were once hewn and fitted in an earlier time when such buildings were erected in wood. But this assertion will not stand even the least technically informed, intelligent scrutiny. The forms assumed by the various structural elements of the two Orders are all imitative of timber construction, truly enough; and, taken individually, they are interpretable as reproductions of wooden prototypes carved in stone. But all this is merely the idiom of their superficial appearance; and these metaphoric shapes have been assigned to them because marble or limestone, of and by itself, when fitted and assembled for walls and ceilings, to enclose and cover rooms, corridors, and porches, possesses only the squared edges and smooth faces of the rectangular blocks and beams to which it has been reduced, being otherwise wholly amorphous and devoid of any other character than an agreeable texture and hue. On the other hand, thanks to the restricting diameter and height of trees, and the dimensions to which adze and saw reduce them in cutting out serviceable beams and boards, and the manner in which they have to be mortised and pegged together, timber is a much more articulate medium and leaves its construction more intelligibly apparent. The builder in stone accordingly drew his formal inspiration from the more expressive vocabulary of carpentry. He did not mimetically reproduce a wooden structure in stone, but created a rather arbitrary repertory of timberlike appearances with which to organize a visually expressive and intelligibly coherent exterior for a structure which otherwise would have been uncommunicatingly bare and blank. In so doing, he was creating and applying tectonic form.

Even so, we are left with no very clear demarcation of this still rather mysterious potency. As already remarked, it is easier to detect than to define. But having once encountered it in its own proper province of tectonic activity, we should be in a better position to recognise its presence elsewhere. The potter's craft (which thus far has been considered only for its graphic ornamentation) in so far as it aspires to be an art is manifestly a tectonic one.

Fig. 17 Lekythos in Providence

It may even assume architectural form, however miniature in scale and however remote technically in its medium and manner of construction.

Certainly, there is an undeniable resemblance between Greek ceramic form and the Greek architectural Orders. In both, the total appearance derives from a calculated assembly of constituent parts so shaped as to make their structural function visibly evident. In both, the proportion of part to part has been carefully considered. And in both, there seems to be involved some sort of appeal to our gravitational sense of stable equilibrium. As in all art, a pertinent example is here more persuasive than much theorizing.

The *lekythos* (Fig. 17) is visibly articulated as a coherent whole assembled out of pertinent parts, with each of these parts possessing a size and shape appropriate to its function. There is a consequent parallel between such a structure and an architectural Order. In the lekythos, the foot is a low flat ring, level and firm enough to make the jar stand upright and wide enough to insure stability. Above this base, and set off from it by horizontal banding, the body rises on a rapidly swelling outline to its maximum diameter and continues to ascend until it is abruptly terminated at a point where a gently curving line of a wholly different geometrical order runs inward to carry a sharply sloping shoulder to a narrow and slenderly upright neck. With equally emphatic suddenness the neck ceases, to be surmounted by a heavy cuplike spout. Perhaps it is not too fanciful to speak of this as a ceramic Order, in which the ring-base corresponds to the column-base, the main body to the column shaft, the shoulder and neck to the entablature, and the spout to the sima-gutter (whose characteristic profile it actually possesses). The comparison is apposite, in that the sense for tectonic form is the same in both species.

As in an architectural Order, it is clear at a glance what the parts of such a ceramic Order are, how they are shaped and decorated, and how their proportionate sizes and contrasting profiles have been heedfully considered. And each of these parts owes something of its size and distinctive shape to the practical function which it fills in containing, funneling, and dispensing the liquid substance for which the vase was intended. It is a frequent experience that those who come fresh to Greek ceramics and for the first time examine their different shapes and patterns with intelligent curiosity discover that, by mere ocular contemplation unaided by specific knowledge of their types and titles, they can define the specific use for which each was created (Fig. 18). A *kylix* can only be for sipping something less bountifully imbibed than water; *kantharos* and *skyphos* must likewise be for drinking, but in deeper draughts; an *oinochoe* however, cannot be for drinking but must be for pouring, and has been designed like the kylix for something less abundant than mere water (for transporting which more casual

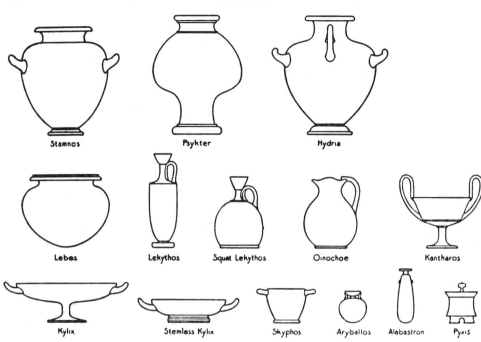

Fig. 18 Standard Shapes of Greek Vases

fluid the *stamnos* and *hydria* are patently designed), yet intended for some
sort of liquid more plentiful and less costly than perfumed oil or honey,
since, obviously, a perfume-pot must be a very different kind of jar to house
its more precious substance and permit it to dribble, drop by drop, from
some smaller-bodied narrow-throated container such as an *alabastron* or
aryballos.

That each type is so distinctive, with its differences so closely adapted
to its utilitarian purpose, and that within each type every structural part is
so clearly set off from its fellows, is partially due to the accidence of everyday speech, the vocabulary of which has already made the analysis put into
visible shape by the potter. Just as in archaic sculpture an eye must be an
eye and an ear must be an ear—irremediably set apart from all the rest,
being isolated by its own distinctively characteristic shape in appropriate
dimensions—so to the potter's mind each feature which he can name must
have its own proper place and proportional size and individual shape and
contour. So vivid and almost violent a contrast of part against part without
loss of harmonious cohesion betokens a strongly imaginative power of visualization. Whoever in his mind's eye can see a pot in service before it has
ever been thrown on the wheel, will recognise beforehand the differing needs
of a lip for pouring, a throat for restraining, an ample belly for containing,

Fig. 19 Red-figure Hydria in Boston

and a stable foot for upholding the thing which his hands have still to shape out of docile but formless clay. And if lekythos, oinochoe, hydria, and the rest are all unconfusedly distinguishable types (each belonging to what one might in architectural analogy call a different ceramic "Order"), the differences which assign each to its species are not arbitrary or capricious or fortuitous, but are due to that peculiar artistic insight and formative intelligence which manifests itself in tectonic form.

A tentative definition for Tectonic Form thence emerges as *the coherent organisation of functionally intelligible parts.* But there is a further property of Greek ceramic design which also enters in. Quite prominently and to a degree which distinguishes Greek ceramic art from that of other times and places, most of the generic types show a high center of gravity.* This observation applies specifically to the *body* of the vase. In many types—the red-figure amphora, the hydria and oinochoē, and very conspicuously the volute krater, kantharos, and loutrophoros—the addition of a high shoulder, long neck or throat, and particularly a pair of elevated handles, will raise the half-way height of the total vase very close to its apparent center of mass (an optical correction usually supplied with remarkable skill and sense of design).

Mathematically, it is by no means an easy matter to determine with any precision the center of gravity for a volume enclosed in curvilinear boundaries such as define a Nolan amphora or a hydria (Fig. 19). But a serviceable approximation may be reached by drawing a network of small squares on the projected elevation of the vase and summing the total area in terms of these squares. The outcome will merely confirm what the eye has already perceived,—that most Greek vases have top-heavy bodies and only remain upright, when filled, because they are stably balanced on their feet. This anthropomorphic analogy to the erect human form can hardly have been deliberate or consciously present to the potter's mind. But if it was never formulated and yet almost universally introduced into his work, it is for that reason all the more remarkable as an evidence of esthetic sensibility.

The appeal to our gravitational awareness of vertical support and equilibrium, which the architectural Orders seem to make, thus reappears in Greek ceramic design. In both instances and in spite of the great difference in massive scale, the appeal operates through abstract and nonrepresentational shapes without visible borrowing from living organic structures.

Whether these are valid instances of that sympathetic projection of human bodily feeling into the unfeeling object of contemplation, for which the term "empathy" has been invented, may be debatable. But the erect balance which in the majority of Greek vases counters an apparent threat of over-toppling, seems to be of the same order of visual suggestion as that peculiar

Pelike and *olpe* are noticeable exceptions to this rule.

(and to the modern eye completely uncalled-for) property of early Doric columns to bulge slightly as though in adjustive response to the superstructure's compressing weight. That this *entasis* in a stone column (barely appreciable in Fig. 20) is an "empathic" transference to an inanimate object may be deduced from the Greek substitution of anthropomorphised supports in place of columns,—the humanised pilasters which we call *caryatids* when they represent female and *atlantes* when they imitate male figures.

Fig. 20 The Parthenon: Southwest Corner

Their intrusion into the inanimate company of abstract structural shapes cannot be due to any imaginative process other than a physically sensed realization of the entablature's weight and the column's muscular struggle to support it.

On any judgment, the abstract formal appeal in architectural and ceramic design could not have been so insistent in classic Greek workmanship if it were merely an invention of modern hypercritical enthusiasm for an imaginary esthetic sensibility. However it was felt and formulated by the builders and potters of antiquity, we must accept it as a measure of their control over tectonic form.

We have treated the canonic shapes and sizes, the areal surfaces and profile appearances, which determine pattern and proportion in the "Orders" of architectural and ceramic design, as though they were due to individual action and depended on the artists' personal judgment and choice. So, in final outcome, they may have been, if we admit such a potency as collective taste and communal decision. For, quite evidently, the individual's contribution to Greek artistic forms was normally very restricted. Once the Doric and Ionic were formulated, no one builder, as far as we know, ever spontaneously invented a new Order in architecture. Corinthian took its place as a third member in the official rank on equal standing with Doric and Ionic only after a long development, commencing with the invention of a new decorative design to replace the mechanically awkward corner-capital in Ionic and followed by gradual modifications in the Ionic entablature above it, until what purported to be a distinctive Order had been differentiated where at first there had been only the substitution of a new kind of capital. So likewise the short-lived Aeolic, which began so promisingly in the sixth century on Lesbos and the opposing shoreland, was not seemingly one man's invention, nor was its disappearance due to merely local disapproval. These major novelties apart, Greek architectural history shows a surprising absence of inventiveness in its visual forms: after a thousand years of use, the Doric Order was still the same canonic sequence of traditional parts.

In ceramic art there prevailed a similar tendency to perpetuate the profiles and proportions which gave each type its distinctive and appropriate character. The potters did not vie with one another in producing novel shapes and types of their own devising, so much as in skillfully reproducing and subtly perfecting those which they had learned. And though those classes of vases which had no Mycenaean or Geometric ancestry must necessarily have been introduced as independent creations at some period and place, we cannot discern their abrupt creation, but find them—like their fellow types of longer heritage—as established shapes only lightly variable under the individual potter's improvization. Such tenacity of type implies a strict workshop tradition and a master-to-apprentice transmission of practical methods and formulas of very considerable precision. Of what nature were these formulas and how were they imparted and applied?

The answers to these questions must be sought in the vases themselves. Particularly informative are the sets of identical pairs, which have survived in considerable numbers (Fig. 21 and 22). To be sure, the twins in such cases are never entirely identical; indeed, it is precisely because they are not so that they are informative. That they were intended to pass as twins may be inferred from their survival together (as in an Etruscan grave), their visible identity of size and shape, and (frequently) the exact duplication of their painted decoration or an unmistakeable stylistic resemblance in the drawing. Deriving, therefore, from the same workshop, produced by the hand of the same potter, and decorated by the same painter, they are not a pair by accident of mass production, but by deliberate intention. Yet when all their dimensions are exactly measured and compared, they always fail to correspond completely in minor details of size or outline. The discrepancies normally amount to less (and rather often to much less) than three sixteenths of an inch in the major dimensions; and as they are seldom appreciable to the average onlooker, we may assume that even to the potters' specialized vision they seemed immaterial.

It is extremely unlikely that such twin vases were manufactured without aid of calipers or linear rule, since the correspondence in every part is much too close to have been attained by mere inspection. On the other hand, it may be taken for certain that no molds were used and no template applied, because the run of the profile is not the same to the degree of identity which these rigidly mechanical aids enforce. It is indicative of the potter's expert mastery of his craft that he could so closely reproduce a curved contour without other guidance than the check on height and width which the application of calipers afforded. The loveliness of such outlines is remarkable; but it is not altogether inexplicable nor yet miraculous, if one considers how it has been compounded of the even speed of the turning wheel and the co-ordinated movement of the potter's hand outward or inward and also upward in a rhythm which much practice made instinctive. The primary impulse is therefore freehand manipulation, while the secondary control is measurement by calipers to a predetermined series of dimensions. These dimensions do not seem to have been fixed by any footrule of constant length sub-divided into equal portions, as the Greek linear foot was divided into "palms" and "fingers," but to have been modular. And by "modular" is meant that the dimensions of a vase were determined in terms of integral ratios between the parts rather than by any constant but arbitrary unit of measurement comparable to our English inch or the European centimeter. Thus, the neck and lip of an oenochoe might be intended to be one fourth as tall as the body from which it was to rise, and the attached handle be intended to protrude above the lip by an equal measure; the body's maximum diameter might be made equal to its height, and the horizontal breadth of lip and foot set at half this amount. In the actual making—in the throwing on the wheel and assembling of the separately formed parts and firing in the oven—these prescriptions might suffer some slight departure from metric accuracy; but if their original intent was to insure desirable proportion and structural harmony, this end had been attained. It is more important that the profile curves should run true to the eye's satisfaction than that a small dimensional deviation should be corrected to satisfy the demands of an invisible and merely measurable exactitude.

The Boston Museum of Fine Arts possesses a group of four oinochoai designed to this suggested scheme of proportion and varying so little in their dimensions and so manifestly decorated by the same hand (even though the painted subjects are in every case different), that they evidently are not only from the same workshop but were intended as companion pieces. They have been very carefully measured and their dimensions published by Lacey Caskey in his *Geometry of Greek Vases* (pp. 140-143). It is noticeable from his table of measurements that not one of the four precisely agrees with any of the other three except occasionally in some single minor detail, but that all four conform within a very small fraction of an inch for the vases' largest diameter. In Caskey's drawings, which show projected elevations at slightly less than half actual size, the eye cannot detect the slightest difference in three out of the four vases in shape or proportions and is scarcely aware of the slightly accentuated bulge in the body of the fourth (due to a slight diminution of height).

These observations, uninteresting in themselves, permit some far-reaching inferences.

Apparently, the potter was tolerant of inaccuracies in his work within the limits of immediate visual detection. The far greater precision with which Greek intaglio gems are cut was demanded by the subject-matter and the medium. Greek coins of good period are similarly precise, though not quite to the same degree. But as the scale of the work increases, the demand for precision declines. Inaccuracy in the cutting of a triglyph will not be as apparent as irregularity in carving the ornament of an architectural molding. In pottery, a warped rim will immediately lead to rejection of the vase; but, as just noted, a failure to attain exact correspondence between companion pieces seems to have passed muster within a tolerance of several millimeters. It may therefore be inferred that a comparable discrepancy might normally have existed between the potter's intended design and his finished product.

Such considerations of the allowable margin of error in various arts are perhaps not very enlightening reading; but they help to dispose of an interesting and extremely ingenious modern theory of design in ancient Greek ceramics, which for a time fascinated many of our best-informed scholars in the field. It was devised by Jay Hambidge, and owed its name of "Dynamic Symmetry" to its dependence on rectangles with their sides related in ratios which, arithmetically stated, are square roots of simple integers such as 2, 3, 5, and 7 (such surds being known as *dynameis* in Greek mathematical parlance). Greek vases were "dynamically analyzed" (cf. Figs. 21-22) by enclosing them within a rectangle tangent to their projected elevations and constructing a network of interior rectangles geometrically related to the prime enclosing rectangle. This network coincided with the structural detail of the vase by determining all crucial dimensions of vertical level or horizontal width. Such analysis was not merely an engaging geometrical exercise for the modern investigator of design (though in the end it proved to be so), but purported to retrace the creative processes of the ancient potters who made the vases.

If this were true, it would raise an issue of considerable importance for the critic of Greek artistic behavior, since it would mean that Greek craftsmen were dependent on invisible sources of power, whose relevance to the visible qualities of their productions they could not have rationally explained. It should be remarked that construction of a vase according to the precepts of Dynamic Symmetry does not determine the curves of its contours, but only the limits within which these contours may move. And although it dictates very precisely the proportions of all the structural parts, it does so only in conformity with the established tradition of typical shapes for each ceramic type. This latter remark is based on the observation that two vases may be practically indistinguishable to the eye and yet purport to have been designed on wholly different "dynamic" systems. Their generic appearance of type, shape, contour, and general proportions must therefore be independent of the particular "dynamic" design employed. But in that event it is difficult to see what Dynamic Symmetry has contributed to the vase.

It would be thoroughly unjust to claim that the Greek potters could not have made these "drawingboard lay-outs" which Dynamic Symmetry demands and for which a T-square and compass are the only necessary tools. The obstacle lies in suggesting any plausible reason why they should have wanted to do so, unless it was through compulsion of some sort of irrational belief in the power of geometrical abstractions over visible form. This is not in the least an impossible assumption, to judge from the teachings of Pythagoras (who ascribed very curious potencies to abstract Number) and the evidence of supersensuous mathematical mysticism in Plato; even so, it would hardly be expected that philosophic tenets of such a sort would have influenced sixth or early fifth century potters in the routine exercise of a traditional craft. However, whether or not they did so is precisely the question at issue; and its importance for any inquiry into Greek artistic behavior is sufficient justification for this digression down a curious byway of artistic theory.

Fortunately for our contention that Greek ceramic art was a forthright creation in visible terms under direct visual control with a purely visual appeal to esthetic sensibility, without taint of irrational superstition or metaphysical mysticism or other transcendental reference, Mr. Caskey's extremely accurate marshalling of the evidence disposed of Dynamic Symmetry as an actual practice of the Attic potters. His detailed confrontation of companion pieces in pairs and larger groups dealt the fatal blow.

In the Boston Museum there are two red-figure lekythoi (Fig. 21) which, in Sir John Beazley's unappealable verdict, "are undeniably a pair, made in the same factory. The paintings are by a single artist." Mr. Caskey adds that "they are of the same height, the heights of all the members are the same; the diameters are also the same except for the largest diameter of the body." But this exception is disastrous for "dynamic analysis" which

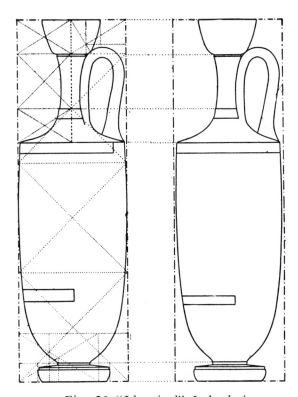

Fig. 21 "Identical" Lekythoi

hinges on the ratio of overall height to maximum width. Despite the visible intent of identical shape, size, and proportions, because of this slight failure to throw the two bodies to the same breadth (they differ by three sixteenths of an inch) one of the pair yields to a rather intricate "dynamic analysis" while the other stubbornly refuses to be analyzed at all. Similarly in the previously cited group of four "identical" oinochoai, two of the series illustrate the same "dynamic" scheme but the remaining two cannot be made to conform to it, each preferring a distinct scheme of its own. Yet to us—as, assuredly, to the potter and his client—there are no distinguishable differences in any of the four. Again, there are in the same museum two panel-amphorai (Fig. 22) of which Mr. Caskey writes, "These two amphorae are assigned to the factory of the potter Andokides, and are decorated by the same painter.

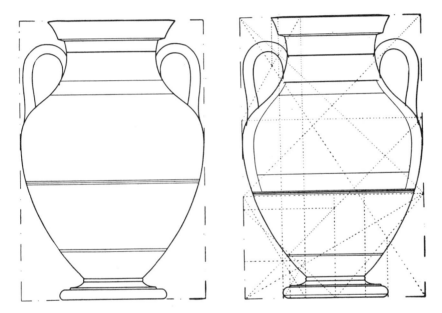

Fig. 22 "Identical" Amphorai

... They resemble one another closely in their main proportions and the forms of details." Yet because one is 21 millimeters taller than the other while its body is only 3-1/2 millimeters wider, the inevitable discrepant verdict results: one of the pair is "dynamically" analyzable (but only on the assumption that the potter was .0016 m. wide of his mark on the height of his vase), while its apparently identical companion piece evades analysis.

These entirely typical instances should suffice to debar Dynamic Symmetry from the Athenian Kerameikos and prove it to be no more than an intellectual pastime of the modern mind. There could be no clearer demonstration that, whatever else it might accomplish, Dynamic Symmetry contributes nothing to the visible appearance of a vase.

But if the proportions of Greek vases were not determined by such a system, either they were created purely by the potter's eyes in conjunction with his skillful hands, or some other (and preferably much simpler) measuring device was used.

It may be accepted as certain that the potters did not determine the dimensions of their vases in accord with a linear footrule such as we of today apply to every variety of need. Measurement of the components of an Attic vase rarely shows any conformity to known metric values for the ancient linear foot. This is only to be expected, since the potters were turning out vases in a great variety of sizes but with rather constant proportions. And since proportion is not a matter of absolute but of relative size, the fixed intervals of a footrule would have no application. But *relative* measures of length, precisely because they are relative, can be derived directly, one from another, inasmuch as they must all be multiples of some common factor or unit. It is this common factor which technical parlance calls a *module*. Being relative to the scale at which a design is carried out, modules can have no fixed metric values except for the particular design to which they apply. Academically employed, a module is very generally taken as a quota part of the total construction; but there would have been no reason for the potters so to treat it. Having thrown the body of a vase to any size deemed suitable, the potter, equipped with a pair of dividers or calipers, could take its dimensions of height and width and lay these off on any available level surface. He could then subdivide these lengths (most easily by halving and quartering) and so construct a scale of proportional parts with which to measure the other elements of his vase.

By the time these various elements had all been fashioned and assembled, what with throwing them on the wheel, lathe-turning them to a finished surface after the clay had hardened, accurately fitting and joining them together, and firing them in a kiln (when considerable and not entirely uniform shrinkage would occur), the precision of the various dimensions and the exactness of all proportions must have suffered, no matter how skillfully the process had been carried out. But if the extent of all such lapses from perfect accuracy still lay beyond the threshold of normal visual perception, neither potter nor public was entitled to find fault. Only modern archaeological investigations ever subjected these vases to minutely exact metric scrutiny.

The relevance of these observations to the behavior of artisans at work in other arts and crafts—notably those of monumental sculpture and architecture—must be immediately apparent. In all of these we shall again encounter the module; and perhaps, with the potters in our memory, we shall know better how to evaluate and interpret its use.

As for Tectonic Form, its pertinence to vase-design should be clear. It must be apparent that it is not created by mathematical formula founded on abstract geometric sanction, but is an expression of perceived rightness in the shape, size, and arrangement of structural parts within an organically cohering whole. What constitutes "rightness," is not easily discoverable; but it derives somehow from suggestions of symmetrical pattern, intelligible gravitational support and balance, continuity and appropriateness of contour, and appreciable conformity of functional part to part by virtue of some commensurable scale of magnitude. If these factors do not complacently yield up any further secret of their virtues and powers, this is because art is not a matter of intellectual formulas, but of esthetic response to esthetic perception. There can be no Theory of Art to instruct us how art must be made. But once it has been made it is possible and permissible to theorize as much as we like, to codify its technical behavior, and to catalog and formulate its visible results.

THE GENESIS OF SCULPTURAL FORM

So far as presently available evidence can inform us, we must hold that no extant example of monumental sculpture from Greek soil may be ascribed to a period earlier than the final quarter of the seventh century. But so advanced a date sets the incidence of this particular art in Greece fully a hundred years later than the beginning of graphic pictorial design. Since there is no readily apparent internal reason why monumental sculpture should have remained unattempted until pictorial art had completed the great technical advance which distinguishes, in vase painting, early Attic black-figure from Geometric Dipylon ware, we are forced to look about for some external reason, some intrusive source of inspiration. And this, beyond reasonable dispute, is to be found in Egypt.

There is a chronological coincidence in the archaeological evidence centering around the event which is very striking and should go far to set doubts at rest.

As far as my own information goes, not only have no objects assignable to the Greek Geometric or sub-Geometric period ever been found in Egypt, but none of the immediately subsequent seventh-century ceramic wares such as proto-Attic and proto-Corinthian has been securely attested there. The archaeological material evidence for a resumption of maritime relations between Aegean Greece and the Delta is thus negative for most of the century. By the start of the reign of phil-Hellenic Psammetichos I, ships from Ionian Miletos and probably from Rhodes began to frequent the western mouth of the Nile; and from about the year 600 onward, Greek traders demonstrably were established at the inland "treaty-port" of Naukratis, not far from the capital city of Saïs. Monumental sculpture—which is to say, glyptic work in stone at lifesize or larger—appears suddenly on the Greek scene; and its earliest occurrence, in so far as this can be fixed with any plausibility, coincides exactly with the resumption of Greek commercial relations with the Nile. This chronological conformity, when taken in conjunction with the indisputably Egyptian character of the earliest Greek *kouros* type of the nude standing male with left foot slightly advanced and clenched hands attached to the thighs, should preclude any hesitation in asserting that the

92

incentive and primary technical understanding for cutting lifesize human figures out of piers of stone came to the Greeks from the Delta. And since Egyptian sculpture at the time (as for a great many centuries previously) existed in a stereotyped phase with many undiscarded archaic traits, an almost intact transmission of its technical traditions to a previously unschooled imitator was possible. In consequence of this direct acceptance of an established workshop procedure, Greek monumental sculpture could be produced without primitive character, having from the very outset entered on an archaic stage of stylistic development. Inevitably, there was occasional more crudely executed work from provincial centers; but the comparative ineptness of these random examples makes only the more strikingly apparent that the normal level of the earliest Greek statuaries is one of fully realized and self-reliant archaic artistry.

Thus undertaken without initial handicap of technical ignorance or purposeless uncertainty of aim, Greek monumental sculpture could begin its millennial career with unhampered vigor and unhesitant ambition.

The distinction previously established between a plastic and a glyptic approach to sculpture is of prime importance for any critique of Greek monumental sculptural art. Specifically, because they were entirely glyptic productions, the early Greek statues in chiselled and polished marble display no plastic character and are without tactual structure or tactile appeal. Having been created under purely visual control, they were subject to the restrictions imposed by the mechanism of human vision; and it is these restrictions, even more than the initial dependence on Egyptian norms, which are responsible for the peculiar characteristics of their style. An archaic phase such as sixth-century Greek marble-work displays is mechanically conditioned and marks an unescapable stylistic state that must recur wherever sculpture is apprehended as an imitative reproduction of physical reality executed in purely glyptic terms.

To understand how this may be and how it is possible for sculpture to be created wholly in visual terms, we must watch the ancient sculptors at work, as their statues reveal their activity. But before doing so we must make sure that we have adequately grasped the difference between pictorial and sculptural vision.

As the exterior world is optically presented to us, its objects define themselves as colored patches within distinctively shaped boundaries. (These, with due apologies for resorting to professional jargon, we shall call "areal shapes"). The other characteristic constituents of pictorial appearances may be generically defined as "projective gradients" of various sorts. These comprise gradations in luminosity, ranging from high light to deep shadow, gradations in color and hue, gradations of pattern, whether of geometrical shape or texture, including gradations of size and of sequence, to name the chief and most conspicuous types. These gradations are either completely essential or very greatly helpful in enabling us to see "areal shapes" as solid objects located in an external space possessed of depth and distance; but they are all purely optical, in the sense that they exist only on the retina or in a similarly focussed image such as the camera or the *camera obscura* can supply. They are two-dimensioned "equivalent conversions" of a tridimensional exterior world. If they are exactly reproduced elsewhere by recording them precisely as they exist on the retina, the outcome will necessarily be a picture. For this reason they may be called pictorial aspects. Their unaltered reproduction at any scale or in any medium is powerless to produce a piece of sculpture, because sculpture belongs to the exterior physical world and all these appearances belong to the optic realm of the eye. Later on, in considering the evolution of graphic form, there will be occasion to examine more closely the nature of these optical conversions of solid shapes into projected planimetric equivalents, since it is they which make up the very substance and being of pictorial representation. For the moment it is sufficient to classify them as "pictorial gradients" in order to set them apart from sculptural representation.

It is a simple matter to prove that such pictorial constituents of vision are of no service to the sculptor and cannot directly concern him in his primary task of evoking a material replica of a solid object. Thus, the luminosity gradients created by illuminating an opaque sphere from a single source of light enable us to see it as a sphere instead of as a circular disk. For this reason a painter can transform a flat disk into a sphere optically by recording on it the appropriate gradation of light and shadow. But if a sculptor wishes to make a sphere, the visible illumination to which such an object may be subject is irrelevant to his task, which consists of shaping an actual material mass to its geometrically correct solid shape. When achieved, this will take care of its own illuminated appearances. Yet how is the sculptor to discover how such an externally actual and physically real object is shaped, when at any given moment he can see only its illuminated hither surface? Of course, if the intended object is as symmetrical and uniform as is a perfect sphere, a mental understanding of its geometrical structure will help him out of his difficulties. But let us suppose that the solid shape is much more complex, so that it cannot be readily formulated in geometrical terms. He can move around it, look at it from a great many different angles, and so perhaps combine for himself a sort of mental notion of how the shape is constituted. But he can never actually *see* it all at once, so that he cannot ever directly copy it from merely looking at it. He can copy its various aspects, but these will not necessarily all fuse together into the true stereometric shape behind the aspects.

Because of the transformation which the illuminated external world un-

[margin note:] not relevant cause we can't see ourselves see

dergoes in its reflection on his retinal screen, there is little of what his eye reports that the sculptor can turn to immediate account. Yet to this there is one all-important exception. The areal shapes of objects, being true silhouettes of their solid form, are geometrically unconverted in vision. To be sure, there may be angles of view from which these shapes may be unfamiliar, uninforming, or even unintelligible, as anyone can demonstrate to his own satisfaction by examining the transformations of the shadow cast upon a screen by an unseen object of complex structure. But among the shifting silhouettes (which correspond to the painter's foreshortened views) there will be some which are fully recognizable and completely intelligible. These are the unforeshortened and hence undistorted silhouettes; and it is these which the archaic draftsman and sculptor will elect to reproduce. And because every areal shape is exactly defined and established by its boundary, it follows that the unskilled artist's prime opportunity for mimetic reproduction lies in recording this defining boundary (or graphic outline, or significant contour, as one may choose to call it). It is this areal silhouette (to give it yet another title) which the primitive sculptor reproduces graphically in order that he may establish an appropriate shape for the unshaped block of stone which he intends to trim into mimetic likeness.

There is, therefore, nothing mysterious in the invariable rule that glyptic sculptural form begins with the assumption of an overall areal shape to impart contour to a hitherto unformed solid mass.

But an immediate difficulty—entirely natural and altogether unavoidable —results from the failure of an areal shape to correspond extensively to the mass which it outlines. For being the projection from a single angle of view, it is valid for that one viewpoint only. This is the great quandary in which glyptic sculpture finds itself at the very start of its career. Its manner of overcoming this formidable obstacle may seem naive, its execution improbable or even technically impossible, its success thoroughly unlikely; but no other solution is available to the sculptor at an immature phase of his art. World over, in all times and places, the same response has been made to this same challenge. That is why all primitive sculpture is fundamentally alike; and that is why archaic sculpture everywhere and always exhibits a characteristic identity of style.

As any solid object is viewed by one who moves around it, its visible silhouette (unless it chances to be spherically uniform in shape) must undergo continuous transformation until a point is reached at which the earlier contour has been completely altered and a new areal shape has appeared. For objects constituted symmetrically as human beings and four-footed animals are, there are four cardinal profiles which yield the least foreshortened (and hence least distorted), most intelligible (because most distinctively characteristic), and hence most serviceable, projected contour-

4 main outline views

they don't make a
round fig.

shapes. All four (which is to say, quite simply, the front view, the rear view, and the two lateral views) will appeal to the sculptor as significant and applicable to his project. These will seem to him to be the master-forms, responsible by their intermingling and mutual interaction for all the intermediate appearances which the object of his interest displays to other points of view. And he will be led to imagine that if he sets these four determinant profiles or master-forms on the four cardinal surfaces of a quadrangular block of sufficient size, he can make these four aspects coalesce into a single solid shape by cutting away the unenclosed and irrelevant matter outside them. A successful outcome to so dubious a project has seemed so unlikely to modern commentators and artists, inured to thinking in terms of plastic execution of sculptural themes, that many have looked on it as an impossible task and hence denied that it could ever have been performed by an ancient stonecutter. Yet the material evidence belies their doubts. Occasional pieces of unfinished archaic sculpture, such as the colossal Ram-bearer of Thasos, still preserve in their blocked-out silhouettes the four cardinal profiles to which they were cut; and even fully finished works, such as the over-lifesize youths from Sunium, betray a similar technical treatment by the unrounded abruptness with which their frontal and lateral surfaces meet.

Admittedly, such a process requires considerable skill for its successful execution. Anyone who will take the trouble to make the experiment for himself, by shaping plasticine or hard wax or any comparable material to a quadrangular pier and then attempting to cut four cardinal profiles inward until they meet, will soon become convinced that the four contours will not automatically coalesce nor maintain themselves without mutual damage. Such an experiment will suggest that the process must not be interpreted too literally nor executed too mechanically. But a stonecutter trained by apprenticeship and practice can perform the feat if he can hold the contour forms visually before him and will work by slow removal of unwanted stone and by constant shifting of his angle of attack from fullfront to side view and back again, being careful never to trespass on either contour by cutting into it or confusing its levels. He will scarcely succeed in this unless he has some rule-of-thumb (which is to say, a rule of rigid yardstick or of plumbed measuring-line) with which to check his levels and keep his proportions exact. In short, the task of harmoniously combining four profile views into a single solid shape exhibiting these profiles is difficult and demanding. But it is easier than any other available method of extracting a sculptural figure out of a blank block because it is the only way to overcome the primal obstacle that the mechanism of human vision imposes.

For the same reason that extension in depth is not directly given in its pictorial projection on the retina, the interior protrusions and recessions within the boundaries of an areal shape elude correct reproduction in glyptic form. The gradients of luminosity, hue, texture, and pattern, with which vision operates, are properties of the visual field, and their exact reproduction could yield only another visual field—which is to say, a picture and not a sculptured shape. For his glyptic record of interior detail the sculptor is again restricted to areal shapes, in this instance to those that may be formed within the total shape, as a zebra's stripes or a giraffe's patches present interior demarcations within the all-enclosing shape of the animal's silhouetted form. Such interior shapes are utilizable by the sculptor in so far as their outlines can be transferred to the surface of a block and made substantive by grooving or scoring or trenching or stepping back the stone. In consequence, interior detail in early sculpture is linear, being of the same order of visual projection as the contour which establishes the silhouetted mass of the block on which it appears.

There is, however, a further property of interior detail which can be directly transferred from vision to sculpture, and that is its color. The gradations of hue which the eye beholds are pictorial conversions; but these (to common-sense experience) have a common source in an objectively uniform color. So the painter (because he records visual conversions) must represent a tree in full summer foliage with many tones of green, whereas more pragmatic and less artistic contemplation insists that every leaf is "really" of much the same tint as every other. It is this unconverted and ungraded basic hue which the archaic sculptor will record and which (since his aim is imitative of the physical object) he has neither right nor reason to omit. On this account, early life-size glyptic work is almost invariably colored, and the colors are applied in ungraded tones of uniform pigment. The sculptor is not concerned to match his colors against the fleeting and changeful tints of optical appearances, but contents himself with any available pigment of approximately similar value, provided it is durable, well-saturated, and effective.

Being debarred from directly shaping the complex stereometric structure of solid bodies by his inability to see them as they exist physically in space, the early sculptor must define the overall solid shape in gross and apply independent interior areal shapes thereon in self-containing outline, superimposing the latter on the former. And because the stonecutter has to work at right angles to the surface of the block, whether he is chipping with a metal point or using a bow drill, he sinks his guidelines by projecting them frontally into the stone while recording the interior detail and, in so doing, cuts straight back without plastic modification. Comparably to the way in which the archaic painter sets a full eye in a profile face, having outlined both elements correctly but assembled them wrongly, the archaic sculptor draws this same full-front eye on the marble surface of a generically blocked-out head and drives its linear contour inward, producing an eye which is

correctly outlined but incorrectly modelled in depth. It is this rigid divorce between voluminal shape and linear design which gives archaic sculpture its essential and peculiar quality. The distinctive characteristic of archaic style is the inveterate property of depictive pattern-shapes to remain
suspended on the surface of the block instead of penetrating it to become an
integral part of its solid substance. And because this trait does not stem from
individual volition or personal choice but from restrictive conditions universally imposed by the mechanism of human vision, "archaic" becomes a
strictly definable critical term with unambiguous application, and an archaic
phase is a necessarily recurrent stage in every artistic civilization which se-
riously undertakes glyptic mimicry of the objective visual world.

The superficial pattern-shapes of archaism breed further patterns by their
unaltered repetition. This is a situation which automatically results from
the nature of these pattern-shapes as noetic schematic forms. What a "noetic
scheme" is may be understood by recalling the previous discussion of the
primitive draftsman's behavior in always drawing the wheel of a car as a
perfect circle. Herein there are two relevant phenomena. Being a mental
construction instead of a direct visual record every schema tends to asume
a geometrically simple shape (as experiments in Gestalt-psychology demonstrate). But it is even more pertinent to observe that every schema which
stands for a seen appearance is derived from an *unforeshortened aspect* of its
subject. The reason for this is not difficult to discover. Only an unforeshortened appearance is judged capable of supplying an object's true and proper
shape, because it alone is intelligibly entire. In every other aspect some element has been abbreviated or distorted or has dropped out, since every foreshortening entails some degree of invisibility along the line of sight. Our
intelligence consequently treats foreshortened aspects as transitory "appearances" of a stable unforeshortened state which alone is "reality." But any
unforeshortened aspect when graphically recorded as an areal shape in silhouette is nothing more than a flat projection upon a uniform plane. As such,
when put to use by the sculptor, it is a purely superficial graphic record which
obstinately resists conversion into solidly modeled form. Originating as a linear projection, it clings to the surface of the mass to which it has been made
to adhere.

Any noetically evolved areal shape must have a fully closed outline; otherwise it would not be a self-subsistent entity. Wherever there is reason for
introducing several such shapes in continuous repetition, as on archaic statues
the curtain of untrimmed hair hanging in back is articulated with a wealth
of bead-like roundels or zigzag chevrons, or the hair parted over the forehead
is covered with snailshell spiral blocks (Plate II), such repetition of contig-
uous but separately contoured identical shapes produces by geometric necessity a compositely symmetrical pattern; and the emergence of such a pattern

acts to stimulate the sculptor's interest in decorative elaboration. Because cutting marble to such patterns demands considerable skill of hand, the archaic artist is prone to believe that a display of accomplished craftsmanship is proof of his fitness to exercise his trade; precision in rendering schematic pattern becomes a mark of professional attainment, especially where the result possesses a peculiarly striking beauty in its own right of decorative appeal. Perhaps such an attitude toward sculpture runs counter to our modern conception of the artist's role. We are habituated to believe that his should be a creatively intrusive personality, imaginatively expressing individually distinctive emotions. But early art does not thus elevate the craftsman above his craft.

Much has been said—and not always wisely—about a mysterious property of primitive and archaic sculpture termed "frontality." It has been observed that, regardless of the pose in which the human figure is presented, an archaic statue displays a central vertical axis rigidly aligned from top to bottom, so that the figure is precisely halved by this axis, with either side the mirror image of the other. In addition, the detail features of face and body are oriented so as to face directly the viewer who confronts the statue. This description of archaic statuary is entirely accurate; but so defined, its properties must seem curiously irrational and arbitrary. Possibly, the phenomena elude comprehension because two distinct but interconnected factors are combined to preclude a simple and single explanation.

Naturally, every artist, however primitive, must be aware of the symmetry of anatomic structure which attaches to all higher organisms, including man, and will grasp the simple fact that in every paired element of bodily structure right-hand corresponds to left-hand by mirror-inversion. Indeed, it is impossible to discover any difference between the two eyes, or the two hands, the feet, or any other of the visible anatomic pairs other than this mirror-inversion of shape. Axial rigidity results from the recognition of this structural relation and its introduction into the noetic image, occasioning exact formal correspondence between the members of every pair of opposites. The second property, of frontal opposition in respect to the viewer, derives from the projection of the various interior shapes in unforeshortened outline upon a uniform surface of solid ground, so that the eyes, the superciliar arches, the nostrils, and lips in the head and the patternised muscular divisions in the torso are all drawn in the same curvilinear plane as constituent parts of a single noetic image. Similarly, the ears in archaic statuary are frontal to the lateral aspect, and the muscular articulations of the back and buttocks are frontal to the rear view.

Perhaps this has been expressed in over-technical language; but it is difficult to see how the phenomena of "frontality" can be given intelligent explanation except by translating them into terms of visual experience. Once they have been so translated, they are seen to be direct consequences of normal visual behavior.

However inevitable frontality may be and however strictly it may be observed during the early phases of sculptural art, the practice of frontality will disappear with equal inevitability as mimetic technique progresses. Axial rigidity will be dissipated as the sculptor comes to recognize that the waking human being keeps itself in equilibrium through constant axial adjustment, not only while moving but even when standing erect or remaining seated. The rigid archaic axis, however applicable to the structural geometry of the human skeleton, is seen to be in conflict with the actual behavior of the living creature. If the man of marble is to seem alive, he must carry himself as a living body does and appear to keep himself erect by maintaining a subtly asymmetric equilibrium of muscular control. On the other hand, frontal opposition, because it is due to linear projection of unforeshortened areal shapes, will be dissipated as soon as solid modeling begins to supplant the purely graphic notation of form details. For example, an eye that has been correctly constructed in depth within a fully hollowed socket will no longer stare out flatly like a painted eye on a panel.

When "living balance" and solid modelling come to be apprehended and introduced into glyptic statuary, the restraints of the archaic phase have been broken through, and a new epoch of stylistic development ensues. But within the confines of archaism, stylistic evolution at first seems to move in quite other directions and to be engrossed in very different interests. To these we must now turn back.

The modern spectator, habituated to viewing sculpture as an art of unrestrictedly variable theme and temper, cannot fail to wonder at the uninventiveness of the archaic masters who for more than a hundred years were content to repeat the same standard type of the nude youth standing stiffly erect with clenched hands held close to his thighs. Admittedly there was other subject-matter in the archaic repertory, notably the draped seated figure of either sex and the heavily clothed standing woman. Yet these, too, exhibited scarcely any variety of pose or act, but were repeated without notable modification as sculptor succeeded sculptor and artistic generations passed. Our surprise at this lack of invention is due to our conception of sculptural art as the representation of any and every manner of living shape without restriction upon theme, mode, or manner, whereas to the Greek master the making of sculpture was quite specifically the enterprise of cutting out, at demand, a nude youth or a clothed woman or an enthroned figure. To him, that is what sculpture was: to turn out a specimen of these established creations was his accepted task, very much as the cabinet-maker's task was to produce tables, benches, bed frames, and chairs in accord with recognized precedents.

If a *kouros* from the later years of the sixth century is compared, detail for detail, with one from the century's earlier decades, the alterations in theme and pose and structural shape will be found negligibly slight; little advance in technical execution will be apparent. And yet a far-reaching difference will be revealed in the depictive accuracy with which anatomic details have been observed and recorded—and this despite a continued reliance on schematic linear form and the surface-projection of areal shape. Judged by the criteria previously cited as distinctive of archaism, a late sixth-century *kouros* is neither more nor less archaic than an early sixth-century one. But its anatomic detail is less noetically abstract and more akin to natural appearances. Within the all-controlling restrictions of the archaic approach to representation, the trend toward realism has exercised virtually uninterrupted sway. For example, as the century wore on, eyes were reduced in size, more correctly shaped, and tilted downward to glance along the nose instead of staring out levelly into space. Ears were not only given correct outline but were modified to show their proper interior conformation. The more subtly protruded muscular swellings in arms and legs were given due recognition; and the anatomic diversity of the athletic male torso, both front and back, was converted to a more complex pattern in closer conformity with physical reality.

There was, in fact, plenty to be learned about the human body's outer appearance for sculptural presentation without overpassing the tenets of schematic form, because an adequately detailed linear record of human anatomic peculiarities is an affair of very considerable intricacy. If much that the archaic sculptor introduced was still a pictorial projection of linear shape rather than a stereometric reproduction of solid structure, this did not preclude his further progress in truthful observation of natural appearances. Only, it restricted this progress within the confines of archaic form.

During the period with which we are at present concerned, Greek social custom considered public display of the feminine nude highly improper. Apparently, habitual behavior had established quite opposite notions about male and female modesty. The onlooker who took not the slightest umbrage at the spectacle of naked boys and youths in the palaestra would have been scandalised at seeing an unclothed woman in public; and his prejudice was transferred even to a carved and colored marble representation. However arbitrary such a code of social decency may seem to those who do not observe it, this discrimination between the sexes was a most fortunate circumstance for Greek sculptural art, since it imposed upon the artists the study of two wholly distinct, but for their art almost equally fundamental, modes of expression. So diverse are the esthetic problems set by the clad and the unclad figure in sculptural presentation that two wholly different disciplines may be discriminated, one concerned with the human body's dictated norm of anatomic structure, the other seeking to impose artistic form upon the unstructural fluidity of loosely adherent costume.

In repeating the *kouros* type over and over, the Attic sculptors manifested an ever more extensively accurate appreciation of anatomic detail with a consequent increasing approximation to natural truth. But the more than thirty surviving Attic *korai* (or draped standing maidens), which were once dedicated to the goddess of the Athenian acropolis and range in date from the central years of the sixth century to the Persian capture of Athens in 480 B.C. (an occasion which led to their overthrow by the invader and subsequent interment on the Acropolis by the Athenians), might induce a different verdict on archaic interest in fidelity to objective truth. Because of the social stricture on the feminine nude, these statues perforce were primarily representations of festal costume rather than of the human form. And since linen chitons and woolen himatia and peploi possessed no set organic structure comparable to the firm silhouettes and predetermined detail of the nude male body, *kouros* and *kore* seem to belong to two completely different categories of art. To be sure, wherever the undraped form was exposed, as in the heads and hands, ankles and feet (which social custom permitted to be shown), there is little distinction in their rendering for either sex and much the same trend toward naturalistic detail. Judged by the heads alone, the Volomandra *kouros* (Fig. 45) and the *"Peplos Kore"* might be brother and sister. But where the sculptor's primary concern was with the elusive structure of loosely worn costume or the baffling texture of waist-long hair, the incentive to decorative elaboration was great and the opportunity for it only too apparent, while strictly realistic representation was well-nigh impossible. Here, then the trend toward mimetic fidelity was thwarted; and technical progress was diverted toward surface ornament without significance for the general evolution of sculptural form.

Ultimately the discrepancy between the ever more correctly rendered anatomic detail and the arbitrarily decorative unreality of the garments must become acutely disturbing to the sculptors. Sooner or later they must choose between the two opposed directions in which archaism had been evolving, between subjective elaboration of two-dimensional design and objective reproduction of tridimensional structure. For an intensely visually minded race with an innate conviction of the reality of the sensuous world the choice was rather completely determined in advance. It was less a question of the end at which to aim than of the means by which that end might be attained.

It would seem that sculpture can remain indefinitely bound to an archaic phase only when its ultimate sanction comes from some other source than the material world of sensuous perception. The superstition of religious beliefs or magical practices, the tyranny of accepted habit and convention, ignorance, incuriosity, insensitivity, public indifference are all arresting forces which can hold art at its archaic (or even a more primitive) level; but none of these forces was powerful enough in sixth-century Greece to arrest the trend toward mimetic truth which necessarily put an end to archaism.

It might be claimed that the *Pouting Girl* (Fig. 23) is an archaic work because the detail is still recorded in schematic linear pattern lodged on the surface without affecting the solid structure. And undeniably some of the rendering—as in the undulant chevrons of the forehead hair and the wrinkled *chiton*—is abstractly decorative. But in most of the garment the brittle loveliness and studied elegance of the earlier Maidens has been replaced by a very different treatment of line. In all of this statue which has survived— the portion between waist and knee having never been recovered—the block has been shaped to the nude form; and the drapery, where not directly incised in archaic manner, has been carved as close-fitting ribbons of cloth without much differentiation into ridge and valley but with enough distinction between light and shadow to lead the eye over the rounded rise and fall of the modeled mass. The novelty is the enforced submission of inanimate surface pattern to animate anatomic structure. The drapery, instead of drawing attention to itself, now draws the eye to the living form behind it. Its function is not to decorate and adorn, but to mould and make visible. If the costume appears to be transparent in many passages, this is a heritage from delineation of detail on the surface according to long-established archaic practice. Much more significant is the discovery of a technique for enclosing the body within the costume without neglecting the textural density of the material. Hitherto, if the body had substance, the drapery had none; and if the drapery had substance, the body disappeared from view. The reconciliation of two contrary demands in a formula which satisfied both was not an easy task. But its tentative and uncertain emergence on the *Pouting Girl* heralds the passing of the archaic phase in Greek sculptural history.

Fig. 23 A & B Athens, Acropolis Museum: the "Pouting Girl"

VI

THE EARLY EVOLUTION
OF PICTORIAL STYLE

What Geometric graphic art most signally lacked, when first the Greek potters attempted the representation of physical realities instead of decorative abstractions of linear designs, was subject-matter. From all the manifold appearances of the rich Aegean landscape around them there was almost nothing that they could reproduce pictorially because—as already remarked—primitive draftsmen do not draw what they see before them, but what they have learned to draw. And of this the late Geometric repertory offered only a meager store. What was needed was new example and suggestion. And these came suddenly, and in abundance, as Greek commerce recommended relations with the older civilizations beyond the Aegean boundaries. Here it encountered a fresh world of decorative art lost to it since Mycenaean times, replete with an array of marvelous beasts and weird monsters that promptly reappeared in Greece on the early Corinthian vases and soon spread elsewhere through Hellenic lands.

Yet for all its fascinating complexity of novel themes, this exotic importation of decorative material failed to supply the Greek artist with that which he instinctively desired most, a mastery over the human form in action, with which to conjure up his own world of events and activities wherein lions and panthers, flying horses and grimacing winged gorgons, bird-bodied sirens and harpies and all the other fantastic notions of the un-Hellenic East had no place.

The painters of the Dipylon jars had already learned to draw rude shapes of men and women, not very correctly, to be sure, nor with any variety of pose or costume or physical appearance, but recognizable nonetheless and indeed quite unambiguous. Yet for all that could be done with them, they were not a very varied company. Then there came—from the same eastern neighborhood which had brought the beasts and monsters to Greek ken—an unforeseen opportunity to expand the painter's repertory of nameless and timeless and placeless men and women to include the won-

105

derworld of poetic legend and heroic adventure and epic myth. Let me
briefly sketch this transformation:

The enormous vogue of epic poetry during the late Geometric period
and its brilliant maturity far in advance of any of the visual arts (because
poetic production is unhampered by physical obstacles and can evolve with
the speed of its own winged words) exerted an irresistible attraction for
the artist who had learned to gather his repertory themes into pictorial incident. The epic spell lured him into diverting his representations of the
everyday and commonplace into the distant magical realm of heroic myth.
The Dipylon paintings, when they illustrated a human happening, dealt
with such contemporary incidents as dances, processions, funeral games
and escorts, the laying-out and carrying-forth of the dead, and, at the last,
ships and their oarsmen crews. But with only a little adaptation and re-
arrangement the same thematic material would bear reinterpretation in epic
terms: contesting men could be epic heroes; the dead man a Trojan or
Achaean slain in the great war for Troy; the cars could be heroes' chariots,
and their horses the talking steeds of Achilles or the fleet coursers of Diomede. So, by attachment to familiar legends the impersonal generic might
become specific and therewith be raised to a higher level of emotional interest. Only—who was to guess, from mere inspection, that such was the
artist's intent and such the meaning of his work? There is a charming little
late-Geometric bronze group (Fig. 12) which represents a man confronting
and gently touching a horse-bodied human who can only be a centaur. But
who is to say whether this pair are a wild creature from Pelion and a Thes-
salian Lapith about to engage in mortal struggle at the wedding feast of
Peirithoos, or Achilles with his foster tutor Cheiron, or merely what they
seem to be, a homeless centaur and a nameless man? Since all representation at that time, whether by painted drawing or by modeled figurine, had
to be compounded out of limited thematic types of wholly generic connotation, the artist could not individualize either his characters or his events.
On the safety-pin previously described and illustrated (Fig. 11) it is impossible to discover who the contestants are supposed to be or even whether
they are specifically intended for nameable persons at all. In the British
Museum there is a late-Geometric bowl of Attic workmanship (Fig. 7A)
which carries as an upper external band of painted decoration a delightfully
naive representation of one of the new swift longboats of that day, with
double tier of twice twenty rowers at their oars. Behind these and stepping
over the vessel's high curved stern, a huge man seizes by the wrist an equally
tall woman who waves a tambourine-like wreath. "Theseus eloping with
Ariadne," say some; "Paris leading off Helen," say others; but "the captain
brings home a bride" would do equally well (and perhaps rather better, in
view of the paucity of legendary themes in Attic Geometric, where the ref-

erence is everyday and contemporary). Much the same scene recurs on a Spartan ivory plaque; but here again the specific interpretation remains a matter for dispute.

At this stage of undifferentiated generalization in the graphic artist's stock-in-trade there suddenly became available to him a simple but entirely effective device for dispelling ambiguity and making clear his pictorial intentions. An illuminating instance will be found on a vase sherd from the island of Aegina, dating from the last quarter of the seventh century. On this there is deftly and primly drawn a procession of unarmored men carrying spears, suggestive of military order in its strict repetition of a single type of figure. Who are these warriors only half-equipped for battle? We should have to decide that they were merely a decorative design without any specific event in mind, had not the painter added behind one of the warriors seven letters to spell the name "Menelas." Instantly the procession of stock figures is converted into a picturing of heroic incident from epic legend,—"*Menelaus führt seinem Bruder die Helden zu, die er in ganz Hellas zum Zuge gegen Troja aufgeboten hat*," one modern scholar explains the scene, using eighty-three letters in order to elucidate seven. Thus, by adding identifying names to the unindividualized types, the written word could make the limited thematic range of graphic resources cover an almost limitless subject-matter. Myth and legend, hitherto the poet's and the storyteller's privileged domain, had on the instant become the painter's picturebook.

From then on, for more than a hundred years, it was common practice for the vase-painters to label their characters. The François Vase from the mid-sixth century is covered with explanatory names (Fig. 24) and even in fifth-century red-figure work, whenever the characters were not too familiar and too well distinguished to be mistakable, the *dramatis personae* were provided with their names. To judge from Pausanias' elaborate description of the wall-paintings by Polygnotos in Delphi, the various figures were supplied with names for the benefit of those who wished to recognize the participants in the storied Sack of Troy and the denizens of the densely peopled Underworld. In the allied art of carved reliefs (which we shall discover to be glyptically materialized paintings) the figured frieze of the Siphnian Treasury at Delphi, from the last quarter of the sixth century, announced its characters' identity in letters of vivid red. But the metopes above the vestibules of the temple of Zeus at Olympia, from the second quarter of the fifth century, no longer informed the spectator who Herakles' defeated opponents were. With time, it became an instinctive matter of the artist's pride to present his scenes so intelligibly that written explanation was superfluous.

The introduction of the written label proved a two-fold source of gain.

Fig. 24 The François Vase, detail showing written names

Primarily, it enabled the painters and relief-sculptors to extend their world from the everyday present to the wider and more varied past. But in giving them this new opportunity and interest, it challenged them to differentiate their types and learn to distinguish pictorially what the written word distinguished semantically.

We do not know how this process of self-instruction was accomplished by the major artists of superior standing, who executed commissions for paintings of lifesize figures in long array on the marble walls of the sanctuaries of the gods and the colonnaded market places of men. But I suspect that we are wide of the mark in setting a query in such terms. We are ill informed when such commissions began to be given; and it is entirely possible that no such major art existed at all until the latter decades of the sixth century, when most of the crucial initial advances had already been made by painters who had no larger wall-surfaces on which to work than those diminutive walls of clay which potters turned on their wheels.

Perhaps we should believe that the art of wall-painting developed in the following sequence of events:

Painted design, having been devised for the decoration of clay vases, was naturally attached to clay as its medium. There was, of course, no compulsion that the curved surface of a vase should be the only ground so decorated. A flat plaque or tablet of dried clay might easily suggest itself as an attractive and more easily manageable substitute. In Ionia, wherever coffins were made of clay their decoration with painted designs required no great inventive imagination; the Klazomenian sarcophagi were the natural outcome. On early Doric temples, terracotta plaques (or alternatively, wooden tablets sized with potter's-white for a ground for color) could be decorated with designs from the vase-painters' repertory and inserted as metopes between the triglyphs. A transition from clay to marble may first have been made on gravemarkers, whose narrow erect shape perpetuated the proportions of the lifesize *kouroi* statues set over Attic burial mounds in monumental sculpture's earliest days. These *stelai* could either carry a painted figure on their smoothed surface or a drawn figure carved in low relief and colored. Since early reliefs were technically closely allied to paintings, it is impossible to determine whether, on these sepulchral monuments, the painted figure was the earlier device or whether (since a carved *stēlē* more closely resembled the statue which it replaced) relief was the prior form. Either way, figures lifesize or nearly so, drawn and colored on a smooth face of marble, had been evolved out of the miniature work of the potter's craft with which picture-making had begun. Thence the transference to a continuous surface such as a temple wall or a sanctuary enclosure or the backing screen of an open colonnade (or *stoa*) presented no obstacle, since it raised neither technical nor mental barrier for the painter's art.

If this reconstruction of the evolution of monumental painting in ancient Greece is substantially correct, it may be asserted that only after nearly two hundred years of preliminary practice and progress as a branch of the fictile art of decorated terracotta (in which, it is of course to be understood, the decoration of vases played an extremely important and perhaps the leading role), painting attained the status of an independent art uncontrolled by the ceramic workshops. It was now the potters' turn to follow instead of leading the way. Those who lament the irreparable loss of the great masterpieces of Greek painting should curb their sorrow for the first two centuries following the Geometric nascence of graphic art: no major works from this period have been lost to us because, most probably, none were ever painted. It is only for the fifth century that the professional student of Attic vases begins to claim dependence of the Kerameikos on the monumental painters and speaks of such things as "Polygnotan vases" or the influence of Mikon and Panainos and others of storied achievement in an art that for us, alas, is little better than a literary legend.

If there were no predecessors to these major artists, our own gain is apparent, rather than our loss. For we shall not need to make inferences from vase-painting, depressed to the status of a minor art, to some invisible paragon beyond our reach. In looking at the seventh and sixth century vases —proto-Attic, black-figure, early red-figure, proto-Corinthian, Corinthian Early, Middle, and Late, "Fikellura Ware," "Delian-Melian," Cairetan, and all the rest of the professional scholars' categories—we are surveying the

unique originals in which the early evolution of pictorial style was consum-
mated. We may therefore turn to them with confidence and with the conviction that whatever critical examination can uncover is genuine primary
evidence for Greek pictorial art.

The inactual question is sometimes raised whether pure outline drawing or solid silhouette is the prior form in graphic art. As in most discussions
which persist as unresolved argument, either position is tenable as long as
the terms of the proposition are not adequately defined. On the Dipylon
vases we have seen that the primitive artist first traced an ideally
constructed objective outline and then filled it in with black pigment to a
solid silhouette. Even if he had applied his pigment directly without first
tracing a guiding boundary-line, the profile of the areal shape must have
been present to his mind. In this immediate sense, outline inevitably pre-
cedes solid silhouette. But whether there were in the earliest Greek art outline drawings which were not filled in at all, may well be doubted, because
a diaphanous object with nothing but its contour to give it substance corresponds to nothing in our visual experience. In this restricted sense, silhouette art is the prior creation, and pure outline drawing a subsequent
refinement.

Blacked-in silhouettes make appeal to that awareness of areal shapes by
which we discriminate objects in the visual field on our retinas. But such
silhouettes are entirely inadequate counterfeits of actual visual experience,
being mere suggestions thereof, more intelligible but hardly more complete
than daylight shadows on a blank wall (more intelligible because shadows
are cast by a heedless sun uninterested in making its creations graphically
communicable).

It is not without interest that there are various ancient literary references to a primal invention of drawing through recording the shape of cast
shadows. Thus, Pliny asserts it to be commonly accepted that Greek painting originated from outlining shadows; and there is an otherwise unknown
Semon of Athens who recorded of himself that "he first discovered the cast
of painted line by smearing the shadow of a horse upon a white board."*
Such anecdotes presumably are utterly fictitious, having arisen out of the
perfectly correct observation that the earliest Greek drawings were solid
black silhouettes which resemble shadows.

If we are to interpret a silhouette at all comprehensively, we must have
some indication of the interior structure within the total shape, and this
the monochrome wash obliterates. Dipylon art did not know how to overcome this difficulty; but proto-Attic and proto-Corinthian devised a means,

*Quoted by Mary Swindler, *Ancient Painting*, p. 138, n. 32.

which sixth century black-figure refined to the utmost perfection. It was a fairly obvious and entirely logical solution.

The normal vocabulary for human physiology comprises a very considerable set of words, such as "arm" and "leg," "chest" and "elbow" and "spine," which bear witness to our power of discriminating objects within objects. Their use is an indication that we comprehend structure by perceiving distinctive parts. This is equivalent to discriminating subordinate shapes within the total shape, as when we are aware of the shape of eyes, nose, mouth, and ears within the larger structure of a human face or head. In graphic imitation there will accordingly be a delineation of interior areal shapes necessarily bounded and defined by their own contours, within the larger area of the total silhouette. Since everything for which the normal man has a spoken name corresponds to some characteristic shape or appearance in visual experience, this vocabulary will demand inclusion in his drawing. Interior line inside the total silhouette is application of contour in order to depict these nominal parts within the whole. For the artist at the Dipylon stage of his art, the technical problem was thoroughly apparent. By their uniform heavy color his solid silhouettes blotted out the interior conformation, just as a cast shadow does. If detail of inner shapes were to be inserted, the difficulty was to make it visible. A different color might have been used, superposing the pigment on the blackened ground. This was a solution actually adopted in certain workshops. At Corinth, where a very light colored clay was plentiful and the potters knew how to prepare a red, a purple, and a white pigment which would stand firing, polychrome details were rather freely added by overlaying or by substituting for black. But this was not an adequate solution of the draftsman's problem, because such altered color was appropriate only for extraneous details such as trappings and harness on horses or minor elements of costume and adornment on men and women. Where the interior shape was organic and integral, as were fingers and kneecaps, muscles and tendons, or folds in garments, a change of color was obviously untrue to appearances and might easily be ludicrous in effect. Some other solution was required which would not take refuge in added pigments.

One attempt at evading the difficulty was to refrain from filling in the silhouette in those parts where some interior detail was especially needed. Thus, a head could be left as an empty area into which an eye or other feature could be inserted. But this "reserved area" technique (as professional jargon calls it) involved a glaring illogicality. If substance and material being were imparted by filling in the contour with solid color, while the ground-tone of the clay was left around and outside it as an equivalent indication of the empty air by which the object was surrounded, then the portion of the silhouette which had been left blank in "reserve" must be no better than transparent, with the sky shining through. Before, the painted figures had been shadows. Now they threatened to become ghosts.

The final method of escape from all these quandaries was as ingenious as it was satisfactory. After filling in his silhouettes, the draftsman took in hand a sharp metal point and with it drew interior lines. By such incision he scraped away a portion of the black pigment and exposed the clay ground beneath to form a line in contrasting color of any desired sharpness and delicacy (cf. the exposition of this method in Fig. 25). He could thus

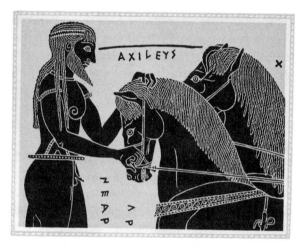

Fig. 25 Modern Drawing to Illustrate Black-figure Technique

add interior detail without any incongruence in color or appearance. The all-important result was a full control both of contour and of interior line. Equipped with these, the painters could devote themselves to the great task of learning how to draw. And the immediate outcome was the conversion of Greek graphic art from a primitive to an archaic phase.

On Dipylon vases, graphic representation consisted of horizontal bands or zones which were limited above and beneath by string-courses of abstract ornamentation but were laterally unrestricted except where protruding handles interfered with their endless continuation around the circle of the vase. This was a perpetuation of the original abstract decorative tradition before pictorial representation was introduced. As a result the earliest pictured scenes were composed as running friezes of marching or dancing men or women or of files of chariots all moving in one direction. On the two seventh-century Early Attic amphorai in New York (Fig. 26), abstract ornament has been largely superseded by pictorial design, which now not only fills the space between the tall handles, but claims more than half of the main body of the vase for its use. Abstract ornament has by no

Fig. 26 Early Attic Amphorai in New York

means been eliminated; on the contrary, it has become a carefully calculated framework to the picture and fills almost precisely the function which,
in architecture of a later day, the moulded ornament which runs above
and below a figured frieze will serve in setting-off and at the same time
enriching the pictorial design. That the same effect should be sought in
two such different media as ceramic and architectural art is a manifestation of the tectonic sense which pervades a ceramic Order as well as its
architectural counterpart. Nonetheless, it may be surprising to encounter
on a vase the structural pattern of the Ionic temple frieze so many decades
before the architects had invented it.

But the further career of Greek graphic art was allied to the Doric
rather than to the Ionic rhythm, to the metope rather than the frieze, because a picture is an isolated incident within the visual field and not part
of the general spatial setting inside of which we see it. (This is why, in our
modern world, paintings are framed and why, when their pictorial content
had great spatial depth and distance, they used to be enclosed by massive
barriers of elaborate gilt carving.) A continuous frieze is bounded only at

top and bottom, whereas a metope is a self-contained panel in total isolation from the rest of the visible field. On the sixth-century black-figure Attic vases one may watch the painters little by little abandoning frieze composition and learning to exploit the closed metope as they come to appreciate the rightness of the framed panel for pictorial presentation. The earlier François Vase (Fig. 24) is all frieze-work, with five superposed horizontal rows of moving figures. Nikosthenes can still set nymphs and satyrs to dance unendingly around the body of a vase. But heroic and mythic scenes—precisely because they concerned a restricted cast of actors in a segregated scene—are usually placed in panels and strictly framed, as on the famous Nessos Vase (Fig. 27) where Herakles (so labelled because

Fig. 27 The Nessos Vase: Neck Panel

not otherwise recognizable) slays the centaur Nessos (similarly so identified) in a closed composition so like that of the typical Doric metope that one would be tempted to suppose that it had been taken bodily from some temple façade, did one not know that at this time it was the temple façades which depended on the vase-painters for their themes.

An extremely interesting by-form of these closed panel compositions, and one which manifestly intrigued the vase-painters, was the insertion of a painted design into the circular medallion formed by the interior ground of a *kylix*. The comparatively flat surface offered a more coherent working-field without the distortion which vase exteriors inevitably occasioned in greater or less degree according to their size. But here the standard repertory of themes had to be adapted to a circle and (like the coin designs which at this same time were more and more occupying the attention of the die engravers) had to be made to conform to a novel kind of symmetry.

The *Slaying of Nessos* was shut in by vertical runs of abstract ornament reminiscent of the older days; but on Nikosthenes' amphora the revel of satyrs and nymphs was not only framed but rhythmically accompanied, above and below, by conspicuous bands of interlacing buds and tightly drawn palmettes over a base ornament of vertical spreading rays which may reproduce the sepals of an opening water-lily. A similar use of ornament may be seen in Figure 28. The spacing and the stylization of all these

Fig. 28 Black-figure Amphora with Floral Ornament

decorative elements is rigid and geometrically abstract; but the sense is animate, to the extent that floral growths are living creatures. With the shift from black-figure to red-figure technique, which ensued during Nikosthenes' active career and permitted a great advance in lifelike rendering of the figures, an interesting change overtakes the ornamental accompaniment, which also takes on a heightened animation. Palmettes still are favorite motives; and often they are still set in rigorous repetition. But more and more they are drawn in freer rhythm and connected with swinging tendrils as though they were growing naturally and not merely stenciled into place. A little later and they will swing lightly on stems which curl and spread and throw out buds on exquisite spiral stalks (Fig. 29). It is as though the painters had ascended through a hierarchy of orna-

Fig. 29 Red-figure Vase-design with palmette and tendril ornaments

ment, starting with lifeless geometric inventions and moving on to more living forms of floral inspiration, treating these at first as though they were still inanimate abstractions, but gradually winning for them the graceful and varied movement of living things. But here the hierarchy of ornament stops short without penetrating the animal world, as though the artists somehow sensed that a picture and its frame must belong to different categories of animate existence. Not until very much later Hellenistic and imperial Roman times will birds and lizards and other small beasts invade the leafy growth of pilaster panels and disport themselves amid the twining *rinceaux* of the builders' frieze, to become, after many intervening centuries, the delight of the master carvers of the European Renaissance. For the moment, on fifth century Attic vases, the enclosing ornament of curling tendril and nodding bud and swinging palmette was more than merely sufficient. Indeed, these may perhaps be rated as the most truly original, as they are among the most beautiful, imaginings of the Greek artistic brain.

The heavy blocked-in silhouette enlivened with incised interior lines prevailed as the accepted graphic method long enough to proliferate an astonishing number of "black-figure" vases. In all of these, by technical compulsion, the silhouetted form is of primary import; and within it, except for occasional supplementation with patches of a few limited colors, there is only incised line to define further detail. If the Dipylon figures were vague shadows, these are shadows made intelligible; but they remain shadow-folk without thickness or substance. They have gained greatly in correctness of outline; and their interior structure may be very elaborately explored. A clothed figure is apt to cast a less intelligible outline for its shadow than a nude form rightly posed. But this was no handicap for the black-figure draftsman because, in daily custom, costume was enriched with woven designs and embroidered decorations; and these provided intricate linear patterns, as though expressly invented for transference to the surface of a vase. In consequence, costume and (to a slightly less extent) armor and other accoutrement became black-figure's favorite topics, responsible for the incomparable sumptuousness of detail which, for example, Exekias achieved in his famous version of *Ajax and Achilles playing draughts.*

All this marks an entirely explicable and wholly normal (perhaps inevitable) phase in the evolution of pictorial style. As such, it was not an Attic monopoly nor any particular workshop's secret, but a universal Greek accomplishment, subject to only minor variation where a polychromatic variety was prized above the rather more intellectual concentration on line alone. But although black-figure ware is ascribable to many other centers in the Greek-speaking world, there were no workshops (unless time's careless chances have misled us) capable of producing anything on the Attic level of taste and skill.

The history of Attic black-figure has been written more than once, most competently and most illuminatingly (most would agree) by Sir John Beazley. The present survey, having no leisure for cataloguing, sorting, and describing, cannot digress to consider schools or workshops or individual masters, nor linger over variations of manner or abnormalities of style. Our task is to discover how graphic art evolved in Greece as the complex organization of individual talents and local traditions combined to achieve mastery over a technique of graphic mimicry of the visual world.

Whatever the workshop from which it comes, and whoever the artisan whose hand created it, black-figure drawing (which is to say, blacked-in silhouette supplemented by incised interior line) must always lack the imprint of reality. In black-figure paintings we contemplate an array of intelligibly animated shapes equipped with enough of the visual properties of the objects which they suggest to be accepted by us as meaningful. But they stand to properly constructed pictures much as the marionettes of a puppet-show stand to flesh-and-blood actors on a stage. We accept them for what they intend to be, but only because we ourselves are willing to make the pretense of believing in them. Therein, I am persuaded, lies a good deal of the charm of black-figure vases. We find pleasure in playing their game of pretense, for which they have worked out the rules and supplied the gaming-board and the counters, with the only stake being our own esthetic enjoyment.

It is easy enough to put our critical fingers on the pictorial inadequacies of such a style. We do not naturally and normally see the external world as a picture, despite the certain fact that it is only a picture of this world that ever reaches us. This picture, cast as an image on our retinas, is—as has been previously pointed out—an astonishingly ingenious structure, in which the ins-and-outs and spatial ordering of material objects in the physical world, beaming to us the focussed reflection of their illuminated surfaces, record themselves as gradient optical conversions from a tridimensional actuality. Intelligent sight is the interpretative perception of these pictorial gradients, which exist only in the retinal image and are not materially present elsewhere. Through them we behold solid configuration and spatial extension. But black-figure leaves them all out. There are no gradations of luminosity in its uniform black pigment, nor yet gradations of hue; no gradations of texture in its even spread, no geometrical gradations of diminishing size or dwindling patterns or boundaries converging with distance. All the pictorial functions which bring us awareness of solid objects in spatial protrusion and recession fail to be recorded, leaving black-figure a flatland of unsubstantial surface-shapes.

As pictorial art matures toward more adequate reproduction of visual experience, the painter's task in mastering technical resources to help him toward this goal consists almost entirely in discovering these optical gradients and learning how to include them in his work. He must do so, because our perception of the world into which we are born and in which we live relies on them: were it not for them, we should seem "to move among shadows a shadow," among objects whose outlines we could see, but whose substance we could learn only by bodily collision and tactile exploration. It is precisely such a world that black-figure shows us; and since we do not have to deal pragmatically and effectively with that world, but only look at it, we enjoy its novelty and find it an enduringly pleasant world to visit.

VII

SCULPTURE IN RELIEF

All archaic sculpture involves a fusion of glyptic with graphic form. It is this simultaneous appeal to two generically distinct levels of visual perception which imparts to the archaic manner its distinctive quality. It also makes possible a third kind of visual art, intermediary between painting and sculpture and dependent upon both. I refer to sculpture in relief, which like a painting is set upon a fixed panel, yet has been given a modicum of sculptural reality by carving.

As long as Greek sculpture persisted in its archaic phase, the most significant formal difference between relief and free-standing statuary was not its attachment to a panel, but its treatment of the dimension of depth. The presence of a background to which the figures are attached is crucial for the spectator in that it prevents him from scrutinizing the work from any but a frontal point of view. But this was not so paramount a consideration for the sculptor, who applied much the same outline drawing for his work whether he intended to cut a relief or a free-standing statue. The enveloping panel served to isolate his design from its material environment, but otherwise made no more significant contribution of an artistic nature than background and frame might add to a painting. For the archaic craftsman the chief consideration in carving relief was not the difference in compositional design, but the treatment of the material dimension of depth.

For the statue carved in-the-round, conformation in depth is integral and essential to sculptural status, since it is its solid configuration which gives it entry into our objective visual world. In archaic relief, on the other hand, extension in depth is physically inactual, being greatly abbreviated and arbitrarily converted to a specific function. This function is to make visually intelligible the spatial recession which unforeshortened graphic representation is incapable of depicting. Archaic relief seeks to overcome the spatial vacuity of archaic draftsmanship by introducing an orderly succession of plane surfaces staggered in depth.

The technical evolution of archaic relief shows an entirely consistent development. The initial phase, in which relief was differentiated from painting and became something else than a colored drawing on a stone

119

panel, was nothing more abstruse or ambitious than the glyptic isolation of the linear design from the medium on which it was drawn. This was achieved by cutting back the panel around the design to give the pictured theme salience above the supporting ground. The artist's concern was not with the ground, but with the representation. The enclosing panel was colored a brilliant hue and therewith became as irrelevant to the subject matter of the graphic design as a cloudless sky is to objects seen outlined against it. The discrepancy in distance between the background and the figured representation raised above it had no other significance. If two "planes of composition" resulted, this was due to the technical accident that the working-levels in such a relief were both smoothed surfaces.

The ensuing formal development of archaic relief was similarly derived from normal visual experience. In order to gain understanding of what comes to our eyes, we organize any and every visual field into discrete areas of significant shape (which we identify as "things") and discriminate their interior structure by the same analytic and synthetic process. It was therefore perfectly natural for the relief sculptor, after he had detached his design from its surrounding by cutting along its outline, to proceed to treat its interior content in similar fashion. The recourse to trimming back the stone, which had been applied to the design as a whole, was now re-employed to differentiate the nearer from the farther elements within its pictured content in order to confer a suggestion of material actuality on that which painting presented only optically.

Early gravestones from the neighborhood of Sparta frequently depict the deceased seated with his wife upon a high-backed chair, in profile drawing. The composition may include further details, but the entire design remains a line drawing which has been converted into relief by cutting back its component contours to produce a steplike recession of detail shapes in proper spatial sequence. In the well-known relief from Chrysapha (Fig. 30), now in Berlin, the original surface of the slab on which the design was drawn survives in the frame of the chair and the hither hand, arm, and shoulder, together with much of the flatly frontal face, of the seated man. The remaining sectors of his silhouetted form have been stepped back into the stone without any attempt to round or model them. All that has been done is to move the original surface of the panel inward in successive stages without altering its level expanse. A slight step into the stone has set the further arm beyond the body, still another step has detached the partial silhouette of the woman behind that of the man (who largely conceals her from view), while a final cutting-back of the panel has set the sharply outlined but smoothly flat head and outstretched arm of the woman in projection above the empty (but once colored) ground around her.

Fig. 30 Grave-relief from Chrysapha

In the far more subtly executed grave-relief of Aristion (Fig. 31),
carved by an Athenian artist who signs himself Aristokles, the principle of
orderly spatial recession in depth has been more extensively applied, in
agreement with a more accurately optical interpretation of solid structure.
In contrast to the Chrysapha relief, wherein subsidiary detail such as the
drapery folds is rendered merely by grooved incision of the surface, on the
relief of Aristion the various areas situated within the stepped-back contours have been gently modulated to suggest a solid conformation. Since
only a very shallow depth of stone was available to the sculptor, if he was
to avoid cutting interior detail deeper into the stone than the overall shape
to which it pertained, this modelling of the surface had to be extremely
restrained. But it was necessary to introduce it because the spatial staircase
of flat treads which earlier reliefs displayed did violence to natural truth of
appearance. In this manner the abrupt gradations characteristic of the first

Fig. 31 Relief of Aristion

attempts at converting graphic design into glyptic form were softened and a more correctly modulated solid shape was given visual suggestion.

It is sometimes intimated that late archaic reliefs, such as that of Aristion, evidence an extraordinary power of rational analysis on the part of the artist, who has been able to reinterpret the spatial continuum of solid mass as an inactual but wholly logical (and hence convincing) sequence of parallel planes compressed within the two major planes of a figured foreground and a uniformly colored background. Such a description of the finished work may be correct, but the imputation of a profound gift for abstruse geometrical manipulation in the stone-cutter is wide of the mark; it overlooks the simple optical fact that the seeing mind makes precisely the same distinctions as these sculptors do, by using intelligible areal shapes as a guide to objective perception. An archaic relief merely re-enacts this habitual behavior by presenting to our inspection the visual analysis as already performed. The archaic artist has accomplished this feat so consummately well because he has merely been reproducing his own visual experience. He was not indulging in geometrical or other logical reasoning nor departing in any way from his basic ambition to reproduce as best he could the real world around him. He was, however, restricted to an archaic manner, because archaism is not a wilful state of mind but an inescapable necessity in the early development of art.

There is a further misunderstanding of the nature of Greek sculptural relief, according to which it is conceived as a *pro rata* diminution of the dimension of depth relatively to the two other fully expanded dimensions of width and height. This is to claim that Greek relief discriminates foreshortening correctly and records its abbreviations exactly as they appear in the retinal image. Such a prescription is certainly untrue of archaic procedure, which does not make so sophisticated an interpretation of pictorial appearance. Recession in depth takes place only at the contours, being a survival of the primitive stepping-back in stages.

It is, however, true that archaic relief mediates between graphic representation and sculptural imitation. It succeeds in so doing because human vision always operates at both the level of pictorial projection (which reaches it in the retinal image) and of stereometric apprehension (which belongs to intelligent perception). By not indulging in esthetic theory but following optical guidance directly, archaic sculptors working in relief were able to fuse appropriately both levels of visual experience and happily escape disaster in either.

In archaic relief the true physical dimension of depth is not taken into consideration. The reconstitution of spatial recession as a sequence of overlapping plane areas produces a series of superimposed pictorial projections, each of which stands out as a plateau raised above its successor. Where

monumental sculpture in-the-round aims to present its subject in entire
solidity, relief in its initial phase of development deals in an analytically
arbitrary abbreviation of the dimension of depth; it contents itself with a
token deployment in space by distributing its thematic material in correct
sequence with each distinguishable part appropriately placed in front or
behind its next adjoining neighbor.

So phrased, such a procedure may sound strangely abstruse and even
unreasonable. But it is the outcome of the simple method by which relief
was evolved out of flat-color drawing. Not only in Greece but in other lands
and at other times, relief may be seen to have owed its origin to the prior
practice of painted design. Thus, in Egyptian tombs of the Old Kingdom,
such as those at Saqqara from the fifth and sixth dynasties, there is graphically no discoverable distinction between a scene executed wholly in paint
upon the plastered wall and one that has been chisel-cut in relief with color
applied thereto. Presumably, Egyptian recourse to carving was due to the
fear that pigment would fade with time and the magic representation cease
to operate, to the detriment of the soul's continued enjoyment of after-life.
By incising the contours and thereby giving material subsistence to the
colored shapes, the durability of stone was substituted for the transiency of
paint. But Egyptian statues in-the-round from this period are formally unrelated to these reliefs. The genetic bond with painting is therefore certain.

Much the same observation applies to early Greek art, as in the bronze
repoussé relief (Fig. 32). The archaic temple metopes and pedimental reliefs from the period before free-standing statuary was introduced into the
gables are glyptically reinforced line-drawings, the thematic material for
which may be found on contemporary vases. In contrast, the earliest sculpture in-the-round with its extremely restricted repertory shows no appreciable connection either with the vase-paintings or the carved metopes or
pediments of the period. Since the genesis of graphic design was older than
the introduction of monumental sculpture in Greece by somewhat more
than a century, the practice of relief carving may well have preceded sculpture in-the-round by a considerable margin of years. Precisely how great
this margin was has proved difficult to ascertain, but whatever it may have
been, the connection between painted design and carved relief remained
unchallenged and undiminished throughout the sixth century. Thereafter,
with the conversion of the archaic into a formal classic style, the direction
of mutual influence between the arts underwent a reversal. As relief became more and more permeated with statuary form, even painting came to
draw inspiration from sculpture. This is already thoroughly apparent in the
"Polygnotan" vases, and there are other slightly later fifth-century vases
(among them, white-ground lekythoi) which vividly reflect the Parthenon's
sculptural manner.

Fig. 32 Repoussé Bronze Relief

It will be readily perceived that, as sculpture attains to more adequate reproduction of the spatial structure of the physical objects which it imitates, the three arts cannot continue in close alliance but must ultimately part company. Graphic art remains wedded to panel-space and the pictorial conversions of retinal images, sculpture in-the-round will recreate solid shapes set apart in exterior visual space, and relief must choose with which of the two it will consort. In Renaissance Italy, some two thousand years after the period we are studying, relief may be seen clinging to the painter's world of pictorial conversions. There are many works—such as the cast bronze altar plaques by Donatello in the church of Sant' Antonio in Padua—where purely pictorial compositions with gradients of depth and distance have been given rudimentary plastic interpretation, with the result that they are little more than paintings cast in metal or carved in stone with most of their proper pictorial adjuncts of gradient color and light and atmospheric envelopment omitted. In diametric opposition to such diversion toward the painter's visual realm, maturely evolved Greek reliefs show an equally close attraction to monumental sculptural form, becoming at times hardly distinguishable from sculpture in the *half-round* (or even three-quarter-round!) displayed against a background wall. Ultimately, as in the gigantomachy reliefs on the socle of the great altar of Zeus at Pergamon, the sculptors went so far in undercutting and rounding the contours of the figures as to give at times the appearance of entire release from the ground in front of which they seemed to move.

In Greek relief there are signs of early alienation from the parent art from which it took its origin. The shift in allegiance may have been partly due to the glyptic nature of carved relief, which necessarily brought it into the stonecutter's workshop and made it a branch of his craft. But the instinctive Greek inclination toward the sculptural rather than the pictorial mode of representation must have been an equally potent factor. In the metopes from the vestibules of the Zeus temple at Olympia, from about the year 460, the attraction toward free-standing sculptural form was so great that it may be said that relief had already shifted allegiance from pictorial to sculptural art.

However, the more pictorial mode of low relief, because it was appropriate to less strongly illuminated positions such as temple interiors, continued to be produced; and in this the enforced diminution of plastic depth kept the execution more closely dependent on graphic design. Thus, the "Phigaleia frieze" in the British Museum, which once adorned the dimly lighted inner room of Apollo's temple in Arcadian Bassai, in thematic material and visual effect stands in closer relationship to contemporary wall-painting than to monumental sculpture in-the-round.

There were other equally cogent reasons why relief could not afford too drastically to sever its connections with pictorial art. The vase-painters' graphic repertory of human and animal motifs had expanded mightily since Geometric beginnings, while monumental sculpture was still confined to a bare handful of acquired themes. And there was nothing which a vase-painter could draw that a relief-sculptor could not reproduce if he chose to do so. Apart from themes that may have been appropriate for a grave *stēlē*, there were numerous other commissions for relief work, such as the carved metopes for Doric temples; and for these the vase-paintings could supply wellnigh inexhaustible subject-matter requiring only slight compositional adjustment to a rectangular field in order to be admirably suited to adorn a temple where they had once decorated the rounded body of a vase.

The alliance with pictorial design, which stimulated the repertory of relief, was destined to be turned to even greater profit by the major art of sculpture in-the-round. Many of the animated poses of the vase-painters, which lent themselves to adoption in relief, and were there worked into glyptic form, proved to be susceptible to further transmission, to become incorporated in the repertory of free-standing statuary. The only immediate obstacle to such a process of transmission was a material one: as long as statues were produced by reduction of a solid block, it was not practically possible to release from such a block the freely moving arms and legs which the painters drew. Painted figures needed no support to keep them in balance, whereas a marble figure must hold its position by close conformity to the laws of gravity. In this regard, relief carving clearly profited by its close resemblance to colored drawing. Its figures, being an integral part of the rigid panel on which they were cut, needed no ground beneath their feet or other aid to keep them from falling. By following the painter's lead, relief could easily outstrip the more laborious and plodding progress of the sculptor working in the round. Herein lies the technical explanation of the early continued dependence of relief design on painting. The statuary sculptor's problem was to keep pace with these freer forms of art and draw benefit from their lead.

That graphic art evolves at a much faster rate than sculpture should not be a matter for surprise or argument. Its speed of production is many times greater because its expenditure of time and energy is so much smaller and its material obstacles are incomparably less formidable. Here again, relief occupies an intermediate position. Although its designs take very considerably longer time to carve than the same design would require to be outlined and colored on a clay plaque or a whitened panel, they occasion far less delay than would their execution as fully detached solid figures. And relief, if it borrows its themes from painting, is not held back by any technical delay, but can keep pace with its sister art as long as that art does not too extensively explore the pictorial realm from which all sculptural presentation is by its own essential nature excluded. Although making much slower progress, sculpture in-the-round will in time reach a stage of development where it has much of value to offer to relief—perhaps at much the same period that painting, by penetrating deeper into its own proper pictorial domain, has ceased to exert any further stimulus. But until this more evolved state has been reached, relief design, with all the freedom of painting's incorporeal evocation of visual appearances converted into pseudo-sculptural equivalents of contoured mass and spatial recession, holds out to the sculptor working in-the-round a tantalizing glimpse of animated themes and energetic poses which he would gladly imitate but cannot. Technical barriers seemed to make this accomplishment impossible. Unless these barriers could somehow be circumvented, they restricted borrowing from pictorial design through the mediation of carved relief to nothing more active or more novel than the closely self-contained figures at rest to which monumental sculpture had long been devoted.

The invention of a process for hollow-casting statues in bronze lifted the technical barrier.

VIII

ATTIC RED-FIGURE

The shift from black-figure to red-figure technique, which was due (it seems) to the initiative of Attic potters, is very generally taken as a landmark in the history of Greek vase-painting. And so without doubt it is, if only because it affords an extremely convenient and quite unmistakeable criterion for descriptive classification. But is is not so indisputable that it marked any clear-cut cleavage between past and future in the minds of the painters who introduced the new method. For us, looking back, the change to red-figure denotes the end of archaism, which might otherwise have endured indefinitely and been perpetuated in dreary academicism. The poor artistic quality of most of the black-figure ware as it continued to be produced through the fifth century—and even much longer on the Panathenaic vases, for which the older technique was a traditional requirement —fully confirms this unfavorable prognosis. Yet is is not apparent that any epochal new ideas for graphic art attended on the invention of the red-figure technique; the painters who first practised it show little sign of having grasped its artistic possibilities or having in any way anticipated its future career. Indeed, it is not entirely evident why the new manner was introduced at all.

Technically considered, it is of course entirely clear what had happened. After tracing the outlines of his figures as before, the painter now used his black pigment to fill in the ground *outside*, instead of inside, the contours. It was now the background which had turned to shadow, while the figures had taken on the lighter color of the red fabric of the vase. As an immediate consequence, the interior lines no longer had to be incised with a pointed tool (which conferred on them no heightened visibility), but could be painted in with the brush, to stand out vividly within the red-bodied silhouette.

All this needs only to be seen to be instantly understood (compare Fig. 25 with Fig. 29). But we cannot quite so immediately perceive what ulterior purpose was served by thus inverting the traditional procedure. Where graphic art was entirely a matter of line, whether for contour or for interior detail, a line laid down in paint seems hardly different from one recorded by incision. It cannot be objected that a brush-stroke is more flexible and hence more accurately depictive than the groove which a graving-tool can cut, because there is no lack of flexibility or accuracy in black-figure incision. And the earliest red-figure productions, such as the so-called "bilingual" vases from Andokides' workshop, show no discernible difference between a painted line and an engraved one, inasmuch as the painter of these interesting exhibition-pieces confined himself rather punctiliously to repeating the same scene on the two faces of his vase, one in black-figure and again in the new red-figure process. No doubt, he was convinced of the superiority of the new manner or he would scarcely have so openly challenged his public to compare the two, but he gives no indication that he understood that the change in technical execution was in any way tantamount to the emergence of a really new style or heralded any drastic difference in the comprehension of graphic form.

I believe that the compelling motive for the change is to be found in an instinctive response to color value. We naturally associate black with the obscurity of darkness, and color with the revealing clarity of light. And in these vase designs, which made no attempt to include any material environment or spatial setting, but set their figures against a blank ground that had no visible content or meaning, it was more appropriate that this empty background should be dark and that the figures should cease to be shadows and acquire the substance on which illumined color attends. It was not that red bodies were truer to natural appearances than black bodies, or red garments more like dyed woolen cloaks than black ones: this would be interpreting the case too literally. It was not the particular hue which counted, but the fact that the delineated shapes had color at all, which was significant. Instead of being dense shadows moving across a screen of light, they now were positive light-illuminated shapes before a negative unilluminated curtain (Fig. 33).

A further and closely related gain was the heightened emphasis which the use of black imparted to the interior lines defining bodily structure. The efficacy of line in its function of presenting material shape was increased by the sharpness with which it stood out in black from the lighter ground. It is no mere metaphor to say that with the changed assignment of the two colors, the clay-red of the vase and the carbon-black of the pigment, the erstwhile shadows suspended on a sunlit wall had ceased to be shadows and had stepped down to stand out as living beings.

The findings of the experimenters in *Gestalt*-pyschology have demonstrated that linear form is largely a contribution of the seer and is not physically present in the seen. But it would be wrong to claim that on this account linear form is unreal. It corresponds consistently and very exactly to

Fig. 33 Red-figure Vase Showing Linear Design

the material configuration of solid objects, even while it is materially inactual in a twofold sense in that, ideally, line is a geometric abstraction from solid substance, and physically, the mosaic of minute patches of colored light which gathers on the retina is not a linear construct but an areal agglomerate. It follows that, literally defined, line exists neither in the visual world nor in the visual field. It is, then, a noetic form contributed by the perceptive mind and by it transferred to art as an essential device for graphic presentation.

In red-figure drawing, line is so largely responsible for mimetic appearances and so little supported or supplemented by any other pictorial factor in vision, that we may say (in accord with our definition of linear form as a mental construct) that red-figure drawing is an intellectualized reconstruction of reality. As such, it was peculiarly appropriate to the highly intellectualized fifth-century Attic mind.

Yet black-figure had also been a linear production, which seemed to place every whit as great reliance on line as red-figure does. Notwithstanding, black-figure line and red-figure line are utterly different in their effect. If we are to understand how Greek graphic art was evolving, we must find some way to formulate this difference and, having described it, must seek a rational explanation for it.

In black-figure work the heavy-toned areal shape (directly descended from the Dipylon solid silhouette) was still the principle element of atten-

tion; and incised interior line, originally introduced to explain the subject-matter represented by a contoured shape, although still used for that
purpose, remained subordinate to the heavily solid black form, being only
its complement for endowing it with intelligible detail. This depression of
interior line to ancillary rank was responsible for its diversion to decorative
enrichment. But with the shift to red-figure drawing, interior line moved
to the fore and disputed with contour outline the primacy in meaningful
depiction of the figured theme. Concentrating on this function, the draftsman's interest was diverted from the decorative to the pictorial significance
of line. Thereby he came to appreciate the axiom that the human figure,
however correctly established by its outline, cannot become fully intelligible until interior line has revealed its structural complexity.

The substitution of depictive interior line for overall solid silhouette
with interior incision had far more important consequences than the in-
novators in this technique could possibly have foreseen. Esthetic theorists,
anxious to exercise their philosophic vocabulary, might explain the situation by pointing out that the adoption of the red-figure technique by the
Attic vase-painters enabled them to explore the "depictive potential" of
graphic line. It would be much simpler (and just as correct) to say that it
gave them the opportunity of teaching themselves how to draw.

Once interior line had been devoted to making formal structure intelligible, it was inevitable that the draftsman should discover that interior
shapes did not necessarily or even normally present themselves in frontal
outline. I mean—and the example will make the general proposition clear
—that the human eye as it appears in a face viewed in profile does not itself
appear in undisturbed and complete frontal shape. Earlier vase-painters
had drawn the human eye as an almond-shaped oval enclosing two concentric circles (which they quite justifiably took to be its characteristic
shape) and persisted in so representing it on all occasions, whether in a
full-front or a profile drawing of the human head. (We have already remarked that primitive drawing thus proceeds with typical outline shapes
which it introduces unaltered wherever it has need of them). It is hardly
remarkable that it should have struck the artists, and presumably also their
public, that in actual visual experience an entire eye does not thus present
itself in any profile view of a face: what is much more remarkable is the
span of time which generally elapses before artists decide that something
should be done about this way of drawing it. In sixth century Greece it was
a very protracted process of gradual correction which transformed the
closed-contour eye of the proto-Attic and early black figure period (as in
Fig. 25) into the open eye in a profile face, perhaps first fully achieved by
Sosias and thereafter destined quickly to become a commonplace in the
potter's art.

However, this is only a particularly glaring instance in a much more general situation, since it is naturally true of almost every object of stereometric configuration that it never presents a simple aspect in which all of its parts exhibit themselves in unforeshortened silhouette. To depict any object correctly as it is presented to visual experience is to register its foreshortenings in the particular aspect which the contour sets. However, the fact that normal vision does not apprehend foreshortening as an alteration of objective shape (we are aware that the object itself undergoes no deformation when we shift our point of view!), but sees it in terms of spatial orientation and extension in depth, acts as a very real obstacle to the inexperienced artist. Even today, with all our familiarity with photographic illustration and realistic graphic art, those of us who cannot "fixate" our visual field as a flat projection against an imaginary screen but see it pragmatically as a world in depth, discover that we have no talent for drawing.

It was the heightened attention to the "depictive potential" of line, attendant on the introduction of the red-figure technique, that led to a mastery over foreshortening by Attic artists at this stage. Lest it should be objected that foreshortening already occurs occasionally in black-figure drawings, it should be noted that a horse drawn fullfront is not *eo ipso* a horse foreshortened; nor does the simultaneous appearance of fullfront and profile aspects within one and the same representation of an object involve this graphic device. Only where aspects in intermediate location between cardinal profiles (the so-called "three-quarter" views) are recorded by altering the contour to conform with the conversions of the visual field—only then is it admissible to apply the term "foreshortened."

It should be taken into account that every foreshortened outline specifically contradicts the typical contour which the archaic draftsman has learned to draw. He must therefore unlearn what he has been habituated to do and, instead, must acquire a new set of formulas, accepting these as abnormalities incident to the changes which schematic form suffers in visual appearance. The accurate reproduction of these graphic deformations denotes a violent intrusion of objective fact upon noetic concept. It should not be surprising that its introduction marks a turning-point in the formal evolution of pictorial art, symptomatic of the dissolution of its archaic phase.

In black-figure design the compositional pattern depends very directly on the silhouetted shapes. These may be disposed in various arrangements and combinations and differ from one another in their elaboration of incised detail. But the areal shapes themselves, being standard in the graphic repertory, do not admit much variation. A horse or an ox or a chariot will always be much the same horse or ox or car, and even human beings in all their different attitudes and occupations will add only a few items to the stock of available shapes. In consequence there tends to be a fixedly unelastic relation between the graphic formula and the pattern which it contributes.

Not that black-figure compositions never show any imaginative invention. The uniquely lovely medallion which Exekias composed, with Dionysos in his vine-clustered ship accompanied by playful dolphins, proves that an ingenious mind could make new combinations from traditional material; but the observation still holds good that, even so, each element must keep to a rigidly established outline: one dolphin is like another, a vineleaf is always the same as the rest, and the pendant clusters of grapes are all much alike; ship and passenger are full profiles, and every detail of construction and rigging may be found unaltered on other vases. The elements out of which the pattern has been put together are therefore inflexible.

No such limitation exists where shapes may be foreshortened to yield a different run of contour and a new overall areal shape. These hitherto unavailable variations from the static norm permit the creation of innumerable new patterns of compositional design. Red-figure drawing thus not merely opened up a new domain of graphic representation through foreshortened appearances, but introduced the artists to an entirely new world of suggestive patterns.

It must be admitted, however, that the Attic vase-painters do not seem to have made the most of their new opportunity in this regard. Initially, the shifting contours and novel silhouettes of foreshortened appearances exercised comparatively little effect on red-figure composition because the painters did not consciously employ foreshortening to create pattern, but to improve their rendering of the living form. Their ambition was to draw things as they looked in physical reality. For this reason the chief significance of the introduction of foreshortening into their work was the emergence of spatial depth to endow their themes with more material substance.

Because foreshortening is perceived as spatial extension in depth, its introduction into Greek art marked the penetration of the hitherto impenetrable dimension which leads behind and beyond the painted surface of a picture. In technical terms, foreshortening acts to convert into a visual world of depth and distance the depthless visual field to which the noetic forms of archaic art are fettered. But because in red-figure vase-painting there was no attempt to include an objective setting to create a total visual scene or "landscape," the figures on the red-figure vases succeed in becoming corporeal and yet remain suspended as though on a shallow stage in front of a dense curtain shutting out all deeper distance.

Every foreshortened outline has a dual nature and, artistically, fills a twofold function. Considered as the linear trace upon the panel, it attaches to panel-space and participates in compositional pattern (all visible pattern being a matter of plane geometry). At the same moment, taken as an element contributing to objective representation, it occasions its own optical conversion to a wholly different outline, which defines a tridimensional structure and is seen as the trace of a solid shape. These twin values of any given contour, as it exists two-dimensionally and as it is apprehended three-dimensionally, are categorically as different, one from the other, as in human speech sound is different from sense. It follows, therefore, that in the painter's art a foreshortened contour-line exists at one and the same moment both in panel-space, where it participates in the compositional pattern, and in pictorial-space, where it contributes to the perception of solid depth and aerial distance. Composition and patternized design in representational painting have artistic significance and esthetic value not so much because they constitute a superficial symmetry of arrangement as because their ordered pattern attaches itself to an otherwise unpatternized gathering of solid objects.

All this was sufficiently apparent to exercise an appreciable effect on the Greek vase-painters. And yet, until they acquired a more extensive understanding of the mechanism of pictorial "illusion" (as we are in the habit of calling the construction of an artificial visual field which the eye can accept as intelligible) and as long as they confined themselves to that limited inducement of spatial perception which is occasioned by foreshortened contour drawing of isolated objects at uniform scale, the artists' ability to create pictorial-space was not very great. Because red-figure painting relied upon line alone, without use of the other pictorial devices for presenting density and depth, such as graduated illumination and geometric gradients of texture and retreating surface and atmospheric envelopment, it exaggerated one element in visual perception by eliminating most of the others. By so doing, red-figure design presents us with a visual world without depth and with no objective content other than an array of animated human and animal performers moving along a shallow corridor in front of an abrupt empty darkness.

This is art of high quality with marvellous tension and great sensitivity, but it is technically an immature art, characteristic of a stage which cannot endure the criticism which every mimetic art must expect to meet—the criticism which results from comparing art with reality—and yet has not learned how to overcome this objection.

The Attic vase-painters were not all equally quick to grasp the opportunities implicit in the new technique. Andokides, who championed the change in what must have seemed to him a persuasive demonstra-

tion of its merits on his "bilingual" vases, often did little else than add
with his brush the same intricate embroidery of ornamental detail which,
in his younger days, he had been wont to scratch with his graver. Epik-
tetos can be singularly charming, but the charm usually emanates from
his preference for the elegance of silhouette over the substance of more
fully suggested bodily forms. Phintias grasps what red-figure drawing
can do, but unfortunately has little knack for drawing. Euthymides and
the Kleophrades Painter have felt the spell of the sculptors' monumental
figures and experiment at making their diminutive nudes look as though
they were lifesize statues more active and more freely posed than stone-
cutters could attempt. The Panaitios Master (Fig. 34) reminds me

Fig. 34 Kylix Medallion by Panaitios

vaguely of Hokusai because he seems to care for nothing in the world so
much as for drawing. Euphronios is ambitious with his themes and,
though he is probably no unusually gifted draftsman, has great feeling
for pattern and understands how to set a scene. With Douris and Brygos
red-figure is reaching the height of its potential capacities, which Makron
is already beginning to abuse. There is still talent aplenty—the Berlin
Painter, the Pan Painter, and the Achilles Painter are leading favorites
di loro che sanno—but the first eagerness begins to slacken, since to draw

animated figures correctly is now no novelty but every painter's privilege. In Meidias, toward the fifth century's close, we encounter the final exploitation of a graphic method which has little more of untried value to offer.

We know that the painter's art did not cease to evolve further at this period, even though the South Italian afterbloom of Attic vase-design seems poorly to reflect its major attainments. During the seventh and sixth centuries it was the vase-designers who had the art of painting in their keeping and explored the paths of graphic mimicry. In the fifth century the leadership reverted from the potter's quarter to the colonnaded market-places and the temple enclosures, where professional painters, who probably would have scorned to decorate a pot, produced figures on a much larger scale for an art almost as monumental as that of statuary. We are persuaded that the fifth century vase-painters were greatly influenced by these superior colleagues; we speak of "Polygnotan vases," and look for imitations of other masters such as Mikon and Panainos, even though their names are better known to us than any work they may have done. But in the fourth century it would seem that "easel-painting" and vase-painting had parted company and the latter had dropped away, to shrivel and to die. There would soon be no more even reasonably well-painted vases, and after that no painted vases at all, except for a few perfunctory survivals such as Panathenaic ware, traditionally prescribed for an equally traditional event.

The demise of the vase-painter's art—which had been no minor achievement, no negligible commercial product, but a true art in its own right—was inevitable, precisely because it was not content to be a purely utilitarian production and could not forget that it had been the first to create graphic art and for two hundred years had led the way in its development and had marketed its masterpieces over most of the Mediterranean and the Black Sea, to be prized and placed as worthy offerings in the graves of Scythians and Etruscans and lesser breeds without the Hellenic law. But restricted as it was to the overly sharply curving clay panels of a commercial product and to the potter's pigments and the chance texture of high-temperature glazing, it could no longer keep pace with an emancipated art which had a richer palette of colors, a subtler spreading and shading of pigment, a monumental scale of representation, and an interest in spatial depth and solidity completely inappropriate to a decorative craft. Unable to produce paintings of the kind and quality and technical caliber which had come to be expected of pictorial art in its maturer phases, it lost status and ceased to be valued or produced.

IX

CREATION OF THE CLASSIC FORMAL
STYLE IN SCULPTURE

The exterior of the human body owes its appearance to its internal structure, which articulates the surface by conforming the elastic covering of skin to the outward pressure of muscle, tendon, and fat. And because all living energy emanates from within, every visible indication of vitality must be due to interior activity. The archaic sculptor who sank anatomical patterns as linear depressions into the block was therefore proceeding in a diametrically contrary fashion to physical reality by imposing these forms intrusively from without instead of imitating the extrusive solidity of shapes created from within. A drastic technical inversion of detail indication was needed, not unlike that from black-figure to red-figure design in vase-painting and strictly parallel to the shift from negative to positive drapery forms which, as we shall see, marked the change from archaic to classic in the representation of costume.

Such a change in emphasis from incised linear pattern, penetrating the surface of the stone from without, to undulant modulation of that surface to present bodily structure from within, is a most significant stylistic symptom in the anatomy of the *kouros*, heralding the advance out of archaism in the early decades of the fifth century.

There was also another and equally essential innovation for vitalizing the nude which the archaic masters had failed to appreciate. Before the inert marble image could offer any convincing semblance of organic life, it must cease to be a dead weight of upended stone and, instead, seem to be animate by manifesting, as though from within itself, visible evidence of the power to stand erect and move about. The formal device which could make this vivifying property apparent was the introduction of what may be termed a pose of "living balance" to replace the lifeless stance of the Egyptianizing tradition.

For the human biped precariously supported upon some sixty square inches of contact with the ground, all moving-about is not merely a shifting of weight from one leg to the other, but a complex muscular adjustment to keep the poised body erect. Even standing still is an overt act of motion, a thwarting of the sleepless pull of earthward gravity by responsive sway through appropriate tension and relaxation. That this is not an inaccurate description should be apparent to anyone who watches a human infant or a fully mature animal such as a bear or dog attempting to keep itself erect on two feet. If the normal adult is unaware of the exacting demands of this everyday performance, this is no proof that its physical intricacy has been lessened. Sculptural presentation, even though it may be imagined to be dealing in superficial appearances only and not be directly concerned with interior mechanism, must include rather complex observations if it would record this living balance.

The first attack on the static rigidity of the *kouros* was directed toward the most obvious feature of the normal erect pose, namely, the uneven distribution of weight which produces an opposition between a taut leg with knee held straight and a relaxed leg with knee bent forward. In the so-called *"Kritios Boy,"* (Plate III) from the decade immediately after the Persian invasion, an unknown sculptor (whose name need not have been Kritios) has attentively considered this feature but has failed to observe the compensatory response in the upper body. Indeed, exquisite as this statue is, the torso is wrongly carried in profile and wholly inactive in front view. In order to include a relaxed knee, the sculptor has taken his quadrangular pier in greater thickness, front to back. In the upper part of the figure he has absorbed the consequent excess of material by curving the lower torso forward from crotch to breast and bending the upper body backward to the shoulder blade, thereby introducing a pelvic tilt quite inappropriate to the male skeleton. But in frontal view there is no corresponding movement or swing; the successive horizontal axes at waist, breast, scapula, and eye level are all undeviatingly parallel. The marble has been worked with magnificent skill to mirror the sensuous beauty of barely adolescent youth, and a surprising familiarity with superficial anatomic form has converted the back, from neck to ankle, into one of the most correctly lovely of all preserved fifth-century statues. But though the pose has drastically broken with archaism, it has not yet reached classic maturity. It is as adolescent technically as its theme is adolescent physically.

All movements of animated contour and shifting surface which the *Kritios Boy* displays—and in comparison with the earlier *kouroi* these mark a very notable advance—were necessarily confined within the solid boundaries of the geometrically simple four-faced block of stone. In order to escape from this rigid imprisonment which the technical process of Greek glyptic sculpture imposed, and in order to win the greater spatial resource needed for themes more energic than the idly inactive standing figure of traditional type, some wholly new technical approach to statuary art was obligatory. Fortunately, that new approach was available.

Monumental statuary in metal must naturally be a rarity in the art of most cultural epochs, not so much because of its great material cost as because of the physical and mechanical difficulties of producing it. Statues of large size (as distinguished from figurines at very much less than natural scale) cannot successfully be cast as solid masses because the sharp contraction of the cooling metal invariably occasions disaster. On the other hand, while hollow-casting very largely avoids this misfortune, it is technically an intricately difficult performance for large figures. Consequently it will be found to be very generally true (except in the Greco-Roman and subsequent European tradition) that metal statues which are taken at lifesize, or on larger scale, have been beaten out in sheet metal over a model which survives as their central supporting core. A few examples of this type have been preserved from ancient Egypt—notably the sixth-dynasty copper statues of King Pepi and his son, now in Cairo.

It was stated in an earlier chapter that Greek acquaintance with monumental sculpture and knowledge of the technical procedure for its production were derived through the Hellenic trading posts established in the Egyptian Delta in the latter half of the seventh century. Intimacy with Egyptian arts and crafts was thus acquired and Egyptian example may well have instructed the Greeks, in addition to the technical lore of sculpture in stone, how to hammer sheathing around a wooden core to produce metal statues on a monumental scale. Among the Greeks, such hammer-beaten images *(sphyrēlata)* appear to have been made in early times, but it is unclear whether any of large size were produced prior to the re-established Greek contact with Nilotic culture. In any case, because Egypt had no adequate knowledge of hollow-casting from molds and made comparatively little use of bronze, monumental sculpture, both in stone and metal, was transmitted as glyptic art to the Greeks. The wooden cores for the earliest monumental bronze statues must have been carved by the same process as the figures in stone, so that the results, being derived from a primary glyptic shape, could not have possessed any very distinctively different character from stone statuary. Later, on the adoption of a process for casting metal hollow instead of beating it out cold, a wooden preliminary figure would still have been required, being as necessary for the casting molds as it had previously been for the hammer-beaten sheathing.

Consequently the new device of hollow-casting (due, according to accepted later opinion, to two craftsmen named Rhoikos and Theodoros working in Samos) did not initiate a new sculptural genus so much as a duplication of the older types in a new material medium. In exchanging metal for stone, Greek sculptural art did not cease to be glyptic, as there was no stage in the manufacture of a hollow-cast bronze to which the term "plastic" had any application. And hence, whatever may have transpired in later times, early Greek sculpture in bronze could not be generically distinct from sculpture in marble, being only a variant of the same artistic form. Dependence on a carved (and not a hand-modeled clay) original for the negative casting-molds, and reliance on graving and polishing after casting had been accomplished, kept the two sculptural media intimately allied. They were variants of a single genus—and that genus was glyptic. Herein the Greek monumental bronzes from the archaic and early classic period differ fundamentally from those of Renaissance and more modern times, since the latter are reproductions of hand-modeled originals in a plastic medium, which the former are not.

We must assume, therefore, that it was the intention of the archaic bronze-casters to produce sculpture conforming as closely to the already well established type of chisel-cut and abrasive-polished marble as was materially possible to achieve. Where the process of casting had pitted or roughened the surface, scraping and burnishing could produce as lustrous and as homogeneous a texture as any marbleworker could impart to stone; and where the sharpness of carving in the wooden model had been dulled by molding and casting, a metal graving-tool could fully restore the precision of the edges and the clear run of shadow in the troughs. Color was less exactly reproducible. The brilliant pigment in a base of beeswax which the crystalline structure of marble absorbed into its pores would not penetrate the closer texture of burnished metal. Here an arbitrary equivalent became the accepted convention, as gilding with gold-leaf and inlaying with metals of various hue were substituted for the more vivid staining in red and blue and yellow which the marble-sculptor applied to his work. This was an unavoidable defect in mimetic accuracy, since the bright pigments of the marble-workers could better imitate dyed garments, even as marble rubbed with the light golden brown of unrefined beeswax more nearly echoed the sun-tan of Hellenic bodies than did the copper-red of freshly burnished bronze or any patina's palette of verdigris or resinous bitumen.

But there was compensation elsewhere. For rendering the interior structure of the eyes of his statues, the marble-sculptor merely scratched circles for iris and pupil with a compass to guide him in his application of color to the surface of the stone; whereas the bronze-caster could much more closely imitate the living structure by using colored glass paste or semiprecious stone and inserting these into a cavity in the bronze as an actual eyeball is incased in its socket. And accessory ornaments such as earrings and necklaces could be genuine specimens of the goldsmith's craft attached or hung in place upon the bronze body instead of being mere painted imitations such as those with which the marble-sculptor was generally content. (But here there may have been some counter-influence from foundry to marble workshop, since the pierced lobes of many of the late archaic marble *korai* indicate that real jewelry had once been added for their adornment).

The formal situation may be briefly summarized. The use of a carved instead of a plastically modeled original for the casting-molds, and the extensive glyptic "cold work" after casting had been completed, with the use of burin and burnishing to parallel chisel and abrasive polishing on work in marble, kept the two sculptural media closely allied as variants of a single sculptural genus—and that genus was glyptic. On this account, all lifesize classic Greek bronzes must be rated, judged, and appreciated as glyptic sculpture.

Nevertheless bronze and marble are such different material media, and hollow-casting as opposed to cutting with mallet and pointed tool is such a distinctive formative process, that unavoidable differences of very appreciable bearing on sculptural manner developed to distinguish metal from marble statuary. For one thing, Greek monumental bronzes were never cast entire within a single mould. Heads, arms, and legs were made in separate castings and then fitted together by a tongue-and-groove method of assembly. Welcome as the confirmation is, we do not need the evidence of the red-figure Foundry Vase to show us in actual operation a technical procedure about which simple ocular inspection of the surviving bronzes can even more fully inform us.

Such piecemeal procedure was dictated to the foundryman by the physical conditions of his craft, since it was beyond his powers to do otherwise. Any consequent artistic gain was an outgrowth of material accident rather than of deliberate intent. But the gain was none the less actual, and its artistic value undiminished. One notable result of this piece-meal creation was the bronze sculptor's release from the spatial restraint imposed on the marble-sculptor by the quarry-shape of his block. Statues which could be assembled out of separate parts were not forcedly contained within the boundaries of a quadrangular pier or any other geometrically simple envelope, but could reach out their arms in any direction into space and stride or lunge or otherwise make free with their unimprisoned legs. In consequence, a considerable share in the variety of poses which the black-figure and early red-figure vase painters had graphically explored could accrue to the sculptor who worked in metal instead of in stone.

That this is not mere academic theorizing on what might or should have taken place, is shown by such a work as the *Discus-Thrower* (Fig. 35) by Myron, originally created in bronze but known to us in an assortment of more or less well preserved later copies in marble. Seen in profile view— and no one can doubt which aspect of the figure is thereby intended, since a single viewpoint has determined the entire composition—the silhouette of the *Discus-Thrower* is precisely such as Myron's immediate predecessor, the Panaitios Master, might have drawn for the interior medallion of a red-figure kylix (Fig. 34). It is a purely linear construction, with that joining of fullfront to lateral views within a single outline which is characteristic of

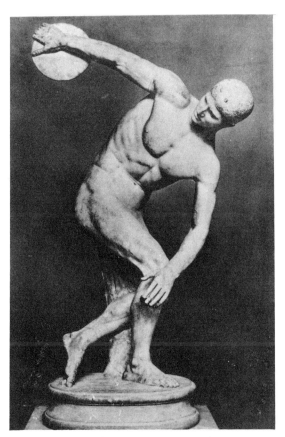

Fig. 35 The Diskobolos (Lancellotti Version)

red-figure drawing before foreshortening had been mastered. Such an outline drawing, when traced on the surface of a marble slab, could have been cut into a relief in archaic style without encountering any technical obstacle. But it could not be drawn on a thicker block and then fully cut in depth to yield a solid figure in-the-round without necessitating the removal of a wholly disproportionate amount of superfluous stone and without leaving the arms perilously attached to the main mass and the support of the entire figure dependent upon a dangerously delicate equilibrium. For this reason the marble copyists of this particular statue, while unable to minimize the waste of labor and material incident to cutting out its tortuous shape from a single block, countered the remaining risks by leaving unremoved various bar-like struts and ties of their own invention in order to strengthen the projecting limbs, together with a heavy vertical support, sketchily carved to resemble the stump of a dead tree, to stabilize the topheavy mass of stone. In hollow-cast thin-walled metal—and we know through Pliny that Myron's original was of bronze—none of these awkward hindrances would have deterred the sculptor. The arms and lower limbs and protruded head, having been piece-made, involved no waste of discarded material or unprofitable work; and the tensile strength of bronze is so much greater than that of marble, and the brute weight of hollow metal so much less than that of its solid marble counterpart, that all risk of breakage and collapse was eliminated. Quite evidently, the bronze-caster could follow the vase-painter's lead in presenting the human form in action, where the marble-cutter had to content himself with it at rest.

At much the same date as Myron's creation of the *Discus-Thrower,* Kritios and Nesiotes collaborated to cast bronze figures to commemorate the heroic pair who had conspired to free Athens from the rule of the Peisistratids; and here too the new freedom of the bronze-caster permitted striding legs and raised arms which the contemporary marble-cutter would not have attempted.

The immobile *kouros* had stepped out of his confining block of marble, and the myth of Daedalus, that statues could be made to walk and run, had finally been confirmed.

A statuary foundry was a costly establishment, very different from the comparatively simple and inexpensive equipment of the marble-worker. All that was needed for the production of monumental marbles was adequate apprenticeship to a properly skilled master, tools and furnishings being of no great cost and the value of the material being defrayed by the sale of the finished product. But to make monumental bronzes much more was needed than energy and good will: a foundry was a factory requiring extensive equipment and the maintenance of a trained personnel. It should follow that the manufacturing centers for sculpture in bronze were much less numerous and geographically much more restricted than those for sculpture in stone. It is probable that all the monumental bronzes of fifth- and fourth-century date were the product of a very limited group of foundries, perhaps not more than a dozen in all. Notable among these were Aegina and Chalkis in the immediate neighborhood of Athens, and Argos and Corinth in the Peloponnese (though the founders in the latter town, where monumental sculpture in marble had not taken strong hold, seemed to have confined themselves to work of exquisite quality but of small size, such as mirrors, tableware, armor, and metal furniture, leaving to their nextdoor Sikyonian neighbors the experimentation in larger metal statuary). In the Greek West, we know only of Rhegium on the Sicilian Strait, whither a certain Pythagoras emigrated from Samos with his experience and perhaps his material equipment and trained assistants. It may, however, be supposed that Cumae at the edge of the Gulf of Naples, as the chief colony of Chalkis on Italian soil, in touch with the rich metallic lodes exploited by the Etruscans, must also have had a well-equipped foundry. At Athens, the practice of cutting a forearm from a separate piece of marble and attaching it by dowel and socket to the main block of a marble *kore* to give it greater freedom of gestural pose, can be traced back to the third quarter of the sixth century and may reflect acquaintance with bronze sculptural procedure at that time. The occasional insertion in marble statues of glass or stone eyes within hollowed sockets—as in the early fifth-century *"Kritios Boy,"* (Plate III) which shows other imitations of bronze technique, Antenor's *korē,* perhaps to be dated as early as 530, and the *Man Carrying a Calf,* which cannot be anterior to 550, *pace* Payne and others—point in the same direction and to much the same date for the first Attic interest in bronze statuary. These may be taken as evidence that the art was introduced into Attica fairly soon after its inauguration at Samos.

Aegina, Athens' early commercial rival and immediate neighbor, seems to have accepted the new sculptural form with equal promptness. We have no indication of any previous devotion to monumental marble-cutting on the island, but considerable evidence for a flourishing and successful production of bronze statues well before the close of the sixth century, with recorded names of outstanding masters, such as Onatas, Glaukias, and Kallon. In reverse of the usual order elsewhere, on Aegina it was experience in making statues in bronze which stimulated interest in the related, yet technically very otherwise demanding, craft of sculpture in stone. The early fifth century pedimental statues from the Aeginetan Aphaia temple are bronze-casters' figures translated into marble. Seemingly, it ran contrary to some habitual Greek sense for material harmony to add metal statuary to a stone temple. Had such heterodoxy been tolerable, here on Aegina, if anywhere in the Greek world, we should have expected to see it. Apparently obligated to marble, yet lacking any firm tradition in that medium, the Aeginetan sculptors copied the freer poses and severely sharp texture of bronze statuary directly in stone, adding bows and spears and swords in live metal, even as they were accustomed to do in their bronze-work. Therewith achieving a boldness and freedom in presenting bodily action without parallel in early fifth century marble-work, the Aeginetans became leaders, instead of the straggling followers which they previously seemed to be, in the development of the marble-worker's style. Unfortu-nately, they do not appear to have persevered in their accomplishment, partly because they were more attracted to the foundry than to the stone-cutter's craft, but also because the political humiliation of the island by Athens at the middle of the fifth century put an end to independent enter-prise. For the further development of the monumental bronze style we must look elsewhere—most especially to Athens and Argos and Sikyon.

Perhaps also to Rhegium on the Sicilian Strait. For on epigraphical grounds it may be permissible to ascribe the bronze *Charioteer* of Delphi (Fig. 36) to the workshop of Rhegine Pythagoras. To such colonial origin may be due the lingering archaism and unreformed severity of its style. Whatever its provenance, it is our only well-preserved example of a monu-mental bronze from the period of the *Discus-Thrower*. That it is so utterly unlike this latter work is not so much a measure of any disparity of man-ner between Myron and "Pythagoras," or between Athens and the Greek western regions, as it is an illustration of two strongly divergent move-ments in early fifth century sculpture—the older tradition of the standing figure at rest, directly descended from the Egyptianising *kouros* type, and the newly introduced figure in action, based on red-figure vase drawings and the thematic material of relief carvings. Uninteresting as is the *Chario-teer's* pose compared with that of the *Discus-Thrower,* it is more informa-tive than Myron's masterpiece about an important stylistic change which did much to put an end to archaism. It is more informative, because drap-ery was a better practice-ground than nude anatomy for this particular innovation, which opened a new domain to the Greek sculptors.

As we have observed, it is characteristic of the archaic phase that linear designs traced on the surface of the solid shape are made materially actual by incision into the depth of the stone, there to survive optically as narrow straight-edged troughs of shadow. Such a procedure runs con-trary to physical actuality for much interior detail wherein (as in drapery, most conspicuously, and in strands of hair) the draftsman's line is intended for a record of *protrusive* features in maximum illumination rather than of recesses wherein shadow is gathered. By sinking his lines into the stone, the archaic master was emphasizing shadow to the detriment of highlight and failing to reproduce the undulant outward and inward surface move-

Fig. 36 The Charioteer of Delphi

ment which imparts to solid shapes most of their substantiality for vision. What archaism needed to discover and actualize in practice (by which act it would promptly destroy itself and put an end to archaism!) was a spatial *protrusion* of surface to give substance to its linear forms. The glyptic sculptor must learn to attack the solid block, not in order to drive his design inward into its surface, but to leave it in projection above it.

Such a reversal of linear function is almost precisely of the same nature as, in the graphic realm of the panel picture, the vase-painters' inversion of black-figure into red-figure, which brought line optically forward from the ground instead of sinking it into it. There is no connection between the two events, not merely because they took place at an interval of some fifty years from each other, but because artists do not approach their tasks and solve their technical problems in terms of abstract principles such as modern esthetic criticism brings to bear. Graphic art evolves at a faster pace than glyptic art. Emergence from archaism is consequently not synchronous for the two disciplines. But emergence from archaism, if it is to take place at all, necessitates the decisive step from a negative to a positive recording of the dimension of depth which attaches to tridimensional shape —and this, in final analysis, is all that these changes in graphic and glyptic styles betoken.

In vase-painting there had been no very clear portents of immanent revolt foreshadowing the conversion to the red-ground technique. Such a change could not well have been made tentatively or piecemeal. But archaic sculpture shows many partial attempts at inverting recessive into protrusive pattern. On the *Pouting Girl* (Fig. 23), while the wrinkles of the chiton and most of the heavier drapery folds are indicated negatively by incision in characteristic archaic manner, it would be difficult to decide whether the sculptor, in his rendering of the hair, has laid more emphasis on the sunken grooves or the raised strands which these outline. And there are Attic *korai* (such as Acropolis 684 and 674) where the solid substance of the hair above the forehead has been even more adequately indicated. Also, there are occasional passages in the drapery of other *korai* in which the artist has been more attentive to the solid fold than to its defining graphic contour. But these are all incomplete and unsure experiments, valuable to the critical beholder because they prove what the uncritical public seldom appreciates, that the transition from the archaic to the classic style is not an abrupt and total severance, but a continuous and logically consistent evolution from one formal level to another. Yet, just as in Greek graphic art if we disregard the bilingual vases and the other early red-figure productions and hold a vase decorated by Exekias side by side with one by the Berlin Painter we are startled by the difference in artistic level and see nothing in common in the two manners, so we are struck by the enormity of the change from archaic to classic in sculpture and see no stylistic likeness whatsoever when we compare the serenely grave Delphi *Charioteer* with a simpering sixth century maiden. Notwithstanding, if we set *Korē* 685 side by side with the *Charioteer,* we shall have to concede that the really effective difference between the two is the conversion of incised into excised drapery (compare Fig. 37 with Fig. 36).

One immediate result of this concentration on the protrusive shape of the loosely fitting Greek costume was a loss of that contact with the bodily form which in archaic work had been the sculptor's first consideration in giving statuary outline to the unshaped block. On late sixth century *korai* the radiating wavy lines which represent the wrinkling of a linen undergarment are often cut into a previously rounded upper arm or shoulder or stretched over breasts already shaped to receive them (Fig. 37); and cloth seems transparent where its folds are incised directly upon buttocks and thighs and calves trimmed to the human figure. But where, as in the *Charioteer,* the drapery has been given material substance of its own, with the ridges standing well out above the deep recession of the troughs, the solid shape is that of the concealing garment itself and not of the bodily form, which visually has ceased to be. The *Charioteer* might almost be the stump of a fluted column raised upon a pair of human feet and surmounted by a human chest and head, so little has his body impressed its shape upon his garment.

Such an outcome challenged the sculptor to reform his ways. If he thought of his art as an evocation of the living form, he must have been ill content with this degradation of it to imitation of an inanimate costume. Through his own quest for strict visual fidelity he had succeeded in destroying his finest theme and denied himself the chief attraction in his strange art of mimicking his kind in metal or marble. For under the more truthful treatment of drapery as a dense envelope of projecting and retreating folds, the *korē* type of a fully costumed figure standing immobilely erect with both feet planted close together now afforded the sculptor little opportunity for anything more than a material study of the shape and texture of woven cloth. The bronze *Dancing-girls* from Herculaneum are as bodiless below the waist as is the Charioteer.

This disappointing outcome may explain the disappearance of the *korē* type from the fifth century repertory. It is true that with the introduction of living balance into the standing pose and its distinction between a taut "weight leg" and a relaxed "free leg," some amelioration was possible, in so far as the forward thrust of the bent knee could break through the rigid curtain of drapery with some slight indication of the human form behind it. Even so, the *"Lemnian" Athena* and the *Cherchel "Demeter"* are dull statuary, however skillful may be the varied lights and shadows of

Fig. 37 Athens, Acropolis Museum: Kore 68

their clothing. And the huge chryselephantine Athena of the Parthenon or the smaller but still colossal *Athena Medici* and the brilliantly adapted *Caryatid Maidens* of the Erechtheion porch justify their stiffly disembodied vertical flutings more by their appeal to tectonic form than by any humanly motivated values. In lifesize figures detached from any architectural setting or suggestion, such bodiless abstractions of motionless garments could hardly have served for long to rouse the admiration either of sculptor or of public.

Far greater interest attended upon the costumed figure if it could somehow be made one with its drapery by carving this close to the body, following its outlines, clinging to its surfaces, and moving with its motion. In the pedimental statues for the temple of Zeus at Olympia, erected after the Persian War from the god's share in the booty from the defeated invaders, the problem of thus reconciling massively defined drapery with the bodily form which it covered was openly attacked and, after several variant methods, was intelligently resolved. Nowhere else in our extant Greek sculptures are we so plainly confronted with artists thinking out their formal problems in terms of trial and error and success.

The five central figures of the east pediment are staid and traditional, erectly isolated figures with drapery (where it occurs) hung vertically in simple folds. At least three of the five have been cut from four-sided piers of quarried stone, like *kouroi* and *korai* of older time. Adjoining these on either flank were racing-cars with their teams of four horses in profile silhouette, deceptively carved in half-round relief to fit the narrow shelf on which they stood. Before and behind the horses were crouched or kneeling figures of grooms and attendants, some nude, some half draped, some fully clothed; and it was here in these statues of lesser size and dignity that the sculptor's progress out of archaism can be followed in Greek sculpture's first formulations of a classic style.

In the opposite or west pediment the central figures are again the least advanced stylistically. Theseus and Peirithoos, striding out from the central protection of an immobile god, with their weapons raised to strike, echo the Attic *Tyrannicides* of a previous decade; while the axial figure of Apollo, for all the well-deserved admiration which the modern world has given it, is rigidly frontal and carries a head sufficiently reminiscent of the earlier *"Blond Boy"* of the Athenian Acropolis to suggest that it may be the work of an *Attic* master (of rather advanced years and set manner) who was in charge of this important commission. As in the other pediment of the temple, innovation and stylistic invention are noticeably confined to the lesser figures nearer the angles, where the cramped space under the descending roof-line has been brilliantly put to account. In the Aegina pediments, however they may be restored, the spectator senses that the narrowing gable has forced the figures into their often very strained poses; whereas in the west pediment at Olympia, for the first time in Greek pedimental sculpture, the figures seem to have assumed their intricate postures by their own volition and because of the actions in which they are engaged rather than from any extraneous architectural compulsion. The triangular gable is now not a distorting and artistically irrelevant cage for the figures, but an accompanying frame to an already marshalled company. And here the drapery of the struggling figures shows a great advance toward a newer (though only apparently freer) idiom of visual presentation. Their sculptors—who must have been younger men eager to seek for untried effects—have realized that drapery must somehow make visible the body which it covers and not shut it blankly away from sight—a major task, and one whose completely logical solution is one of the triumphs of the Greek artistic genius.

But how could this be accomplished? If drapery was to be cut in substantial thickness in order to give it material semblance, it would claim for itself the exterior of the block to a depth of several inches and thereby, as we have seen, deny to the sculptor's chisel all contact with the bodily shape beneath the costume, imaginable perhaps, but wholly unformed within the dark depth of stone. If this most serious and most awkward situation was to be remedied, body and drapery must somehow be fused into a single entity, so that to see one was to apprehend the other. But how could this be done? At Olympia, in the statues from the pediments of the temple of Zeus, we may watch the sculptors at grips with this problem and see how they found a solution to its difficulties.

But rather than analyzing their only partially successful efforts at perfecting an effectual formula, it will be more expedient to pass them by and turn directly to a fully evolved example of the classic idiom of formalized drapery.

However, a few definitions and illustrations of certain typical devices are a necessary preliminary to any exposition of this extraordinarily sophisticated and self-conscious style.

The first device to be considered is the traditional one, inherited from mid-sixth-century archaism, of illusionary transparency achieved by carving sparse and clearly spaced drapery folds upon a fully modelled nude form. The archaic masters had unintentionally stumbled upon this paradoxical device by incising their schematic drapery patterns directly upon the surface of a marble block that had previously been shaped to an overall bodily outline. Both the nude body and the costume upon it thus appeared together, even though in different visual categories, the former appertaining to the statue's solid structure with the latter suspended upon it as a sort of linear envelopment. The spectator confronted with this twofold representation was obliged to interpret what he beheld in terms of a body beneath and a costume above—in short, the drapery seemed transparent. Fifth century art heightened this casual and in its origin accidental effect into a deliberately calculated art of visual illusion.

A second and very different formal device of late-fifth-century drapery seems not to have been known to the archaic sculptors and was only brought into general use as a result of experimentation with stereographic optical suggestion of the sort which the younger collaborators on the Olympia pediments had been attempting. Indeed, the idea of such a device could hardly have occurred to the sculptors until they had learned how to disengage drapery from the body sufficiently to make it possible to treat it as independent material hanging free of the wearer's body instead of being imposed upon it in superficial linear attachment, as early archaic drapery had been. In describing sculptural drapery analytically we may speak of *one-point attachment* when only one end of a strip or piece or panel of cloth is firmly affixed to the wearer while all the remainder hangs free, to form rigidly vertical furrows when the figure is at rest or to flutter and stream away when it is in motion. We may further distinguish *two-point attachment* when both ends of a strip or panel are held firmly in place on the body, leaving the intervening material free to sag in a looping curve. Geometrically considered, all sagging curves which so originate are closely allied in type and are technically classed as catenaries (a term which, as the word implies, denotes the class of curve which a flexible chain, or *catena*, will assume when suspended, whether its two terminals lie at the same or at different level). To the Greek sculptors interested, as were the fifth-century Attic masters, in the intelligent exploitation of formal resources, catenary drapery was an invention of extreme usefulness. At its points of attachment the underlying form was necessarily close to the surface; but elsewhere the loop of hanging cloth could serve to make the form seem to retreat within the stone to any desired depth, dependent on the thickness to which the catenary was cut into the block. The varying strength of shadow therewith at the marblecutter's disposal, ranging from the palest twilight of transparency to the full darkness of deeply undercut folds and pockets, was a further aid of great utility for defining the bodily structure within the costume. The inanimate garment clarified the physical form while it enshrouded it.

A third device—which may first be seen winning recognition in the experiments of the masters of the Olympia pediments—is indubitably the most important, far-reaching, and stylistically significant of all. It consists in carving ridges and furrows of drapery to serve as an optically intelligible commentary to the body in order to make more immediately comprehensible its directional changes of surface, its plastic disposition,

154 GREEK ART

its modeled structure. This linear accompaniment of light and shadow might be made to run parallel with the bodily contours; but it functioned most effectively when it moved transversely across the modeled form so as to present to the beholder its curving rise and fall, thereby making visible the modeling in depth which foreshortening distorts or conceals. In verbal description such a process probably seems far from clear. For that reason it is time to turn to its visible embodiment in a work of sculpture.

The Seated Goddess of the Terme Museum (Plate IV) is a coldly mechanical copy from some late-fifth-century work of the Attic School. Its harshness of execution, by exaggerating the contrast between light and shadow, makes it an ideal demonstration piece for the formal classic style.

Besides being implicit in the readily intelligible pose, the anatomic structure is explicitly presented by the rounded breasts and the kneecaps, which are fully modeled without any concealment by the drapery (here shown as transparent), while the correctly shaped lower limbs are only lightly glossed with an accompaniment of low narrow ridges running in traverse over the modelled surface and looping down in deep catenaries across the lap to form heavy pockets between the knees and shins. Still ampler catenaries originate from a gathering point on the seat of the throne beneath the right thigh, to drop downward across the ankle of the leg and thence rise to a terminal attachment at the other knee. Upon the abdomen the drapery folds are treated as flat ribbons in vertical career; these part to left and right in gentle curvature to model the form on which they move and with their even illumination set off the more heavily enveloped limbs beneath from the deeply shadowed overfold of the garment above. This latter feature resumes the horizontal movement conspicuous across the thighs, but reverses its curve from a sinking to a rising arc, transferring to the visible plane the otherwise scarcely appreciable rounding of the body. From the brooches which fasten the garment on either shoulder the drapery ridges spread fanwise down around the breasts, joining in catenaries below the neck and trailing aside without attachment over either flank. Neutral regions where no bodily form is to be imagined behind the garment, are carved in straight vertical folds of strongly contrasting light and shadow without anatomical reference, thus announcing themselves as out of employ for the modeled form. In general, the deeper shadows accompany recession in the stereometric form of the block, while the shallower attend its protrusion; but where the drapery is clear of the body it becomes geometrically indifferent, displaying no variety but acting as an inarticulate foil of vertically pendant streamers.

The description has been carried into such detail in order to emphasize the high degree of idiomatic inflexion which characterizes fifth-century formalism. It is no exaggeration to claim that the quality and direction of every ridge and furrow has been dictated to the sculptor by the anatomical surface structure of a human body placed in such a pose. His option is always within the restrictive terms of a formulation which he has accepted as correct and therefore cannot violate. His art is not an imaginative creation of something hitherto unseen, but an evocation in poignant vividness of an entirely familiar experience. Through sculpture, as the Greek mind understood that art, we apprehend with fuller sensuous perception the living shapes of our own race and kind and under the spell of a visual harmony of sculptural formulation assign to them a sensuous beauty which only art can supply.

Poses of the human body *in action* had been derived by the marble-workers from the bronze-casters, who had taken them from the repertory of painted design. Initially these animated poses had been confined to masculine themes, because graphic art had elected to make such studies in the nude and because an idiom of sculptural drapery had first to be invented before the feminine figure could be shown in action. The difficult task of inventing such an idiom was undertaken by the group of sculptors collaborating for the pediments of the Parthenon in the thirties of the fifth century when, to judge by its rather experimental character, the requisite formula seems to have been still a novelty. By that time the various devices for draping the figure at rest had become thoroughly familiar and were being applied in a perfection never afterwards surpassed, as on the seated and reclining divinities of the east pediment, destined to be among the most admired of the Elgin marbles. But, so far as we can control the evidence, out of the total number of some forty human figures in the two pediments only five were shown draped and in active movement. These were the colossal Athena besides the central axis of the west pediment, the charioteer of her car, the accompanying figure behind Poseidon's car, and in the other gable the Athena emerging from before her enthroned father and the running goddess commonly known as Iris but better identified as the divinity of childbirth, Eileithuia. On all of these, one and the same formula for drapery in motion was used, with long ridges and accompanying furrows drawn out in near parallel into sweeping ogival curves.

This S-shaped flowing line subsequently established itself as the standard formula for presenting active bodily motion through suggestion by drapery. The device will be found repeatedly in use throughout later classical times. Thus, it may be seen on the frieze of the Maussoleum from the middle of the fourth century, on the *Alexander Sarcophagus* from that century's close, and in the classicizing renaissance of the mid-Hellenistic Age on the great Pergamenian altar frieze and the *Victory of Samothrace*.

And yet, for all its effectiveness, the formula had one extremely inconven-
ient characteristic when applied to marble statuary in the round, resulting
from the purely physical obstacle that stone drapery could not be cut to
the thinness of actual cloth. Because of this hindrance, wherever a garment was represented blowing or fluttering free, the marble-cutter was
forced to give it unnatural weight and bulk in order to forestall breakage.
Thus, in Paionios' airborne Nike from the year 421-0, once mounted on top
of a slender thirty-foot triangular shaft in front of the temple of Zeus in
the Olympian sanctuary, one and the same piece of garment makes abrupt
and unexplained transition from clinging, thinly transparent texture on
the half-nude form into thickly ponderous masses of densely billowing
ogival folds. Drapery upon the body and drapery free of the supporting
figure had to be (in marble, at least) two materially different substances
if it was to be submissive to the formally distinctive patterns of the transparent modeling-line upon the nude and the opaque motion-line beyond
its contours.

These, then, are the four generically different geometric devices for
drapery in the Formal Classic period: shallow and intermittent folds on
the molded nude, to induce an illusion of transparency; close-clinging
modeling-lines in ceaselessly shifting curvature, to make the body's stereometric articulation intelligible; controlled but marvelously adaptable
catenaries, to give depth and balance to the solid form on which they were
hung; and long swinging S-curves reaching out beyond the body, to add
an illusion of movement to a figure posed for action. Out of these four
disparate resources, somehow combined in harmonious cooperation, the
wonderful drapery style of the late fifth century was compounded.

There can be no disputing that sculpture under such strict dictation of
fixed formulas cannot escape the charge of being a highly artificial creation. It was, however, artifice in the etymological sense of the word, as
something which art had made. And it was universally valid because it
relied on generic optical devices rather than on the arbitrary preferences
of individual or local taste. Its manners are not mannerisms; and its carefully calculated effects are sensible to every interested spectator without
need of allowance for differences of culture, race, or period. The strength
of classic art is this dependence on universal principles of intelligent perception: its weakness is its restriction to their unvarying demands.

It should therefore be carefully considered how these geometrically
abstract devices for representing drapery were combined in fifth-century
practice to produce a concordance of patternized linear form with physical
bodily structure. For it is this concordance between solid shape and applied interpretative pattern which more than any other factor is responsible for the harmonic unity of the classical draped figure. And to this in large

measure is due the mysterious quality of "Classicism" which adheres to these statuary forms. If this quality may be defined in concrete terms of artistic behavior rather than in vague esthetic generalizations, the formal analysis of fifth-century drapery will point the way to its intelligent comprehension.

However, any such analysis is necessarily restricted to the draped figure; whereas Classicism, whatever this may prove to be, is an equally recognizable property of the nude "Apolline" tradition in Greek art. It might seem that for the sculptural representation of the unclothed male body an artificially imposed harmony of abstract devices, such as was invented for drapery, must be wholly impracticable. Remarkably enough, this was not the case.

In view of the persistent trend toward mimetic accuracy in Greek sculpture, a major critical problem is presented by the abstract ideality of the classic nude, the quality so greatly prized by its confirmed admirers and so bitterly impugned in the current reaction against classicism. It is this trait which imparts to the typical fifth-century male nude and to fifth-century heads of either sex that aloofly impersonal unreality of ideal perfection which aroused the enthusiasm of Winckelmann and Goethe when they encountered it in the intensified formalism of mechanically produced Roman copies. For its interest as an example of West European response to the ideated Greek conception of sculptural representation, I venture to quote, without presuming to translate, a passage from Goethe's *Italienische Reise:*

"Umgeben von antiken Statuen empfindet man sich in einem bewegten Naturleben, man wird ... durchaus auf den Menschen in seinem reinsten Zustande zurückgeführt, wodurch denn der Beschauer selbst lebendig und rein menschlich wird ... Alles unser Denken und Sinnen ist von solchen Gestalten begleitet, und es wird dadurch unmöglich, in Barbarei zurückzufallen ...

"Den ersten Platz bei uns behauptete Juno Ludovisi ... keiner unser Zeitgenossen, der zum erstenmal vor sie hintratt, darf behaupten, diesem Anblick gewachsen zu sein."

After his return to Weimar, Goethe was presented with a cast of this colossal head, which he displayed in his reception-room with such general approval that the chamber was thereafter known as *"das Junozimmer."*

Our present-day familiarity with genuine Greek originals may incline us to dismiss such late-eighteenth-century appraisals of classic style as ill-informed and irrelevant. Yet the cold *Ludovisi Hera* head merely exaggerates a quality which indubitably first-hand work by the fifth-century masters, for all its greater warmth and intensity, also displays. Such typical examples as the head of the *Barberini Suppliant* or the *Laborde Head,* both now in the Louvre, which might be selected to replace the *Ludovisi*

Hera in today's better-founded judgment of the classic manner, possess much the same ideated unreality of formalized abstraction.

I am persuaded that the most cogent explanation for such a continuance of ideated formalism into a period of fully conscious interest in natural truth is to be found in the existence of what may quite properly be called a cult of mathematical mysticism among the fifth-century sculptors, operating to prevent any concession to the asymmetry of structure and irregularity of shape which they could not have failed to discern in human facial features and bodily forms as they occurred in nature.

A faith in the efficacy of integral Number as a sort of esoteric assurance of perfection in representing the human form in art is not an unfamiliar phenomenon, either in esthetic theory or in actual artistic practice; but its dominating influence on Greek sculptural style during the second and third quarters of the fifth century is not always sufficiently appreciated.

Numerical rules of proportion are indispensable to the glyptic sculptor. The artisan who works on a monumental scale to produce statues out of single blocks of stone must have at his disposal some simply formulated and easily applied mnemonic rules of proportions, because without their aid it would be impossible for him to cut out a human form with all its parts in correct size and position. Since stone once removed from the block cannot well be replaced nor, in general, a faulty cutting be remedied, a glyptic medium virtually precludes extensive correction of errors of execution. On this account the craftsman must know in advance where every element of the final figured shape lies within the block and how much rough-blocked matter must be reserved for it. Such preknowledge can be most serviceably stored and applied if it has been formulated as a schedule of approximate proportional measurements. And since measurements cannot be recorded and applied except in terms of linear distances, an arithmetical schedule or "modular canon" in integral or simple fractional units will be the inevitable outcome. Thus, the topmost sixth or seventh part of the total block may conveniently be reserved for the material lump of stone which is to become the statue's head, whereas it would not be practical or appreciably more accurate to set 13/80 or 11/75 as the proper norm.

It may be taken for granted that instruction in the use of canonic measurement formed part of the technical knowledge which reached Greece from Egypt. On the wall of the tomb of a noble of the New Empire, a certain *Sw-m-Nwt,* there is still to be seen a drawing of a standing man laid out upon a network of squares. Because the lines of this guiding framework intersect the body at crucial points such as forehead, base of neck, armpit, navel, crotch, knee, and ankle, the purpose of the graph was not merely a mechanical transference of a standard copybook sketch in enlarged size, but the attainment of correct bodily proportions in agreement with some traditional norm. If similar guides were employed by the Egyptian sculptors also (and we have some confirmatory evidence that this was the case), the source of Greek dependence on sculptural canon is apparent. If it be objected that the earliest Greek *kouroi,* such as the one now in New York, do not follow any known Egyptian canon and give no clear indication that any preconceived scheme of proportionate measurement controlled their ill-considered elements, it may be replied that at least the notion of assigning measurable sizes to the various parts of the bodily structure had taken hold and only needed to be developed through trial and improvement into a routine workshop formulation. The *Tenea "Apollo"* in Munich gives the impression of having been fashioned in accord with a fully formulated canon (though I have never had an opportunity of subjecting him to the minute scrutiny of caliper and meter-stick). But however much or little Egyptian precept may have been acquired and transmitted, by the fifth century the use of a modular canon, expressible in simple integral numbers, had become firmly fixed in Greek sculptural practice.

The presence of such a canon of simple integral ratio is instantly recognizable to the accustomed eye, especially in the facial features of a statue, because here even a slight departure from the physical norm becomes apparent and artificial symmetry of pattern is particularly intrusive. Measurement performed on an enlarged photograph of a canonic head in strictly frontal view will usually reveal the modular ratios. Thus, the head of the *Kritios Boy* (to take one example out of many) has been constructed in strict conformity to a modular canon, and the terms of this canon are easily discoverable. In order to be of much practical utility, a canon needs to be expressible in fairly simple integral ratios, with the result that its accurate embodiment—and every good artisan takes pride in accuracy—must produce areal shapes and intervals between them which are so strikingly symmetrical that they do not need to be remeasured by the spectator in order to be detected. That the eyes shall each have a length exactly equal to the distance between them, that the bridge of the nose shall be half an eye-length across, and the end of the nose precisely an eye-length in width at the nostrils, is not a physiological necessity to which all living human beings conform; but these extremely simple and easily remembered relations are sufficiently close to the common norm to insure the sculptor who employs them from miscutting his block or otherwise working out of scale.

And yet, although the original purpose of employing these modular prescriptions was the purely practical one of preserving the stonecutter from ruining his work by miscutting, and useful or even indispensable as

modular canon may have been, it is difficult to believe that the traces of its
employment would have been left so conspicuously apparent in the *Kritios
Boy* if "Kritios" had not approved the outcome for its own inherent beauty
as well as drawn advantage from its purely technical convenience. Since it
would have been perfectly possible in the final stages of work to modify these
precise ratios sufficiently to disguise them, it is hardly probable that they
would have been suffered to remain so evident had they not seemed to
possess some especial merit in their own right, some earnest of visible loveliness to justify their workshop practicality. Canonic rules originating at the
level of the craftsman's need thus became elevated to esthetic principles
for his art.

It is true that proportions such as those just stated may be closely
approximated in actual life (the writer has more than once encountered
"canonic" features in living guise), but mere approximation is not geometric precision. The sculptor who adheres to a simple integral canon,
however narrowly its prescriptions may conform to anything observable
in his race and period, will never produce an individually characterized
face, whether true portrait or plausibly possible likeness, but only a geometrically ideated abstraction (Fig. 38). The so-called "idealism" of classic art is not simply due to a generalization of the type by omission of individual characteristics and regularization of the contours, but more than
all to this deliberate substitution of integral ratio, intact and entire, for
the chance approaches to it discoverable in nature's own structural symmetry. The difference in meaning between our word "symmetry" and the
Greek "*symmetria*," from which it is descended, defines very exactly the
difference between *ideal* beauty as we conceive it and *ideated* beauty as
Greek sculpture created it by applying a modular canon.

It may be accepted without further debate that in the post-archaic formalized style simple integral ratios were applied not only to the features of
the face but to every one of the individually shaped and structurally distinguishable parts of the body. It will be recalled that piecemeal accretion
of separate detail is characteristic of early art, so that such a procedure of
discrimination between part and part, as separately defined elements in
a total design, was entirely congenial.

From considerations such as these we may appreciate the force of the
famous passage in which the physician Galen quotes the third century philosopher Chrysippos as asserting that "beauty consists in the proportions
... of the parts, that is, of finger to finger and of all the fingers to the palm
and wrist, and of these to the forearm, and of the forearm to the upper
arm, and of all the parts to each other, as they are set forth in the Canon of
Polykleitos, who supported his theory by producing a statue in agreement with its prescriptions" — a statue (according to another reference to

Fig. 38 Bronze Head of a Boy, Munich

it by Galen) "which derived its name and fame from the exact commensurability of every one of its constituent parts." Whatever may be the explanation of our difficulty in recovering a series of simple integral proportions by applying caliper and meter-tape to our marble versions of the Polykleitan *Doryphoros,* we are obligated to admit the existence of an all-penetrating and all-controlling system of canonic form in the mid-fifth-century sculptural rendering of the male nude body.

The passage from Plotinus which Miss Richter has prefaced to her

Handbook of Greek Art expresses Galen's contention with equal precision
and even greater emphasis. I venture to offer a slightly different translation of the text, to read:

"What is it, then, which stirs the sight of the beholder and turns and
draws it toward itself, to make him delight in its contemplation? . . . . Virtually all authorities agree that it is the commensurability of the parts to
one another and to the whole, with fair use of added colors, which creates
the beauty in visual contemplation. In the case of these, as indeed for
all other objects, that they are beautiful is due to the presence of pre-
measured harmonic responses."

In the light of such wholly unambiguous statements, when we read
Pliny's appraisal of Myron as *"numerosior in arte et in symmetria di-
ligentior"* we are entitled to interpret his unclear and not too Latin phrases
as signifying that Myron was "more addicted to the use of number and
measurable proportion in his art."

With Myron active in the second quarter of the fifth century and Polykleitos in the third quarter, we have authority for sculptural devotion to
canonic Number during at least the central decades of the century. Since
some sort of sculptural canon must have already existed as a mechanical
aid to glyptic technique, the exact period of its conversion from a workshop rule-of-thumb to an artistic and well-nigh metaphysical formula of
perfection is not easy to determine. That it lost its hold on sculptural practice as stricter imitation of physical truth proved its factual inaccuracy may
be accepted as certain, but the chronology of this event, too, remains un-
fixed. Perhaps fourth-century progress in veridical portraiture was partially responsible for its rejection, since any scheme of integral numbers
which pretends to apply to human physiognomy in all its intricately individualized perversity becomes too involved to be artistically workable.
Whatever the actual timetable of the events may have been, it remains
indisputable that the Greek sculptors' canon, originating as a purely mechanical aid and thereafter elevated into an esthetic principle of great
significance for classical art, was finally dismissed from service, having
been discovered to be a fallacy *para physin,* "contrary to nature" because
untrue to life.

In brief, then, the reign of Number over Greek sculpture was essentially a fifth-century episode. But because that century was a crucial formative period for the classic style, the episode left an enduring mark on all
ancient sculptural art by creating an artificial formal idiom for the treatment
of the nude almost as abstract as the contemporary devices for sculptural
drapery. It is this numerical conception of a visible anatomic harmony of
its forms which distinguishes the Greek classic nude and sets it apart from
all subsequent treatment of this perennial sculptural theme.

X

THE FURTHER DEVELOPMENT
OF PICTORIAL STYLE

Down to the close of the fifth century, vase-paintings are our only extensive original witnesses to the evolutionary career of Greek graphic art.
Fortunately for us, they supply reliable first-hand testimony. But in order
to pursue our study into the period which literary tradition acclaims as the
Golden Age of painting in Greece, we are forced to look elsewhere for
information. From the early years of the fourth century onward the decoration of vases fell into rapid decline as a serious artistic activity and soon
thereafter so nearly disappeared that it offers us little or nothing of interest for the technical development of Greek painting. Except for such
partial glimpses as white-ground Attic lekythoi can give at the fifth century's expanding palette of colors, or the huge Campanian amphorai at
a staging of figures in horizontal tiers to suggest (very inadequately) spatial distance as an acquirement of the early fourth century, we search
virtually in vain for any authoritative first-hand evidence on the evolution of pictorial form. Since no original work by any of the great masters of
the fifth and fourth centuries has survived, and it is in the highest degree
unusual that we can cite an authentic copy of any of their lost productions,
it is no easy matter to discover how pictorial art developed beyond the
"linear depictive" state so brilliantly exploited by the red-figure vase
painters.

The situation is not entirely hopeless.

To show us what panel paintings by the major artists may have been
like in the period before easel-painting and vase-painting had parted company, there is a marble plaque from Herculaneum (now in the Naples
museum) with a surprisingly well-preserved encaustic painting of two
kneeling girls who play at knucklebones while three others stand over
them (Fig. 39). The work is signed by Alexandros—as copyist, one pre-
sumes. It has been asserted by a modern critic that "the drawing, which is

163

Fig. 39 The "Knucklebone-players"

fairly fine, does not equal that of some of our better vases." This may well be so, and might perhaps be turned to account to prove how very good the best vase-paintings are. But there is something else in such a painting which even the finest vase-paintings hardly show—a calm greatness of mood and a magnificent aloofness from everyday reality, which are derived from fifth-century sculptural forms. These figures were not drawn from living models, but from the sculptors' workshops. And more than any other factor it may have been this sculptural orientation in monumental painting (which the small scale and limited resources of vase-decoration did not encourage) that split the major and the minor art irretrievably asunder.

For comparable information on the evolutionary stage of painting slightly more than a century later, there is the remarkably finely executed *Alexander Mosaic* (Plate V), from Pompeii (now likewise in the Naples museum). There is every reason to accept this mosaic picture as a punctiliously accurate reproduction of an Early Hellenistic painting. (It should be observed that in Roman times mosaics were "floor paintings," executed in stone in order to withstand the wear-and-tear of human traffic. It was not until Byzantine and Early Christian times that mosaic was conceived as an art with distinctive characteristics of its own, in which profitable account could be made of the rigidity of line, the homogeneity of tone, and the broken luminosity imposed by the *tesserae,* the tiny squares of color which yet are not small enough to duplicate the finer mesh of our retinal screen. A classical mosaic is formally a painted picture).

For evidence on a slightly later technical stage of Greek painting there are the two mosaics from Pompeii signed by Dioskourides of Samos, one of which presents a group of gossiping women in comic masks, evidently intended to picture a stage scene from the New Comedy, while the other (Fig. 40) more engagingly depicts a strolling band of street musicians.

There is little else of importance wherewith to fill the lacuna intervening between late fifth-century Greek and first-century Roman graphic art, unless something may be derived from the Pompeian wall-paintings. These, to be sure, exist in remarkable abundance and in not too badly damaged condition. Amid their great range of stylistic modes and pictured themes they supply us with a very considerable number of compositions that on internal evidence may be held to be direct copies (though of mediocre execution) or adaptive versions or greatly altered re-creations of older Greek originals. The difficulty is to discover with any degree of certainty to which of these very different categories they should be assigned. Here every decision is beset with ambiguity and more than merely casual doubt. Since there are no signatures (beyond the altogether exceptional naming of the executant artisan), it is impossible to discover what older master may have been copied or adapted. Where several examples of an identical theme occur, the differences in compositional detail and technical manner prove that all cannot be equally faithful reproductions and invite a suspicion that none need be reliable. Comparison with independently original paintings from the late period in which these copyists were active raises (but does not solve) the further problem of how much of the chiaroscuro illumination, atmospheric envelopment, spatial suggestion, and thematic detail in their "copies" is ascribable to earlier Greek attainment and how much is due to an intrusion of subsequent technical practice. Considerations such as these have made a discouraging task out of any attempt to reconstruct a valid history of later Greek painting where

Fig. 40 Mosaic by Dioskourides

assumption, surmise, and arbitrary decision must supply what factual document and critical appraisal of actual specimens ought to have provided.

There is, however, an Ariadne's clue through this vexatious labyrinth. If (as we have insisted) the sequence of styles in painting is not an arbitrary monument to individual tastes and talents, but corresponds to a physiologically and psychologically conditioned evolution through obligatory steps and stages, it should be possible to identify these same steps and stages in some other better documented cultural period than ancient Greece. Having thus acquired by interrogation elsewhere an insight into their nature and the reasons for their enforced sequence, it should then be possible to interpolate these phases into the history of classical painting. On the assumption that Greek painting must have followed a comparable evolutionary schedule, it should be possible to re-arrange the evidence gleaned from Pompeian and other documents in proper chronological order and determine what features have been taken intact from older sources and what are alterations and additions from more advanced technical manners. If we could thus distinguish between accurate reproduction, conflation, adaptation, technical correction, and outright perversion of earlier masterpieces, we should be able to form some rational conception of the stylistic level attained by the earlier classical painters.

Amid all accessible material for such a comparative study of stylistic evolution, Italian Renaissance painting offers the most copiously preserved series of documented examples from which to deduce an ordered sequence of phases for the formal development of pictorial style. The bulk of the evidence is enormous; yet the career of stylistic development emerges clearly and can be reduced to manageable proportions. But before we turn to Renaissance Italy, we must make brief excursion elsewhere.

Everyday pragmatic vision is highly selective. This is partly due to the restriction of mechanical focus under muscular control which forces us to blur much of our field of vision; but much more extensively it is the result of wilful mental attention. We fail to examine and identify the major content of any visual field, not because we lack available time or mental facility, but because we have no need or desire to do so. We deal only with what immediately concerns us (and this is, of course, a very variable quantity, according to who and what we are and how we are disposed toward our environment). In addition, whatever atttracts our attention within the complex structure of a visual field is not perceived as what it is optically and physically—a gathering of minute points of colored light assembled in changing pattern—but as a spatial array of objects external to us. So entirely do we convert the visual field in any act of perceptive apprehension that it disappears completely as a visual field. A lecturer confronted by a seated audience in a lecture-room sees very nearly nothing of room or audience while he is absorbed in reading or speaking. If he pauses to examine his collection of captive bipeds, he sees persons seated in rows and shut in by walls, a floor, and a ceiling. This is largely a nominalistic perception, consisting of raw optical awareness very extensively eked out by conceptual understanding. A Kodachrome film, stimulated by a focused lens and a flashlight bulb, would record something entirely different by producing an intricate structure of flat patches of varying colors, in which the individuals whom the lecturer had supposed that he had seen have been reduced to fragments and appear as illuminated areas arranged on a gradient scale of diminishing size, with the smaller ones staggered on top of (and not behind) the larger ones. Many more strange transformations have taken place, of none of which the lecturer has been in the least aware, despite the fact that a pair of miniature Kodachrome pictures of the scene has all the time been in his possession, inaccessibly lodged behind the irises of his two eyes.

A primitive artist, desirous to represent such a scene, would produce a graphic construction corresponding much more closely to the lecturer's notion of what he had seen than to the camera's version of the affair. On the other hand, a technically fully evolved painter would reconstruct a complete visual field with all its complex content and could produce a colored panel in remarkably close accord with the photographic record.

Here are the two termini in the technical development of mimetic pictorial form. We have already considered the earlier one in examining the Dipylon vases. The later one, the final phase in a long series, in spite of its apparent complexity can be formulated in very simple summary terms: In order to make an optically adequate picture, all that is needed is an enlarged reproduction of a visual field, recorded accurately and fully. The strange thing is that this should be so difficult to make. There are only two major obstacles; but these, it would appear, are tremendous. Normal vision, being a practical performance, so thoroughgoingly perceives the visual field as an external visual world that it is unnatural for us to be aware of anything other than an exterior environment of solid objects in spatial extension and ordering. Only if we can *"un-see"* this visual world, can we discover the very different properties of the flatly two-dimensional appearances which must be reproduced if we are to supply to other eyes than our own the material for beholding an objective scene within the pictures we paint. This is the first difficulty, that it is almost impossible to "fixate" what we see before us, in all its intricate structure and without perceptual interpretation or conversion, having projected it in-the-flat upon an imaginary ground or screen or panel. The seemingly unperformable feat of the late ice-age painters, who drew startlingly accurate outlines of wild animals on thoroughly unsuitable surfaces of wall and roof of unlit caverns, is probably to be explained as due to such a power of "eidetic fixation." It is symptomatic that only the animals are here represented, almost always disconnectedly and never with ground beneath their feet or any accompanying setting of place or material circumstance, and that they are attached to any sort of surface, however irregular or discolored, even where previously occupied by other drawings, as though they had been arrested and limned by the painter while they floated luminously before his eyes.

The second major obstacle to direct and literal reproduction of the visual field within the eye is the disintegrating analysis of conceptual recognition which breaks up the continuum of colored light into familiar objects whose shifting outline and infinite gradations of illumination, hue, and surface texture we ignore as soon as we have made an objective identification. Anyone who has not had considerable practice, and happens to be endowed with little talent for drawing, need only ask himself to visualize the precise outline of a dog walking obliquely toward him or to put on paper how a trotting horse lifts and puts down his feet or to match with pigment the variegated colors of an unweeded garden path half-screened by shrubbery, in order to realise how much there is which our normal visual behavior dismisses unperceived and unrecallable because the practical requirements of seeing do not concern us with it.

Noetic control—by which I refer to the mind's dictation directing and over-riding the merely passive acceptance and recall of visual experience —is markedly conspicuous in Egyptian paintings from the early dynasties. In such a masterly piece of work as the *Oryx-feeding* in the tomb of Khnem-hotep (Fig. 41), the two antelopes and one of the two attendants show very remarkable accuracy of outline but complete disregard for any accompanying objective environment or spatial setting. But what is truly extraordinary about this drawing is the likelihood that the painter's intent was not the representation of two separate animals, each with an attendant, but a rehearsal, by means of two simultaneously present moments of one continuous action, of the forced feeding of antelopes in general, which involved grasping them by their horns, pressing down on their withers in order to ground them, and thereafter forcing open their mouths and cramming them with food. Very much as the spoken phrase "feeding antelopes" does not specify or even consider how many antelopes are to be fed nor when or where the feeding takes place, so this picture too is a generalized abstraction, but in visual instead of in verbal terms. It is an idea made visible, rather than the illustration of an actual incident.

Late medieval European religious art has much of this noetic or conceptual character. The Madonnas and saints envisioned without mate-

Fig. 41 Egyptian Tomb Painting: Oryx-Feeding

rial setting against the heavenly blue or glittering gold ground of mosaic or the blank surface of a plastered wall may indeed have been deliberately intended as celestial appearances untrammeled by association with the ordinary world of sense; yet it may be suspected that their aloofness was primarily the conceptual isolation of a technically unadvanced graphic art and that they are herein akin to the mammoth and bison and reindeer afloat on the ceilings of the paleolithic caverns.

But medieval religious art was often narrative and not purely iconic in its themes, intent on recounting the life-histories and not merely showing the bodily image of the martyred saints; and few narratives are so confined to the human actors that they can be intelligible without some sort of local setting and objective scene. There was no need to add much visual distance to such a presentation because the persons in the story completely filled the foreground of attention; yet even these demanded for themselves some sort of space in which to move or stand. The strictly delimited aerial depth—one might say, the "token space"—which medieval painting found adequate for its narrative scenes is a remarkable compromise between depthless mental abstraction and the disposition of a true visual field. Objects intended for more distant localization are placed higher on the panel, and nearer objects eclipse farther ones, all of which is optically correct, but scale seldom conforms to the requirement that size must dwindle in direct proportion to distance. Instead, the artist employs *emotional scale,* which decrees that whatever looms large in the mind because of its importance in the story shall be drawn in greater absolute size on the panel. So Giotto, inheriting his representational schemes from the frozen wreckage of Roman pictorial tradition, made Anna and Joachim as tall as the city gate of Jerusalem before which they hold their meeting, and in the scene of Joachim and the Shepherds he shrank the sheep to their histrionically proper unimportance.

One may speculate why it was that a graphic tradition which had maintained itself for so many centuries and had apparently been perfectly satisfactory as an artistic convention, should now rather abruptly have been rejected by Giotto's successors. Only one explanation commends itself. With Duccio and Giotto, painting ceased to be a perpetuation of iconographic tradition and became an interrogation of actual sensuous experience. It had been deriving its entire sanction from its own past performance; from now on, it turned its attention to the living present. For many hundred years it had been copying only itself in transcendental self-sufficiency; now it began to copy the materially actual world around it. Why the change came when it did, rather than at some earlier or later time, is probably not a question primarily for the art historian, since the answer must be rooted deep in the change from medieval to modern mentality which affected all human activity. But once the painters had committed themselves to representing visual appearances in lieu of iconographic conventions, they had given themselves an unavoidable measure for success or failure. Under its sanction, whatever *looked right* in a picture had been *painted right* by the artist; whatever did not look right must have been painted wrong. In the long run of time, if this criterion maintains itself through many successive generations of artists, the only possible end-term and final goal of technical progress is a full and accurate control of all the pictorial conversions of the visual field in the retinal image. Under our definition of a picture as an externalized retinal image, a technically perfected picture must include, in all their complex peculiarity, all the component elements of the normal visual field. Under this criterion, the whole evolutionary career of pictorial form may be summarized as the progressive discovery and reproduction of these characteristic qualities. Their acquisition and consolidation in the technical repertory is not haphazard, but appears to conform to a prescribed sequence. As we have already seen in Greek graphic art, the earliest acquirement is significant contour and the silhouetted areal shape which contour defines. Within the various outlines thus established, solid color will be applied without discrimination of interior variations of hue or intensity. This undifferentiated uniformity of tone is a result of conceptual identification of the entire shape as a discrete unitary thing, distinct from other things. In this early stage, painting is essentially a coloring of outline drawings. And it is remarkable that this uniformity between color and the shape to which it pertains main-

tains itself long after painters have become conscious of the chromatic complexity of illuminated surfaces. Even so advanced a technician as Raphael still
drew a linear cartoon to which he applied his pigments, so sharply does the
mind divorce structural shape from chromatic value. No doubt this is the
case because, even by non-metaphysicians, shape is identified with physical
reality, while color is deemed to be an accessory accident. To comprehend
that the entire visible world is nothing more and nothing other than a disposition of luminous color is as great an achievement for the painter as it is
for the thinker.

To the draftsman who has acquired a knowledge of foreshortening,
the inaccuracy and consequent inadequacy of flat monochrome coloring
becomes distressingly apparent. Under foreshortening, the surfaces of objects cease to appear spread out in the flat and begin to acquire recession
in depth. Graphically considered, this is purely a matter of linear representation, but visually it betokens a penetration inward into spatial distance. And in everyday visual experience the extension of an object in
depth is characterized by chromatic variety because of the varied incidence and reflection of light. Contrary to the early artists' ordering of
events, it is the gradation of luminous appearance rather than the linear
conformation which is primary in enabling us to perceive solid structure.
A wrinkled cloth or a hanging curtain or a fluttering cloak displays extension and recession of surface in terms of variegated illumination, but
when this variety is eliminated under uniform illumination, all movement in depth vanishes from perception. Differences in illumination
reach us as graded changes of hue. Whatever is openly struck by light
reflects a brighter tone; whatever recedes into diffused illumination shows
a darker tone. And these changes remain equally operative for cloth, curtain, or cloak dyed to a single and uniform color.

To meet this situation and record this tonal effect, painters working
at an unadvanced stage of their art introduce three gradations of hue
in place of the single flat color of the earlier phase, thereby distinguish-
ing high-light, half-light, and full shadow. Thus, Cennini in his cele-
brated treatise on the technique of painting (ca. A.D. 1400) speaks of
coloring costume or drapery "with the three gradations." So drastic a
simplification of the tonal range between *"chiaro"* and *"oscuro"* fails to
agree with ordinary visual observation. Cennini's tonal trio is a purely
logical trichotomy such as the mind instinctively makes when we divide
any continuous process into Beginning, Middle, and End. Much the
same dissection of a continuum into a series of rigidly discrete elements
attends on the popular conception that there are seven distinct colors
in the rainbow's continuous spectrum. In a painting, this simplified res-
olution of illumination into high-light, intermediate value, and shadow

produces a very striking effect, not altogether unlike the frozen arrest which the camera's momentary glimpse of a continuous movement substitutes for the actual event. In Italian painting after the opening phase of completely monotone coloring, it is evident that each separate color for costume or other material has been prepared in three tonal "strengths" and applied as described.

In ancient Greek painting, gradations of tone appear on red-figure vases, where the unpainted ground represents the brighter tones, black pigment the darker ones, and a diluted wash is added for certain intermediate values. But this latter is chiefly intended to show texture, as of hair or beard, and does not correspond to the phenomenon under discussion, which involves three gradations of the same hue applied to a single substance such as a piece of drapery. On the white-ground lekythoi, which should more closely resemble wall-paintings with their use of several colors on a white slip, the only trace of graded tones is a similar dilution of the glazed pigment to a wash; however, this is not used to show grades of luminosity, but merely to enrich the palette with new tints. It is possible that the extreme preoccupation of fifth-century graphic art with linear form dulled the painter's perception of the contribution which color makes to modeling. However, on several Pompeian mural pictures which on internal evidence seem to be based on Greek originals of fourth-century date, chiaroscuro modeling in three tones of a single color is employed both on the nude and for the drapery. Our problem is to discover, if we can, whether the device was already in use in the original painting or is a modification from later technical practice introduced by the copyist or some intermediary.

The painting of the *Knucklebone-Players* (Fig. 39) seems to have confined modeling to two tones—that of the material ground in lighter value and that of the drapery lines in darker. But in *Pentheus and the Maenads* from Pompeii (Plate VI) there is clear differentiation between high-light, intermediate illumination, and full shadow. In the *Alexander Mosaic* (Plate V) the simple twofold distinction between light and shadow is widely employed, but there is also considerable recourse to triple gradation of hue. The *Street Musicians* by Dioskourides (Fig. 40) very conspicuously reduces the solid color of the costumes to three strongly contrasted gradations of hue. Here, in view of the obvious virtuosity of the executant craftsman, it would surely be erroneous to ascribe the restriction to three tones to a want of stone *tesserae* in greater chromatic variety. Because the drapery patterns reflect early "baroque" sculptural styles, the date of the original painting reproduced in mosaic by Dioskourides should fall somewhere around the second quarter of the second century. If this is correct, we are entitled to conclude that the technical device of three gradations of illumination was a thoroughly established tradition in that period, whereas continuously graded chiaroscuro, merging each tone into the next, was either unknown or perhaps (for lack of sufficiently dramatic contrast) not in vogue at that date.

In Italian Renaissance painting, the next step consisted in fusing the three graded tones by brushing the pigments into one another across their dividing boundaries, thus producing a more nearly continuous transition from fully to partially illuminated surfaces. Such a practice is very common in the Pompeian wall-paintings, as in subsequent Roman work (where still more complex optical blending of colors is attempted). But whereas the introduction of the technique can be closely observed and strictly dated in the Renaissance, it is at present impossible for lack of dated material to assign an even approximately close date for its first occurrence among the Greek painters, since its use at Pompeii is not reliable evidence for the original sources from which the wall-decorators took their themes. If we may trust to analogy with Renaissance invention, the device should have been introduced into Greek painting before Mid-Hellenistic times, but the Greek insistence on linear definition of form, which is such a conspicuous characteristic of all Greek art, may have retarded its adoption.

It should be added to this account that the Renaissance painters evolved a most ingenious technique which obviated the preparation of three or more graded hues for each color on their palette. By first recording the luminosity gradients in terms of *"grisaille"* or some other monochrome, and then covering this "underpainting" with flat pigments thinned to a transparent glaze, a cartoon could be illuminated with flat colors and yet appear to have been executed in full tonal variety of hue. It goes without further comment that because such a device involved transparent oleaginous varnish to carry the pigment, there could hardly have been any comparable phenomenon in antiquity with its reliance on an encaustic medium in colored wax or the application of opaque tempera.

The painters' scrutiny of the play of light and shadow over the costumed figure, to the benefit of an expanding repertory of pictorial devices, must inevitably have attracted their attention to a different type of shadow—that idle attendant on every one of us which dogs our every step and gesture whenever we venture into the sunlight. In Italian painting, Fra Angelico's angels cast no shadows. This is very well for such celestial beings, since it leaves unclouded the radiance of their presence. But in the Annunciations by slightly later masters the angel casts as dense a shadow as Madonna herself. It was not any conviction of heavenly incorporeality which swayed the painter-monk, but a fortunate immaturity in his outlook on visual fact. Inevitably, as the naturalistic trend continued, the shadow cast by the illuminated figure must sooner or later become part of pictorial equipment. But it does not appear in earlier phases as long as the noetic control by which the draftsman constructs his graphic shapes devotes itself to the object and fails to take account of its presumptive environment. (Seemingly, the shadow which an object projects is not accepted as an inherent part of that object: it would be interesting to know whether the shapes which people our dreams ever cast shadows!)

In Greek painting, the *Knucklebone-players* (Fig. 39) cast no shade, nor are there any shadows on the whiteground lekythoi (which do not appreciably overpass the fifth century); but the *Alexander Mosaic* (Plate V) makes consistent use of them. Since its subject-matter, the defeat of the Persian king by Alexander in the battle of Issos, refers to a late fourth century event and we know from ancient sources that an extremely famous painting of this historic episode was made by a certain Philoxenos of Eretria for King Cassander, whose reign fell in the generation immediately succeeding, there is general agreement that the mosaic should be accepted as documentary evidence for a late fourth-century pictorial style. The use of the cast shadow should therefore be postulated for this period. Since it occurs also in *Pentheus and the Maenads,* it may well be of still earlier invention.

Naturally, the painter's interest in effects of illumination would not have been confined to chiaroscuro and shadows but have extended to other phenomena of lighting. Among these the high reflectivity of polished metal must have attracted his attention with its property of creating mirrored images of surrounding objects. For the general esthetic history of painting, the recording of reflections—whether from burnished metal or silvered mirrors or windless water—is not an incident of great importance. We are impressed by Velasquez' skill in mirroring persons otherwise invisible to us in the room where we behold him at work at his easel, and we admit that in interior scenes by Dutch artists metallic reflections have as sound a claim as anything else to be included in the scrupulously exact cataloguing of household furnishings. But it can hardly be asserted that artistic worth is notably enhanced by a detail which must strike us as primarily a parade of technical ingenuity. However, for a reconstruction of the formal evolution of pictorial art it is of moment that the *Alexander Mosaic* should have introduced as a prominent feature the skillfully blurred reflection of a fallen Persian's face and upper body in the obliquely foreshortened surface of a polished bronze shield.

If their presence and actions are to seem plausible, the characters in a painted representation must have some sort of objective environment and material setting. Yet Greek graphic art, intent only on its human themes and (as we shall note) very greatly under the influence of sculptural form with its almost unavoidable concentration on the spatially isolated human figure, was little inclined to construct pictorial space around its characters. In this respect Greek art contrasts strongly with Italian painting, upon which sculpture by-and-large exerted far less influence and in which the inclusion of an environmental setting was an inheritance out of the Roman past, surviving as a stereotyped iconographic tradition through the intervening Early Christian age. The expansion of this airless and spaceless scenic setting into a realistic environment of depth and distance was at first restricted to the immediate zone in which the chief figures were presented, but culminated in a complete mastery, in optically correct terms, of a homogeneous recession of visual space from its nearest visible beginning in the foreground to its ultimate termination at a remote horizon. The entire development may be observed in full and fascinating detail in the Italian painters.

Cimabue may paint a Madonna seated upon a throne, but the throne is nowhere, because it has no spatial context. The silhouette of figure and throne conform quite closely to the contours which in the living world such objects might assume in a retinal image, but the areal shapes thus defined lack solidity because they are without modeling for depth. There is no difficulty in explaining this insubstantiality in their appearance. We only need list the optic factors which the painter has left out of account. Except for some strictly conventional high-lights inherited from earlier iconic formulation, the only illumination of the picture is the extraneous light by which we ourselves behold it: there is no illumination from within. Although there is brilliant color aplenty, this is not graded for luminosity or textural pattern. The costumes in early figure-painting are often adorned with woven or embroidered designs, but these are always spread out in the flat over the panel, so that the garment is without movement in depth because the patterned design shows no gradient distortion as it follows the folds in and out. Finally, and most prominently of all, the figure is not localized in visual space because there are no attendant objects exterior to it to give it spatial setting. In Cimabue's painting a mental concept has isolated his theme from every visual environment; in consequence as much of the panel has been given over to it as the theme could be made to cover. The result is a huge figure in the unmediated foreground of a shallow space devoid of distance.

A correction of this conceptual isolation in depthless "noetic space" could most readily be achieved by surrounding the theme with other extraneous objects distributed to orient and localize it within a pictorially constructed spatial setting. To do this would serve to translate the representation from the Nowhere of iconic imagination to the Here and Now of normal sense-experience. Such a translation became one of the chief interests of succeeding painters, but the visual realism at which it aimed could be attained only through a long series of discoveries. One obligatory step was the recognition that visual space in everyday experience does not begin with the objects on which we concentrate our attention, but extends much closer to us as a disregarded intervening foreground. (As a matter of physical fact, visual space begins for all of us with the tip of our own nose, however completely we are habituated to ignore this unhelpful intruder into vision.) The painter who is aware that objects which are more distant in the exterior world assume a vertically superior position in the visual field, has the key to the technical problem of indicating spatial recession. In order to create foreground space all he need do is raise his theme above the bottom margin of the panel: the more it is raised, the farther will it recede into distance and the more of frontal space will intervene.

For the early painters this is no mysterious lore. There is, however, a further observation directly involved. Everyone knows (or if not, can easily discover) that as an object becomes more distant in the visual world its size will dwindle correspondingly on the visual screen and at the same time its location on the visual panel will alter by moving upward. It is extremely interesting to note that the ancient Egyptian painters properly record the second but tend to ignore the first principle. In the Egyptian murals, whether merely painted in the flat or carved and colored as reliefs, a higher position on the wall may betoken merely a change of subject to a new theme, but very often it is to be understood as an indication that the object is situated farther away in space, even though it may show no diminution in size. In fifth-century Greek painting, the so-called "Polygnotan vases" present figures at various horizontal levels on the panel and show them posed on undulant lines which must betoken broken terrain. Since the upper figures are at times partially eclipsed by these undulant lines, there can be no question but that their disposition conforms to the optic law that location in height on the visual screen is correlated with distance from the viewer. And yet, precisely as in Egyptian painting, the size of the figures undergoes no change in scale! The huge Campanian amphorae from the early fourth century still adhere to this inactual formula, which an obstinate Greek interest in the human actors, rather than in the scene in which they are engaged, has elevated into an unchallenged convention. Nevertheless a rudimentary visual space has been introduced.

In the *Knucklebone-Players* (Fig. 39) all five of the figures are grounded near the bottom of the panel, whereas in the Pompeian version of *Pentheus and the Maenads* (Plate VI) the leading figures have been set sufficiently far above the bottom of the panel to give them recession in pictorial space. The treatment of the resulting narrow strip of foreground as a correctly tilted "visual ground" may be due to the copyist, as may also be the cast shadows and the exaggeratedly powerful illumination. But since the foreground strip itself could not be eliminated without materially altering the compositional pattern, it should be accepted as an original feature.

This same use of a foreground strip at the bottom of the panel immediately beneath the figures re-appears in the *Alexander Mosaic* (Plate V), where it has been treated as a tilted visual ground leading the eye depthward into space. And because other pictorial devices which in Renaissance painting are of considerably later introduction than the tilted foreground also occur in fully developed manner in this mosaic, it should follow that the elevation of the figures above the bottom of the panel in order to create their recession in visual space must have been fully established by Hellenistic times. On comparison of all the available evidence it transpires that it is presumably an early fourth century accomplishment.

By thus moving them up the panel, the size of the figures was necessarily diminished. To make them occupy the rest of the panel by bringing their heads close to its upper margin (as spaceless earlier drawings tended to do) would have nullified the spatial recession introduced beneath them. Besides, Polygnotan superposition had already automatically produced figures markedly smaller than the total panel. It was therefore inevitable that as the figures came to be set higher above the bottom of the panel, their heads would at the same time be brought down lower from the top. In short, as the figures were made to recede farther away in visual space they were diminished proportionately in size. This is the reason for the abandoning of megalography (as the rendering of figures in terms of panel size is sometimes called). In Dioskourides' mosaic of the *Street Musicians* (Fig. 40), while the foreground comprises a narrow horizontal band tilted to represent a curbed sidewalk along the exterior wall of an urban dwelling, the head line for the figures has been dropped so low that they scarcely extend more than half the height of the panel, And in Pompeian paintings wherein landscape is a prominent feature the human figures are frequently drawn in truly diminutive scale under pressure of the optical law that size and distance vary inversely.

The mere staggering of figures of the same size at different levels in the Polygnotan manner is spatially ineffective (cf. Fig. 42). There may be abundant sky above the figures; but empty sky contains no spatial grad-

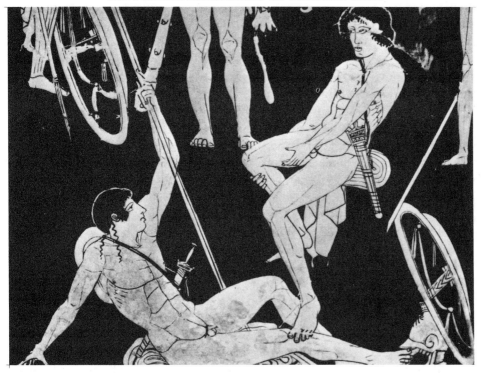

Fig. 42 Detail from a "Polygnotan" Vase

ients to make distance visible. In the *Alexander Mosaic,* although the headline for the figures has been lowered greatly, there is no content in the broad strip of panel above them except sky and the gnarled trunk of a single tree and the leaning spears of the charging horsemen. One figure hides another in very skillful suggestion of still others unseen behind; but even so, the visual space is, as in all Greek art of the classic phase, only the space created by the figures themselves to contain their poses and admit their movement. It is, in short, sculptural rather than pictorial space. Without an objective setting of landscape to fill the depth of aerial distance it is well-nigh impossible to construct visual space in painting. The Italian painters of the Renaissance were not so deeply engrossed in their characters that they could not interest themselves in the inanimate world. By learning how to depict landscape they acquired a command over spatial depth and distance into which, after much practice, they were able to insert their figures in an unbroken visual expanse extending from the nearest visible foreground to the remotest horizon-meeting of earth and sky. How they accomplished this, and by what preliminaries they passed to final mastery, is an enthralling study for which there is here little pretext for entering at length. But a summary may prove pertinent to Greek art.

As long as the major figures took over most of the panel for themselves, there was little room for any spatial construction more extensive than an abbreviated glimpse at a distant background scene such as could be depicted in miniature scale like the back-drop curtain of stage scenery. Such glimpses of distant meadows with copses and streams, or wooded hills overtopped by mountain peaks against a clear or clouded sky, demanded no perspective or other geometrical construction to arrange their contents in depth, but could be presented in outline drawing of superimposed shapes in constant focus and uniform illumination. They were in fact quite literally drop-curtains which left out of account all intervening spatial extension.

But when the construction of an immediate foreground space had been mastered and the thematic figures grew more solidly substantial as foreshortening and chiaroscuro and other visual gradients were introduced, the unfilled lacuna between the immediate foreground and the remote distance became uncomfortably apparent. Unable to introduce the missing intermediate space, the painters sought to justify its omission by hiding it from view. Hence the huge velvet curtains hanging behind Bellini's Madonnas and the blank walls shutting off the scene with only tiny windows opening on landscapes judiciously remote. Delightful as these are, they avoid the issue in seeking to disguise a technical insufficiency. About this time, the introduction of triaxial linear perspective to scaffold pictorial space within an architectural framework emphasized the discontinuity between the artificial hither-space of theoretical construction and the more naturalistic farther-space of normal visual projection. It is at times extremely diverting to mark the inevitable collision between these two types of spatial construction, which cannot be made to blend because they are of different geometrical orders. Only with the rejection of the abstract rigidity of triaxial perspective—in which an exactly level ground or floor and strictly vertical uprights must be shown, in combination with a converging cone of radial lines aimed at an arbitrarily located "vanishing-point"—did it at last become possible for the painters to connect foreground with background continuously and concordantly. The same Giovanni Bellini who dodges the issue in his iconic altar-pieces has penetrated the secret of continuous spatial recession in his great many-figured compositions, such as his *Feast of the Gods* (now in the National Gallery in Washington) and rather more painfully, and hence more enlighteningly to the enquirer on his method of solution, in the somewhat earlier *Transfiguration* in the Naples Pinacoteca.

None of all this development appears to have any very cogent parallel in ancient painting. It may be a matter for surprise that a civilization so deeply versed in geometric theory as classic Greece should never have made any application of it to pictorial representation, such as the mathematicians of the Renaissance supplied to the painters of their day. But it may be that the Greeks were too keenly sensitive to visual actuality to have been misled by so specious a substitute for normal experience. For in the everyday world of sense the objective world before our eyes expands steadily into ever wider reaches toward a more greatly extended horizon zone instead of folding itself together upon a distant point, as the theory of triaxial linear perspective insists. In developed Greek painting after the fifth century the axial lines of composition very generally spread fanwise apart and obliquely outward to create expanding, instead of contracting, spatial distance.

By neglecting and rejecting the study of inanimate nature, Greek graphic art deliberately debarred itself from further progress toward the technical goal which may be academically defined as "the construction of a correct retinal image in all its complexity as a flat visual field mechanically projected by a spatially extended exterior world." By concentrating their attention on the human theme, Greek artists make us suppose that, in their eyes, this was art's immediate and sole concern. Here may be a weakness in Greek art, but it certainly was also a source of tremendous strength. By refusing to explore further the spatial forms of the visual field and confining itself to the representation of human forms in a foreground focus of restricted visual attention, Greek painting allied itself to sculpture, which by its physical nature is restricted to a similar visual range. It may, I think, be claimed with full justice that classic Greek painting and Greek sculpture are twin aspects of the same conception of art as the emotionally evocative presentation of the human form in visual isolation from the rest of the sensuous world. If these had any spiritual counterparts in West European art, we may perhaps look to Mantegna, Signorelli, and Michelangelo to supply them.

The further parallels in technical formal evolution between ancient and modern painting fall in Roman times and lie beyond the purview of this study.

XI

THE TRANSITION TO NATURALISM
IN SCULPTURE

The artists who evolved the classic idiom of formal drapery incurred the risk of becoming absorbed in its calligraphic appeal and thereby being diverted from the study of natural truth to the exploration of abstract beauty of design. The peril most especially beset the worker in relief, not only because he was apt to draw on the painter's repertory of linear forms, but because the linear character of formal drapery was much more obtrusive in relief. By sharply abbreviating their recession in depth but fully recording their extension upon the panel, relief gave pictorial intensification to the formal devices for drapery while diminishing their spatial actuality. Calligraphy, which dwells on beauty of line for its own sake, apart from objective content, requires projection upon a plane surface. Sculpture in-the-round, possessing tridimensional appeal, was therefore less well-adapted for its display, while relief, exhibiting design in-the-flat, was ideally suited to its presentation.

From the carved marble parapet which once protected the precinct of Victorious Athena beside the great entrance gateway to the Acropolis, there has survived the incomparably skilled relief of the winged Nikē stooping to unlace her sandal. The standard formulas for transparency, linear modeling, and catenary design have been combined in adaptation to a single pictorial plane. But the depth of carving with resultant variety of light and shadow has been so adroitly modulated that patternization in-the-flat does not supervene to destroy statuary depth. What is in physical actuality largely pictorial representation appears to be fully actualized sculptural reality.

The masters who collaborated on this parapet frieze were not all equally skilled at harmonizing modeling in-the-round with linear design in-the-flat. Thus, the sculptor whose style reflects Paionios' Nike at Olympia and the relief of the kid-slaying Bacchant in the Conservatori-Museum in Rome overrode the modeling of the nude with long-drawn

182

Fig. 43 From the Nike Parapet

flourishes of ogival motion-lines (Fig. 43). "His manner is flamboyant and dramatic, he loves line-play, and his sense for linear design is much stronger than his feeling for plastic form."

Perhaps a decade after the Nikē Parapet had been set in place, four of the collaborating artists again worked together to carve reliefs for a large circular pedestal, twenty feet in circumference, presenting a sequence of nine slightly less than lifesize maenads engaged in postured dancing and Bacchic revelry in an unsurpassable virtuosity of draped design. None of the nine has survived to our day (unless the *"Kid-slayer"* in Rome should prove against all probability to be one), but most of their company was copied or adapted innumerable times in antiquity. The figures were generally taken at considerably reduced scale, being applied to ornament marble candelabra bases, urns, household altars, and similar productions of artistic commerce, but occasionally they were more accurately reproduced at full size on flat plaques for insertion in villa or palace walls. As a rather unexpected, but mechanically unavoidable, outcome of the transference of a carved relief from a curved to a level surface, the design of the figures could be reproduced exactly on these plaques, but the cutting in depth had to be supplied by the copyist at his own discretion. Through mere economy of labor, the carving was skimped, much of the plastic illusion was lost, and a more purely superficial pictorial rendering resulted. Unaware of this, many of the earlier critics in modern times maintained that such flamboyant and unsubstantial treatment of the draped human form could not possibly have originated in the High Classic period, but must be an invention of later times, the product of an artificial classicizing mode comparable to the calligraphic perversions of archaic to which the term "archaistic" has been applied. Fortunately for our understanding of fifth-century sculpture, other copies of the Maenad Base at fullscale and on correctly curved panels have survived—notably the *"Kid-slayer"* of the Conservatori in Rome and a much damaged but almost complete series discovered on the site of the Hellenistic city of Ptolemais on the North African coast. From comparative study of these it has become possible to identify the sculptors as members of the same group of Attic artists which had carved the Nikē Temple parapet, and thus assure ourselves that it was indeed during the late fifth century that the formal devices of classic drapery were raised to a pitch of decorative ornateness that rivaled the elaborate schematic patterns of the late-archaic phase exactly a century earlier. Where we then spoke of a "florid archaic" decorative trend prevailing over tectonic structure in the Attic *korai,* we must now employ a similar term to describe a "florid formal" intensification of the late-fifth-century idiom of drapery into deliberately calligraphic ornament.

This, which may very pertinently be called the flamboyant phase of the classic formal style, seems to have endured into the initial decades of the fourth century. We know the names of some of its practitioners. Such was Timotheos, who in his sculpture in-the-round for the acroteria and pediments of the early fourth-century temple of Asklepios at Epidauros in the Argolid has provided evidence for the loveliness and unsapped vitality of the style and shown its suitability for other than relief-work. The *Leda-with-the-Swan* in the Capitoline Museum has often been taken to be a further example of his picturesque (or better, pictorial-linear) manner.

The disappearance of this attractive and by no means effeminate mode may have been due in considerable measure to a disintegration of the Attic workshops after the disastrous outcome of the thirty years' war with Sparta. During the brief pause in the struggle that Athens thought to have successfully terminated in 421, but was unwisely induced to resume in 417 to her own ultimate destruction, Attic sculptors had been engaged in numerous commissions to commemorate their city's and her allies' victories. The reliefs for the Nikē Temple parapet at home, and the statues of Nikē by Paionios dedicated at Olympia and Delphi by the Messenian settlers of Naupaktos at the mouth of the Corinthian Gulf (where there had been important naval engagements) were conspicuous examples of these War Memorials. But after Athens' utter defeat in 401 it was Sparta which commissioned and set up the monuments for victory, and it was quite naturally Peloponnesian and not Attic sculptors who executed them. At Delphi the great bronze company of gods and naval commanders participant in the sea fight off Aigospotamoi was an imposing (and undoubtedly very costly) production by the pupils and successors of Argive Polykleitos. While the starving Attic marble-workers emigrated to Rhodes, Cilicia, Phoenicia, and the South Italian West in search of a livelihood, the bronze foundries at Argos and Sikyon flourished. Throughout mainland Greece the marble traditions of the Pheidian-Agorakritan-Kallimachan succession were replaced by work in bronze by the Polykleitan school, and interest in consequence shifted from the brilliant virtuosity of drapery carved in stone to the more contained, but no less demanding, representation of the nude male athletic form in cast and chased and inlaid metal. In order to understand the sculptural trends of the second quarter of the fourth century it is necessary to revert to the Peloponnesian art of the mid-fifth, with its transformation of the *kouros* into the victor-athlete type.

The accepted paradigm for this event has already been briefly mentioned. It is the *Doryphoros* (or "Spearman") by Polykleitos, probably the most frequently copied of all classical statues throughout Greco-Roman times. It will be recalled that it was surnamed "The Rule" (in

Greek speech, *canon*) not so much because it embodied a physical consummation of athletic strength as because it reconstituted the male athletic nude in formal perfection of sculptural presentation. As Galen reported —and as we have already noted—"it derived its name and fame from the exact commensurability of every one of its constituent parts."

The *Doryphoros* of Polykleitos is a commonplace in all the art histories and sculptural handbooks. It should suffice here to call to mind the "chiastic rhythm" which results from opposing a raised arm above a relaxed leg to a lowered shoulder above a leg set tautly straight. With the corresponding muscles on either side of the body thereby distinguished in alternate tension and release, the static symmetry and axial rigidity of the archaic *kouros* were dissolved into a more lifelike pattern of immanent muscular action. When to this vitalizing change in pose was added the substitution of protruding rounded surfaces for the grooved depressions of archaic linear boundaries, there resulted a suggestion of innate physical energy and contained power of balanced movement which transmuted the lifeless image into a living form.

Equally significant was the change in bodily contour. In lateral view, the relaxed leg carried its bent knee forward but set its foot behind the taut leg, while the sharply crook'd arm performed a similar function for elbow and hand. In consequence there was no longer, as in the archaic *kouros*, a single profile carried uniformly through from one side of the figure to the other, but a change of outline in depth, articulating the bodily elements and making them visibly intelligible in much the same manner as a "stepped" relief. If Pliny was to record a complaint that Polykleitan statues were four-square *("quadrata")*, the remark was based on the entirely accurate observation that only the four cardinal aspects were the sculptor's concern, to the neglect of intermediate appearances. And if Pliny's source further complained that the Polykleitan figures were too much alike *("paene ad unum exemplum")*, this was the inevitable price of a fixed canon of proportions with its inelastic prescription of harmonic perfection.

To Greek philosophic thinking as Plato typified it—wherein arithmetical Number had little significance except as it was concretely incorporated in visible geometric appearance—beauty was the visible presentation of an intellectually intelligible harmony, and harmony was a concordance of Number. All beauty of the human face and body must accordingly be a manifestation of abstract geometric concord and as such be accessible to geometric analysis. In philosophic imagination the Supreme Deity (who was something other than the household head of the Olympic community of gods) was "the Eternal Geometer" who geometricized all his creative activity and therefore could not fail to have embodied and materialized geometric thought in living creatures. The artist's task and opportunity was to uncover this geometric intent and set it forth for others to see.

In Greek metaphysical theory, while the ideal form was One its material incorporations were Many, so that if art insisted on presenting the ideated form rather than its individual variety, it was taking position with the One against the Many. Yet the One, the harmoniously geometric form, is an intellectual apprehension beyond sense and sight, and any representational art which pretends to deal with the seen world of appearance may not for long be satisfied with the unseen. Many men other than the ancient Greek thinkers have held that beauty is intelligible and not merely sensuously affective. But whether its invisible transcendence can be made to attach itself in visible guise to the living form of man or boy or womankind by introducing geometrically harmonized ratios and proportions into everyday physical reality may well be doubted. But that the fifth-century sculptors believed that it could is not open to doubt.

Preoccupation with the mathematics of an implicit, ultimate formal structure—for such is what Polykleitos' search for the "many numbers" in the human body signifies—may be more harmful than helpful to representational art. In Italian Renaissance painting there is an entire period, extending from Paolo Uccello to Tintoretto, when the geometrical conception of visual space as a triaxial construction in terms of precisely plumbed verticals, exactly level horizontals, and a uniform convergence of all linear extension in depth toward a common focal center, imposed an almost intolerable rigidity on the pictorial construction of visual space. The geometric scaffolding of a grandiose outdoor banquet scene by Paolo Veronese can be exposed by setting a straight-edge to its elaborate architectural framework of floors, tables, stairways, piers, lintels, and cornices. Here is a logically exact parallel to Greek sculptural *symmetria*. When Leonardo da Vinci opened his treatise on painting with the warning, "Let no one who is not a mathematician read my work!" he was championing an esthetic principle of very dubious validity, yet one which would have found a congenial response from the old Argive master, who might well have given much the same warning in committing to writing his treatise on the sculptural Canon.

In Greek sculpture the application of strict numerical response undeniably introduced a fuller harmony to the structural pattern, but at the expense of lifelike illusion. Cicero's stricture on the works of a certain early Greek sculptor that they were *"rigidiora quam ut imitentur veritatem"* may be applied to all "measured" statues.

The only feasible escape from the tyranny of Canon is greater recourse to natural truth. For, even though Number and geometric concord are implicit in most organic things ("Nature's Harmonic Unity" was the title given half-a-century ago to a treatise on the mathematical symmetry inherent in the shapes of crystals, plants, shells, diatoms, insects, and higher animals) the living individual eludes any straightforward integral formulation of proportionate sizes and symmetrical structure. The forces of organic growth may work for uniformity, but material accident and other external influences impose complexity and a subtle irregularity of imbalance. Just as there never has been actual costume which, if precisely translated into marble, would have passed muster as Greek late-fifth-century drapery, so there never have been human faces and bodies that, if faithfully reproduced in bronze or stone, could be mistaken for fifth-century Greek statuary. Rodin's *L'Age d'Airain* more nearly reproduces the appearance of a living body cast in bronze. Inspection of it will instruct every perceptive onlooker on the magnitude of the classic sculptor's reformation of anatomic fact.

This, then, as we have described it, was the Polykleitan tradition "of chiastic balance and studied muscular response, of tempered proportion and harmonious outline, of expressive pose for the body at rest in a moment of suspended action, of the athletic nude in heroic strength."* It was this tradition which the numerous and active group of his apprenticed disciples expanded into an idiom of formalized naturalism during the early decades of the fourth century to fill the commissions with which they, and not their Attic former rivals, were entrusted. Inscribed marble pedestals with the footprints of lost bronze statues, and numerous references in Pausanias' *Guide to Greece,* bear witness to their productivity. But if these works were ever copied in marble in Roman times, we today have failed to identify them except for a few isolated instances such as the *"Oil-pourer"* of the Pitti Gallery in Florence or the *"Standing Discobolos"* in Rome (which may—but also may *not*—have been taken from a bronze by Naukydes, brother of the sculptor who bore the great master's name). The bronze originals themselves have all perished, with the notable exception of a single statue recovered in dilapidated condition from the Aegean near a tiny island below Cythera, twice re-assembled from its fragments and now, superbly reconstituted, on exhibition in the National Museum in Athens (Fig. 44 and Plate VII). As our only original monumental bronze from the first quarter of the fourth century, it deserves our utmost attention.

Nevertheless, despite the comparative paucity of documents with hardly any originals among them (because these were almost all in bronze, and bronze has a poor chance of survival) and a rather puz-

*Quoted from my recent book, *Greek Sculpture,* by permission of the University of Chicago Press.

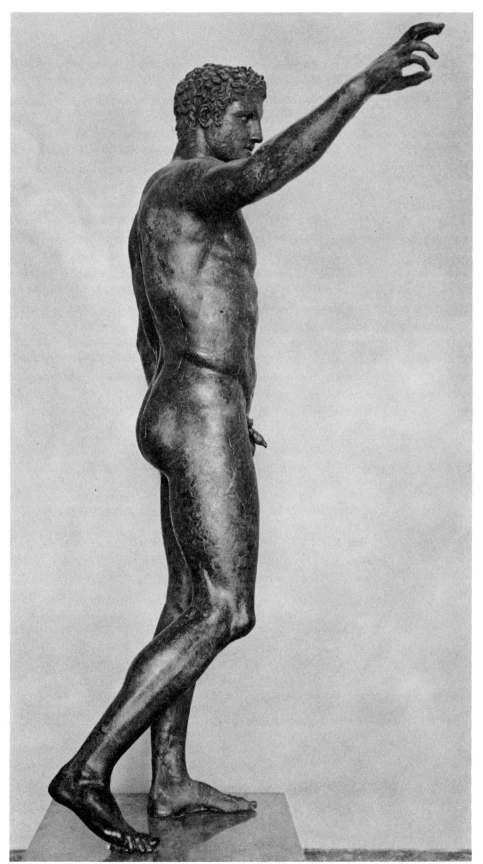

Fig. 44 Athens National Museum: the "Ball-player"

zling absence of authenticated copies from the Polykleitan school, with
nothing at all to any degree of certainty ascribable to Skopas and little
to inform us very extensively on the evolving mastery of his incredibly
productive contemporary, Lysippos,—it is entirely possible to trace the
gradual degradation of the number-ridden Canon from its dictatorial
control over the nude to a vaguely applied and only half-heeded influence on anatomic design. There is neither typographic space nor
appropriate leisure to permit the inclusion here of an investigation which
could not avoid being extremely discursive. But its omission is not dam-
aging to our study of the evolution of sculptural form, because the process was thoroughly consistent, almost undeviatingly continuous, and is
susceptible of being epitomized in a single and simple formula. Persistent
and increasingly detailed observation of natural appearances on the part
of the practicing artists led to repeated modification of the inherited
tradition of the workshops in order to bring it closer to physical actuality,
and this is the simple formula to which the Greek sculptors conformed
through the late fourth and early third centuries. How serious was their
study of visual anatomic fact—never quite the same as the superficial
anatomy of the human body which the medical profession envisages—is
shown by the famous passage in which Pliny records of a sculptor in
bronze, active in Lysippos' famous foundry at Sikyon, that

*"Lysistratus, a brother of Lysippus, initiated the practice of taking im-
pressions of the human form in plaster from the living model and pouring
wax into these molds* [to produce wax positives] *for correcting* [sculptural] *
representation."*

One is reminded of the late-nineteenth-century controversy over
Rodin's *L'Age d'Airain* concerning whether this nude figure of a boy had
been previously formed freehand in clay by the sculptor or mechanically
reproduced from negative molds taken directly from a live model. This
incident is not cited in order to suggest that Lysistratos (any more than
Rodin) cast his statues from molds mechanically formed on the living
flesh—the wording of Pliny's text precludes such an interpretation—but
rather to draw attention to the high degree of fidelity to natural appearances attained by Rodin (certainly) and by Lysistratos (presumably).

There is nothing in Pliny's account to justify the assumption, only
too frequently made in modern archaeological writing, that Lysistratos' innovation consisted in making life-masks of the human face. (The
term *facies* in the Latin is wrongly taken to refer to the countenance, but
the word is as ambiguous as French *"figure,"* and there is no suggestion
of any employ of life-masks discernible in early-third-century sculptural
portraiture, still less in normal statuary.) Inevitable as it may have been
for the sculptor's interest in naturalistic representation to have been ex-

tended to the features of the face and not to have confined itself to the rest of the bodily anatomy, our modern attitude toward the role of facial expression in statuary inclines us to misunderstand the ancient Greek conception. A brief review of the evidence should clarify the situation:

The Egyptian mortuary statue was intended as a refuge for the released soul of the embalmed body in whose tomb it was stationed. On that account the statue's facial features must bear some sufficient resemblance to the dead person's individual appearance. But there is no indication that the Greeks ever considered a *kouros* statue to be an actual person's duplicate image or looked on statues as possessed of any other inner life than that which visual mimicry might confer upon inanimate stone and metal. It would be difficult to discover to what extent the common folk may have imagined that the gods were bodily present within their images in their temple-dwellings, since here religious superstition could have supervened on commonsense appraisal; but since the gods were held to be invisible to mortal eyes, their images were by necessity even more inactual likenesses than were statues of human beings. At any rate, the *kouros* and *korē* were artistic abstractions without suggestion of a personal human relation between spectator and work of art. We may confidently assert that the Greeks viewed statuary objectively with complete awareness that it was a mimetic re-creation of living appearances which should not and could not be confused with reality without jeopardizing its existence as art. The "archaic smile" which animates the late-sixth-century *korē* is not a coquettish advance of endearment made by an elegantly dressed and bejewelled young woman to those whom she sees approaching her. In whatever sense her public is aware of her, she is in every sense unaware of her public. If her lips are drawn upward at the corners of her mouth, this is a purely physical indication of inner well-being, intended to remedy the morose lifelessness of the earlier straight-lipped representation. Her eyes are carefully painted so that they will seem physically fitted for seeing, as her ears are properly shaped for hearing, but it is not the spectator who stands before her that she is imagined to see or hear. She may look full at him if he places himself so as to intercept her gaze, but she will not see him.

Modern statues, after late-Gothic times, have been given blank and orbless eyes lest they become too interesting to their human visitors in a purely subjective communication of emotion. The Greeks, not being prone to this commonplace sensibility, felt no need to deprive their statues of the physical appearance of sight. That the artists of the Renaissance were misled by the empty eyes of the ancient marble heads which they found washed and bleached clean of painted iris and pupil, and through reverence for supposed classic precedent omitted such indications from their own statues, is a historic accident; but the persistence of the tradition into our own times is not the continuance of a chance error but the reflection of modern artistic convictions and esthetic needs. What Pater had to say of Mona Lisa would never have crossed a fifth-century Greek mind, since a Greek statue could look abroad, unheeding of its admirers, without being suspected of harboring thoughts ineffable. In the fifth-century Greek conception of statuary art the facial features were *bodily* features which, like the remaining anatomic structure, gave visual comprehension of the body's inner vitality. A well-shaped midriff was every whit as spiritual as a well-turned ear or a correctly fashioned eye, and the modern public which instinctively looks first at a Greek statue's face and dwells but casually upon its other parts, is misapplying a social behavior derived from everyday communal life and woefully failing to do justice to the ancient sculptural intent.

The recourse to simplified schematic shapes without regard for incidental irregularities such as are normal to every individual being, and the symmetrical arrangement of these shapes in precise correspondence of part to part for every paired feature in face and body, conspired together to produce the abstract ideality of the archaic types. In an archaic head any lack of exact correspondence between its paired elements is due to technical accident and not to deliberate intent (cf. Fig. 45). But as time passed and mimetic accuracy steadily increased, the same naturalistic observation which led to modification of rigid structural symmetry in bodily pose and substituted the calculated asymmetry of living balance for the lifeless precision of the older noetic concept affected also the rendering of the facial features. In these the need to differentiate each element from its mirror-opposite was particularly apparent because the features of living men and women are never precisely in balance either of identical size and shape or relative axial location. Where the sculptural theme was divine or mythical or otherwise remote from daily experience, it might suit gods and heroes to be ideally fashioned in the abstract perfection of noetic form, but where it concerned itself with ordinary human beings—whether athlete or warrior or statesman— ideal symmetry came to be tempered with deliberately introduced irregularity. Where this is not immediately apparent to the unaided eye, the following simple photographic expedient will reveal it:

An exactly frontal photograph of a sculptured head is divided into two halves along the vertical axis through chin, mouth, nose, and forehead. A separate print is made of each half, and each of these is then completed by turning the negative over in reverse to add its own mirror-

Fig. 45 Athens National Museum: Archaic Kouros from Volomandra

image. By this purely mechanical process, two different pictures are produced and any asymmetry of shape or position between corresponding left-hand and right-hand structure becomes instantly apparent. Figures 46 and 47 illustrate such an experiment performed on one of the surviving copies of a head highly popular in antiquity and variously identified as Vergil or Menander. After close examination, a distinguished neuro-surgeon has reached the conclusion that its erstwhile living prototype must have suffered in his early years from a "sensory type of hemiplegia in the parietal area with a mild motor component" (more briefly, cerebral palsy?). It would be rash for a layman in matters medical to suggest that such an inference wholly misinterprets the situation. Nevertheless it would appear that, under such diagnostic scrutiny, most of the distinguished men of later classical and early imperial Roman times must have suffered from physical abnormalities of one sort or another,

Fig. 46 Mirror-image Duplication of Left Half of Head

with their afflictions increasing in intensity according as they lived in the fourth, third, or second century before the Christian era. Those of the fifth century, however, would prove largely immune to this threat of physical malady because fifth-century sculpture displays no intentional irregularization of the features (cf. Fig. 38). Even where the subject purported to be some specific individual the noetic symmetry characteristic of the archaic phase was maintained during the formal phase of sculpture, and it was not until the fourth century was well advanced that calculated asymmetry becomes generally discernible—as in the portrait heads of Plato, derived from an original due to the contemporary artist, Silanion. But from that period on, portrait heads were asymmetrically individualized in order to detach them from the abstractly ideal tradition of earlier art (which continued to be employed for more generic, heroic, or divine themes).

Faith in the esthetic efficacy of the numerical canon acted as a deterrent to realistic study of the human face. And the traditional conventions of glyptic practice, such as the notorious "Greek profile" produced by leaving the bridge of the nose unstopped in the plane of the forehead (a technical accident whose origin will best be understood by examining the still-featureless face of the Ram-bearer of Thasos), conspired with canonic measuring to make accurate personal portraiture impossible in the fifth century. The herm inscribed "Perikles" may in some distant way have recalled that statesman's appearance to those already familiar with it, but it could not possibly have looked very much like him.

On the other hand, it should not be overlooked that the red-figure

Fig. 47 Mirror-image Duplication of Right Half of Head

vase-painters had interested themselves in depicting elderly men and old hags, and the introduction of these themes into the graphic repertory led to their adoption by the sculptors, as in the wrinkle-faced slave women couched in the corners of the west pediment at Olympia or the *Drunken Hag* by Myron, which has survived in copies and because of its simple block shape and its mid-fifth century drapery forms should not be dissociated from the older Myron of the *Discus-thrower*. Lucian refers to a statue by the (early-fourth-century) Athenian sculptor Demetrios, which represented a certain Corinthian general as paunched and bald, with beard and garments in disarray and veins prominent on his exposed body. There has been considerable question whether a description so appropriate to the advanced Hellenistic age does not imply considerable literary exaggeration on Lucian's part or even (less plausibly) an outright error in his ascription of the statue. However this may be, and despite the fact that there had always been a powerful undercurrent toward realism, during the high classic phase it was openly evinced in sculpture only in less exalted themes, as likewise in the minor art of caricature in terracotta figurines. For their major commissions the fifth and fourth-century sculptors in general resisted its intrusion, even though they could not have remained wholly unaffected by it. For, as we have continually insisted, the trend toward naturalism runs underneath all Greek art, and this, slowly but surely, promoted the possibility of turning the acquired sculptural resources toward fully individualized portraiture. Yet, so long as these resources remained purely glyptic and the sculptor actualized his forms only as he worked inward into an unmodeled block of marble, the extreme intricacies of surface-modeling in minute ever-shifting planes which are characteristic of the maturely developed human countenance and are responsible for its uniquely individual appearance, seem to be beyond the power of chisel, rasp, and abrasive to reproduce. Fully realistic portraiture, as we of the modern world have understood it since the Renaissance, was obliged to await the introduction of plastic freehand modeling of a positive image in wax for casting in bronze. And this did not take place until the third century had ended and the classic phase of Greek sculpture had been overpassed.

It remains to consider this passing of the classic phase in order to discover, if we can, what were the factors which determined the decline of formalism in Greek sculpture.

Reduced to the most general terms, these factors have already become abundantly clear in the course of this study. The reaction against ideated form was grounded in the very simple and forthright objection that it was unnatural precisely because it was formal, and in so far as it was formal it was to that same extent unnatural. Aristotelian philosophy manifests a strong repugnance against everything that is contrary to the natural state—*para physin*. If this prejudice extended to the artists as well as the philosophers, it gives us the key to stylistic evolution in ancient visual art. Just as in philosophy the transcendent idealism of Plato gave place to the scientific naturalism of Aristotle, so in sculpture much the same transition led from the ideated form of the Polykleitan period to the scientific realism of the Lysippan school.

Formal drapery, it will be recalled, was functional to the optical suggestion of solid form. But where drapery is also understood as the representation of actual human costume—(and unlike the "classical drapery" in more modern usage, which is a thoroughly inactual commodity, the *chitons* and *peploi* and *himatia* and *chlainai* and *chlamydes* which appear in Greek statuary art were representations of normal contemporary clothing)—its formalization could not fail to be sensed as sculptural artifice. If we may make a rather arbitrary distinction between "drapery" and "costume" by restricting the former term to the formal modification and the latter term to the physical actuality of human garments, it would be possible to epitomize a very long process in Greek stylistic history by saying that, under the pressure of the naturalistic trend, drapery evolved into costume.

In much the same way and for exactly the same underlying reason, the abstractly generic structure of the features of the human face became modified in statuary art in the direction of veridical portraiture or portrait-like realism. Similarly the formal features of superficial bodily anatomy underwent an identical metamorphosis from ideated into naturalistic rendering. To apply a distinction like that previously suggested between drapery and costume, the Nude of abstract invention was modified into the Naked of physical actuality.

There was, however, a much more arduous and subtle advance toward natural truth which sculpture was obliged to make if it was to persevere toward a fully realistic state. This advance was deeply involved in the physiological distinction, on which this study has so insistently dwelt, between the characteristic structures of the visual field and the visual world, between optical appearance and external material reality. In final analysis, this distinction determines the basic difference between pictorial and sculptural representation, but it is also the source of the difference in sensuous apprehension between seeing and touching an object, as likewise between two-dimensional and tridimensional reproduction of structure. The formal devices of the fifth century were designed and adopted in order to make the sculptured shape *appear* to be tridimensionally existent; however, out-and-out realism requires that the sculp-

tured shape shall not merely *seem* to reproduce, but shall actually reconstruct in full material counterfeit the solid structure of the represented
object. It may be objected that already by the third quarter of the fifth
century such a statue as the Polykleitan *Doryphoros* presents every element of the human body in fully solid shape. There is no skimping or
misrepresentation of the dimension of depth such as there is in a fifth-
century relief. Arms are correctly rounded, fingers and wrists are solidly
entire, and however much its superficial appearance may have been formalized, the torso occupies the same extension in space that the living
body possesses. Where then, it may be demanded, is there any tridimensional inactuality? To this it should be replied that the inactuality does
not reside in the separate elements of the body individually considered,
but in their correlation and assembly. It is the total disposition in aerial
space which is faulty because the pose has been compressed within four
cardinal aspects in projected silhouette. There can be no question that it
is perfectly feasible for a living model to assume the pose of the *Doryphoros,* but in so doing the model will be subjecting himself to a pictorial
restriction and resigning his natural behavior as an organism free to dispose himself without such restriction, physically at ease in the spatial expanse
of the world of which he is part.

From the work of Polykleitos' pupils and successors there has survived
to us only a single original bronze statue, but this fortunately is of superb
quality. After the vicissitudes of having been sunk in a storm-wrecked
cargo ship to the depths of the Aegean, of having been recovered through
the exploratory activity of deep-sea divers in search of sponges, and thereafter reconstituted from a great number of fragments, to be displayed at
last in accurately reconstructed shape in the National Museum in Athens,
the *"Ball-player"* has become our most precious document for the nude
athletic victor-statue of antiquity (Fig. 44 and Plate VII).

In any unilinear progress toward a fixed aim or end, every move por-
tends the future as clearly as it reveals the past. It is therefore no marvel
that the *"Ball-player"* at one and the same time recalls the style of Polykleitos and foretells the manner of Lysippos. The "quadrature" to which
Pliny took exception in the work of Polykleitos has been partially dissolved by bringing a raised arm forward of the body so as to cause the
torso to revolve slightly on its vertical axis, while the head has been
turned to direct its gaze toward the laterally displaced and outwardly
extended right hand. The *"Ball-player"* is not hurling a ball, but is sighting
his aim in preparation for the throw. The pose presents a "Myronic moment"
of pause similar to that of the Discus Thrower. Through this device the upper
body no longer faces in the same direction as the lower limbs, and four-point
cardinal frontality has been broken. In this important innovation the

unknown sculptor of the *"Ball-player"* proves himself in advance of his master, Polykleitos, and at the same time an immediate precursor of his great successor, Lysippos. The pose of the *"Ball-player"* requires only the slight modification of lifting the slackly idle left arm and bringing it across toward the other hand to bring it into almost total agreement with the Vatican *Apoxyomenos* (Fig. 48)—the statue which (in spite of much uncertainty occasioned by the discovery at Delphi of the very differently composed *Agias*) must still be accepted as a paradigm for the mature style of Lysippos.

But even the evolved Lysippan formula, as it is embodied in the *Apoxyomenos,* the *Bow-stringing Eros,* and the *Seated Ares* of the Ludovisi collection in the Terme Museum, does not fully solve the spatial problem bequeathed by the practice of cardinal frontality. Considered geometrically as a proposition in applied optical theory, the elimination of frontal silhouette by bodily torsion has not been carried to complete effectiveness by Lysippos. A brief review of the situation will make this clear:

In the canonic Polykleitan pose we are too attentive to unforeshortened outline appearances to gain much direct perception of solid structure. Spatial depth is largely unapparent because its informative optical conversions are not sufficiently indicated. Admittedly, the *Doryphoros* in uncorroded bronze would not have seemed wholly flat and unsubstantial, because the luminosity gradients of its strongly reflective surfaces would give it modeling, but it would fail to convey properly its density, its physical actuality, its structural conformation as a balanced mass suspended in visual space. The Vatican *Apoxyomenos,* when set side by side with the Delphic *Agias* (as is possible in plaster cast or in photograph), very vividly demonstrates the great advance in stereometric suggestion from the standard Polykleitan formula which Lysippos employed in his earlier work to the sculptor's own improved solution in the later. Where the *Agias* stands flatly frontal, a magnificently outlined form emphatically silhouetted as though carved in relief and projected upon a uniform plane, the *Apoxyomenos* eludes such projection and dulls the graphic force of his contours by compelling us to see him as a solid figure leaning outward into space and free to move his limbs, even though the suggested movement is one of horizontal rotation rather than of locomotion.

It was this device of horizontal revolution on the body's vertical axis of support which Lysippos' followers developed into an intelligently calculated formula for eliminating all frontal rigidity of silhouetted pose and liberating the sculptured form from the last traces of graphic restraint. A number of bronze statues have survived—all apparently recastings (or reworkings at reduced scale) from originals that have perished—which conform very exactly to a compositional formula of spiral torsion. In these,

Fig. 48 The Vatican Apoxyomenos

"the horizontal axes which might be imagined as passing through the two ankles, the knees, the hips, the shoulders, and the ears, point like a compass needle revolving through a quadrant of a full circle, so that the uppermost lies at a right angle to the lowermost. All frontality of pose is destroyed by thus confronting the entire circuit of possible viewpoints everywhere with both silhouetted and foreshortened aspects in coherent relation. In consequence, the spatial configuration of the presented object remains visually intelligible as solid form from every point of view."*

The *Seated Hermes* and the *Dancing Faun*, which are well-preserved bronzes extracted from the buried Vesuvian sites, exhibit bodily proportions and anatomical detail in close agreement with the Lysippan norm. And the formula to which their poses conform is too strictly applied as an abstractly intellectualized theorem to be a casual discovery of later Hellenistic times. There is good reason, therefore, to ascribe it to the Lysippan School and assign its use to the early years of the third century. It must rank as the last of the significant formal devices which distinguish classic Greek sculpture and set it apart as an abnormally intellectualized genus of representational art. That the other formal inventions of the classic phase appeared on the scene at a considerably earlier date (most of them being introduced during the course of the fifth century) is due to the different category of visual apprehension to which they belong. There is a consistent shift of esthetic level from the incised linear notation of archaism through the modified surface conformations of the classic phase to the fully stereomorphic conception of poses in spiral torsion.

"With tridimensional spatial presentation, such as the *Seated Hermes* exemplifies, the long process of stylistic evolution from pictorial vision to stereomorphic reproduction of material structure reaches a culminating stage.... The great era of formal development consequently ends after three and a half centuries with the Lysippan School of the early Hellenistic Age."*

The scrutiny of Greek sculptural style does not end at this point (even though Pliny seemed to think so, since he said of the early third century, *"cessavit deinde ars,"*—sc. *ars toreutice*), because every great action must have an epilog, and no art with so much vital energy as the Greek could ever have stagnated so early. But with the attainment of the last of the great High-Classic evolutionary phases it may be worth a paragraph to consider the Classic Manner itself, viewing it not as a purely local event or a restrictedly Hellenic incident, but as an aspect of Western Man's emergence into cultural self-consciousness.

*Passages in quotation marks followed by an asterisk (*) are reproduced from my more extensive survey in *Greek Sculpture: A Critical Review*, by permission of the publisher, the University of Chicago Press.

Keeping to the physiological and psychological perspective which this study has applied, it may be said that we normally behold the surrounding world very imperfectly because it is inadequately presented to us in sight. It is not because the world "is too much with us, late and soon," but because it is too *little* with us, that so "little we see in Nature that is ours." The representational arts can remedy this defect by presenting us with a fuller visual apprehension than everyday experience brings. It is not merely that "every thing is spoilt by use" because daily habit dulls our senses to a purely serviceable minimum of awareness, whereas esthetic contemplation, being unpragmatic, enables us to notice what pragmatic sight overlooks. This is undoubtedly the case, but, in addition, art is able to present the visual world to us in a more assimilable and hence more intelligible form by clarifying and strengthening its "optical potential." It is only on this ground—I believe—that the extreme artificiality of the Greek high-classic idiom may be justified and the futility of reintroducing it in modern times as a current mannerism may be made evident. As a device for overcoming the optical inadequacies of the archaic approach and ameliorating the rigor of Early Formal abstractness it was a magnificent success: as an academic prescription for general use in order to sublimate mimetic realism with an ideal component of classic transcendence it has little to recommend it. Removed from its historical and genetic context, it is without bearing on present-day esthetic interests.

Notwithstanding, in the land and among the people of its own proper origin it found a spectacular reapplication. For in that environment it was not the stilted and affected manner which it cannot fail to be in an alien setting where men and women wear wholly other costume and respond through other emotional outlets to the contemplation of the heroic athletic nude. As already pointed out, during the course of the third century naturalism completely dominated sculptural style; so that, having led to its predestined goal, the path of technical progress now opened up no further prospect of advance. It should be taken into consideration that naturalism in Greek art, because directly evolved out of formalism, carried a certain taint of idealism and formal restraint. It was not a robust, nor yet a strongly imaginative, manner. And it should be further remarked that Naturalism, as I have employed the term, is not Realism as very generally understood in literary criticism where it has been applied to emphasis on the more brutal and unpleasant aspects of life to the neglect of all that is more delicately appealing and more sensuously attractive. There is, therefore, something slightly commonplace and emotionally undemonstrative in this phase of Greek sculpture. Its serenity failed to reflect the intensity of Mid-Hellenistic political and civil life with its dramatic reversals of fortune and its worship of the goddess Tyche as the sole effective agent in men's destinies.

It is impossible to tell how much the evolution of artistic style, with its technical determination from within, may be influenced by external human events and moods. For that reason it is impossible to determine to what extent it was the temper of the times and how far it was a reaction induced within the technical framework of the art itself, which led to dramatic reuse—verging on misuse—of the older High Classic devices. On this phenomenon there will be occasion for descriptive comment in a following chapter, wherein it will be briefly touched upon as an epilog or aftermath of the main evolutionary course of Greek sculptural style.

XII

EVOLUTION OF ARCHITECTURAL FORM
—THE DORIC ORDER

Except for such passing notice as a discussion of tectonic form occasioned, the builder's art has thus far been neglected in this survey. The omission was not in the least due to any misappraisal of classic architecture as a minor or otherwise negligible achievement of the Greek genius. But the nonmimetic character of architectural form completely dissociates it from sculpture and painting in any formal study of the evolution of style. If stylistic change in these latter arts was conditioned by an innate trend toward imitative accuracy in reproducing visual appearances of material objects and living things, little profit can be expected from involving architecture in the discussion of their behavior. So completely does the builder's range of interest diverge from this essential preoccupation of the graphic and the glyptic artist, that if Greek architecture shows any evolutionary sequence of phase, form, or fashion, its development must depend on some wholly different trend toward some categorically different objective. That architectural style is subject to change will of course be admitted by everyone, but whether its changes can be ascribed to any controlling influence other than shifting taste and casual preference remains to be discovered. In painting and sculpture, as we have seen, the technical goal is set from the start and is lodged outside the artist in an external world which he has no power to modify but must accept as it is. On casual inspection it seems highly improbable that the architect is subject to any comparable influence from without. His actions are not dictated to him by natural appearances, since he is imitating nothing that already exists apart from his own activity. The natural world contains no structures which he has set himself to copy, and the visual forms with which he endows the products of his craft have no prototypes elsewhere than in his own mind or in the past of his own profession. He is subject to strong material restrictions in so far as he is a builder and a constructional engineer, but in so far as he works beyond

204

these restraints to produce tectonic shapes with esthetic significance, he seems to be exercising a purely mental activity, dealing not in imitative (or mimetic) but in abstractly creative (or noetic) forms. The prime question for our enquiry, therefore, is whether noetic form displays any evolutionary trend comparable to that which mimetic form so clearly exhibits.

Before essaying an answer, Greek architecture must be more closely defined within the wider realm of possible modes available to a builder. In the Aegean territory the material medium was stone and timber and sun-dried brick, and the stone was more especially marble, which was almost everywhere accessible and very generally of superb quality. When a different grade of stone was employed, such as (among very few other acceptable substitutes) uncrystallized limestone in its various states of harsh shell-conglomerate, soft *poros,* and the more finely levigated and close-grained deposits from strata accompanying true marble, it was nearly always hidden from sight in important buildings. If used for foundation work, it was buried under earth, and where it formed an integral part of the visible construction, it was carefully coated with fine stucco of marble dust to give the appearance of the marble which it should more properly have been. Brick was chiefly confined to domestic and minor public structures, and was very generally plastered or stuccoed over. Being employed without formal articulation, it has little or no significance for a survey of Greek architectural form. As a highly organized and self-conscious discipline, Greek architecture is therefore the art of building with marble.

But marble was also the sculptors' much exploited medium. The material source of supply was the same for temples as for statues (in the Parthenon there is no apparent distinction between the Pentelic marble used for the walls and columns and that which served the sculptors for the pedimental statues, and the carved metopes and wall-frieze are an integral material part of the structural fabric). The technical methods of extraction from the quarries and of reduction to serviceable shape and size were essentially the same for building blocks as for statuary; much the same tools were used to dress the marble, the same abrasive was applied for final finish, the same wax pigments added for brilliant coloring of detail. It is therefore hardly surprising that the same skilled artisans were in the employ of both the builder and the supplier of statuary, or that Greek sculptors could also be architects and Greek architects enjoy repute as sculptors. The Polykleitos who is named as architect of the magnificent theater and the incomparably executed *tholos* at Epidauros must be a lineal descendant of the famous sculptor of that name and can hardly be other than the sculptor mentioned by Pausanias as a pupil of

Naukydes and distinguished by us as Polykleitos the Younger. Skopas, whose renown as sculptor rivalled that of Praxiteles, is stated to have been the architect responsible for the new temple of Athena Alea in Arcadian Tegea after the older structure was destroyed by fire. Pythios, famed for his temple to Athena in Priene and his collaboration on the Maussoleum, is said to have carved the marble horses and car which topped the Carian prince's spectacular tomb. And it is difficult to imagine that anyone not fully at home in the sculptor's workshop could have successfully directed the building of a Greek temple, which was put together out of accurately trimmed and superbly fitted blocks of marble with every detail of the Order carved in the solid stone. When these blocks had been assembled and so carefully fitted that the joints were virtually invisible, the result might almost have been a single intricate piece of carving, more complex than any statue and yet, like a statue, a unified glyptic form with abrasive-smoothed surface and brilliant painted detail.

This kinship of Greek architecture to glyptic sculpture can hardly be exaggerated by the modern critic, so deep an imprint did it make on ancient architectural thought and sensibility and so insistently is it apparent in all that has survived from the classic centuries. Greek architecture, like Greek sculpture, is a tectonic rendering of glyptic form, whose technical perfection depended on skill in cutting, fitting, and decorating marble.

The Siphnian treasury at Delphi is an illuminating demonstration of the extent to which a Greek builder could rely upon the sculptor's craft. The tiny structure consisted of a single chamber preceded by an open vestibule with which it communicated through a large doorway. For the two columns normal to such a vestibule there were substituted twin statues of archaic *korai* standing on statuary pedestals and carrying elaborately carved basket crowns in lieu of capitals. The figured frieze above them dwarfed the intervening blank epistyle, borrowing the latter's crown-moulding for its base and adding an equally conspicuous head-moulding of exquisitely carved leaves to frame it in above. This figured frieze with its accompanying ornament was not confined to the façade, but continued as a wall-crown around the remaining three sides of the building. In front, the gable was filled with statuary, and its three angles supported other statues as finials on the roof against the sky. The eaves around the building were carved underneath with lotus and palmette; the gutters above them drained through carved lion-heads. The wall-base carried a large barrel-molding of bead and reel, and the exposed wall-ends on the façade were marked as pilasters by projecting leaf-molding. **Within the open vestibule behind the simpering *korai* the door frame was elaborately outlined with palmette and pointed leaf and beading.**

And although in actual area the blank marble surfaces of the floors within, together with the vertical walls, inside and out, considerably exceeded the surface given over to this intricate adornment in colored carving, they were of no moment artistically except as smooth panels against which the bright glory of the sculptors' handiwork could be displayed.

This treasury of the gold-rich Siphnians was no doubt a pretentious show-piece designed to impress the other communities of the Greek world. There could not have been many examples of such a lavish sculptural incrustation of a structurally simple building. The great temples could not have tolerated so jewel-like a treatment of their bulk. The Zeus temple at Olympia showed blank exterior metopes and little glyptic adornment below the cornice line. Similarly, the Parthenon counted greatly on its purely architectural structure, its sequence of marching columns and rhythmical repetition of the elements of its Order. Yet the sculptural contribution to this temple was no mean affair with its ninety-two exterior metopes of four-foot slabs carved in highest relief, its forty free-standing statues (including several at colossal scale) within the pediments, and its more than five hundred running feet of exterior wall-crown carved in low relief with figures at nearly half lifesize. (The gold and ivory colossus of Athena within the temple is hardly to be assessed as part of the architecture—and here, no doubt, it was the architect who helped out the sculptor by building for him the thirty-foot interior scaffolding on which to support his figure.) The nearby Erechtheion is as notable for its exquisitely carved moldings, which run everywhere along its walls and surround its several doorways, as for its better-known but no more deftly carved Caryatid maidens. In Asia Minor at Ephesos and Didyma the huge temples in Ionic Order may have had somewhat less of applied sculptural adornment; yet the carved column-bases from the Ephesian temple must have ranked among the great achievements of mid-fourth-century statuesque relief; and the buildings themselves were no less a stonecutter's triumph of precisely hewn, closely fitted, and exquisitely surfaced marble, whether the blocks were simple ashlars for the walls, or complex key-pieces in the close-knit entablature, or parts of the coffered ceilings, or drums of the tall, tapering, and precisely fluted column-shafts. Indeed, it is not so much the directly sculptural contribution of meticulously carved string-course ornament or the figured friezes and pedimental statues in-the-round or the open-mouthed lion-heads draining the roofs or the swift-moving roof-top statues against the sky—great as their contribution was to the total architectural effect of the Greek temples—but the sculptural treatment of the various abstract motives of the Orders and the strictly sculptural conception of the mason's task of preparing, shaping, fitting, and finishing his structural material, which is the most unusual characteristic of Greek architectural art in contrast to the building practices of other lands and times. In Doric columns such as those of the Parthenon (Fig. 20 on page 83)—with their minute convexity of parabolic curvature working counter to the diminishing diameter of the ascending shaft, and the ever-changing concave curve of their fluted hollows growing sharper as the arrises draw closer together in the ascent—there were tasks set to the stonecutter demanding greater skill and more expenditure of time and labor than builders have ever again been able to command. The Doric columns of advanced Hellenistic, Roman, and more modern times are seldom more than perfunctory simplifications of the Periclean prototype. The Ionic capitals of the Erechtheion, with their triple-stringed spirals and sharply delicate floral necking-band and braided cables picked out in colored glass, are triumphs of intricacy in which the sculptor rather than the mason has had the major share. And even an ordinary Ionic capital in the more usual tradition of the Order, if it is not a veritable marvel of sculptural deftness, may be stigmatized as a poor example of its kind. (Thus, the huge capital from Sardis on exhibition in the New York Metropolitan Museum, because it has a miscalculated spiral for one of its volutes, must derive from the imperial Roman rebuilding of the Artemis temple and not from its original undertaking. A better example is shown in Fig. 52).

Where a circular plan was substituted for the normal rectangle of temple or treasury or shrine—as in the *tholos* at Epidauros with external Doric and interior Corinthian colonnading—it is hardly possible to exaggerate the difficulty of the stonecutter's task in trimming the faces of the blocks to fit the concentric arcs on varying radii which apply to every step-block and floor-block and wall-block in the structure and to every member of the entablatures, the rhomboidal coffering of the ceilings, and the interlocking tiles of the sloping conical roof.

The famous Sidonian sarcophagi are purely sculptural productions, carved out of blocks of marble, but in their insistence on treating the body and lid of the coffin in architectural terms—the *"Mourning Women"* sit or stand in the intercolumniations of a fully detailed Ionic temple carved in relief—they testify to the essential oneness of the two arts as the Greeks envisaged them.

Such an attitude on the part of its practitioners is, in and by itself, hardly sufficient reason for anticipating that architectural and sculptural style must have run similar evolutionary careers. But if we may assume that the Greek master-builder regarded his productions in much the same way as did the sculptor, there may be some justification for inquiring whether there was anything in common in the formal development of these two arts so intimately allied in Greek conception.

If we recall how in archaic sculpture the interior solid mass was only vaguely affected and scarcely at all penetrated by the articulation of detail on its surface, and if we further remind ourselves how in an archaic statue the solid pattern shape was dependent on four cardinal profiles to the neglect of intermediate aspects, we shall discover a striking similarity to the classic architect's presentation of structural mass and surface detail in the standard peripteral temple (cf. Fig. 49). Here too, as in archaic sculpture, all visible appearance is constructed out of four cardinal silhouetted contours enclosing intelligible details in frontal projection upon the exterior of a visually inaccessible mass. The hidden interior remains spatially undefined by the exterior Order and uninvolved in its patternized articulation. Perhaps this could be expressed more simply by saying that the Greek temple was intended to be viewed *from the outside* as a rhythmic linear movement of a columned Order about the four sides of a rectangle. This rectangle was only externally defined, being spanned

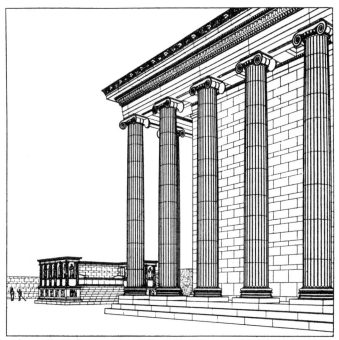

Fig. 49 Priene, Temple of Athena: Reconstruction

by a covering gable roof but otherwise offering no visible indication of
its interior structure or disposition or appearance or purpose.

In this rather specialized sense, within the limitations of a definition
based on a purely formal analogy, *Greek architecture throughout the entire classic age may be defined as archaic,* because it failed to overpass
that stylistic phase from which Greek painting and sculpture so effectively emerged. Even the strictest application of canonic proportion,
which caused Vitruvius to compare the Greek Orders to the processes of
Polykleitan statuary, did not induce in architecture the vitalizing effect
which it had on sculpture. The builder's canon, for lack of any organic
living prototype to guide it, remained an abstract assemblage of man-
made parts and arbitrary patterns.

And if the colonnaded temple resembled block sculpture in-the-
round, the colonnaded stoa with its rows of columns in double rank before a smoothly continuous background wall equally strikingly resembled
an archaic stepped relief in parallel planes without fully presented visual
depth.

If all this is anything more than a fanciful analogy between two arts
of widely divergent aims and interests, it should be possible to suggest
the formal step which Greek architecture might have taken to pass from
archaic restraint to a more evolved phase comparable to that which
Greek sculpture reached in fifth-century formalism. That transition, it
will be recalled, was characterized by a conversion of negatively incised
into affirmatively excised drapery and a conversion of graphically outlined anatomy, externally patternized, into modeled shapes indicative of
interior bodily structure. Although the sculptor necessarily continued to
attack the marble block from without, he succeeded in suggesting that
the exterior appearance of the clothed or the nude form was due to forces
operative from within. In this way the superficial expanse of archaic pattern was transformed into solid indices of interior condition. A comparable transformation is at least imaginable for architecture, and indeed
just such a conversion to an exterior articulation of the interior voluminal
disposition is displayed by Byzantine buildings of the Greek Christian
Middle Ages. In the typical mid-Byzantine church, every structural element by which aerial space is defined and enclosed in the succession of
walls and piers, arches and pendentives, roofs and domes of the interior,
extrudes some indication of its location in plan and its function in support, so that the entire interior disposition is apprehensible from its
exterior formulation. This is very generally (and no doubt very rightly)
applauded as a supreme virtue of the Byzantine ecclesiastical style. It
should be observed, however, that it is a completely inelastic stylistic dictation in conformity with geometrical principles corresponding very

closely to the rigid optical formulas of the late fifth-century Attic sculpture. So comprehensive are the formal restrictions of such a mode that individual imaginative invention is virtually precluded.

It is significant that the Byzantine formal idiom was bred on classic Greek soil. Elsewhere, the imperial Roman architects, with their use of a plastic medium in poured concrete and a wide range of utilitarian commissions to stimulate their inventiveness, had already advanced to much freer spatial manipulation and extricated themselves from abstract formal restraint. The parallel with sculptural style is obscured at this stage because realistic naturalism, which succeeded formalism in early Hellenistic sculpture, has no meaning for architectural style. But there is again a resemblance in the succeeding phase. In Greek sculpture, by overclosely copying the unexciting world of everyday reality to which humanity naturally conforms in physical appearance and costume and behavior, third-century naturalism had created a placid and esthetically unexciting manner which only great technical skill rescued from becoming commonplace. Growing restive under the monotony of this merely mimetic achievement, in the succeeding second century the sculptors looked about for some more expressive treatment to their work and, struck by the suggestive power of the formal devices of the earlier masters, revived these devices, not for their original purpose of stereographic representation, but in much more arbitrary manner as visual stimulants to emotional response. Where fifth-century motion-lines were introduced, they were now applied not so much to activate an otherwise static pose as to stir a moving figure into swirling frenzy—as the Victory from Samothrace leans against the imaginary blast of wind sweeping her on the war-ship's prow upon which she has alighted. Where in the fifth century the modeling-lines, because of the purpose for which they had been invented, maintained strict accord with the bodily form beneath, in the second-century revival they were used without relevance to the body's modeling and diverted into unfamiliar and extravagant patterns of intersecting lines and broken lights and shadows—as in those fantastically gowned women from Pergamon and Magnesia and other Asiatic seaboard towns, which seem to belong not merely to a different century but to a different artistic era from the restrainedly serious figures of classic Attic and Peloponnesian art.

If we define such an unlicensed style as a phase of "free emotive form," we mean that the formal devices for sculptural presentation were now free to be applied in whatever way appealed to the artist's fancy instead of being straightly confined to the functions for which they had been invented, and we mean that these formal devices, when so employed, were "emotive" in the sense that their diversion from their proper sphere of making sculptured form intelligible to the eye caused them to evoke new

modes of emotional response as the sculptors turned them to exciting
and unfamiliar effect. This dramatically exaggerated experimentation with
the formal resources of the art, which ran its course during the second
and third quarters of the second century only to succumb to its own con-
tagion of meaningless disorder before the century was out, has often been
referred to by modern critics as "baroque." The term, though frequently
applied, has almost as frequently been criticized as an unjustified ascription to antiquity of a uniquely modern phenomenon. But if our analysis of
second century Greek sculpture as a phase of "free emotive form" is justified, it follows that the title of "baroque" is entirely deserved. For, on
analysis, it will be discovered that the conflicting praise and disapproval
so generously showered on European baroque derive from discordant judgment on the propriety of just such "free emotive forms" in architecture and
the representational arts. What else are the huge corner scrolls beneath
the dome of Santa Maria della Salute in Venice except "free emotive
forms"? and what else are the visually stimulating but functionally repre-
hensible contrivances of the more luridly baroque architects, one-and-all
and everywhere?

   This alignment of European baroque and second-century Hellenistic
sculpture as parallel phenomena in the formal development of two very
different arts is not based on any purely fortuitous coincidence. For it is significant that in each case there succeeded on baroque extravagance a submissive return to traditional formulation, a penitent neo-classic revival
more conspicuous for academic correctness than for imaginative novelty.

   Admittedly, a highly pertinent objection to this temporally distracted
comparison between the stylistic history of five hundred years of sculptural
development and nearly twenty-five centuries of much interrupted architectural accomplishment, is the glaring chronological discrepancy. The reply to this objection is the equally pertinent observation (already made
several times in this enquiry) that the various arts develop at differing rates
of speed conditioned by such external influences as production-time, economic cost, and public demand — a saddening commentary how earthbound
is the Daedalid flight into the artist's empyrean! If account be made of the
span of years which the average Greek temple or similar major architectural
enterprise demanded for its completion, and the rarity of such structures in
every community, compared with the throng of statues and the even more
prolific graphic work of drawings on vases and paintings on colonnaded
walls and wooden panels, a very great lag in formal architectural evolution
will have to be admitted as inevitable, a delay sufficient to put it wholly out
of step with other more rapidly and more abundantly produced types of art.

   After having thus detected an agreement in formal development between sculpture and architecture in their final phases, if we next turn our

attention in the opposite direction from later developments toward initial stages, we shall discover divergence rather than convergence of behavior in these two arts.

To begin with sculpture: if the poses and themes and stylistic devices which the advanced fourth century currently employed be traced back to their respective origins in earlier work, from which in one way or another they had been evolved, the range and variety of these will be found ever lessening as we proceed backward in time. Divergences fuse and disappear within fewer and more schematic types and technical modes. Already at the transitional period from archaic to early formal we are confronted with a greatly restricted inventiveness of form and when we reach the mid-archaic phase, there remain effective only three or four accepted poses, a limited stock of schematic representational devices for facial features, hair, and costume, and a single anatomic pattern for the nude. On the other hand, if we turn to architecture and proceed in similar manner to trace its stock of available building forms backward in time from the high classic period to its earliest beginnings, the outcome will be exactly the opposite. Later uniformity will be seen to expand into fluid variety instead of contracting into fewer norms. Fixed precepts of canonic tradition are dissipated in heterogeneous experiment and amorphous abnormality. It must be a matter of considerable astonishment to the unarchaeological practitioner of architecture, taught in his early training to regard the three Greek Orders as an invariable code of sequence, proportion, and design with strictest regulation of shape and function in every part, to encounter for the first time the rank growth of orderless profusion which archaeology has unearthed in its exploration of the earliest architecture on Greek soil. Where he had learned a single standard norm for the ancient Greek temple—restricting its plan to a rectangular room (with or without a second ante-room) flanked by symmetrical vestibules and surrounded by an open colonnade in single or double file treated as a single consecutive Order of invariable prescribed elements in the Doric, Ionic, or Corinthian scheme, rising from a stepped platform and surmounted by a uniform gable roof—he will look in vain for any such canonic structure before the sixth century. Instead, he will be shown long, narrow buildings with naked walls unmasked by colonnading, with promiscuously arranged rooms of arbitrary proportions, at times ending in apses or hairpin curves, with relief sculpture in unexpected locations, with roofs pitched steeply or laid perfectly flat, with interior wooden column-posts aligned on the major central axis or vaguely scattered about where their support seemed needed—in fact, a builder's hodgepodge without authority or established fashion, without agreed behavior or secure tradition, floundering in artistic helplessness. Out of all this groping uncertainty, by some astounding concen-

tration on what was fitting and right in Greek eyes and rejection of what
was inappropriate or vague or valueless, somehow or other—and it is very
strange that we have nothing more precise to record about the process—the
two Orders and the standard norms for temple, stoa, council-house, and
entrance gateway emerged and, after having been fittingly reviewed and
perfected, were accepted as mandatory by all self-conscious Greek communities. This is not to say that there was no variety and no changeful
vitality in classic architecture, once it had become normalized, but the
variety is *within* the norm and the vitality is organic and internal, implying
conformity to type rather than transgression beyond it. Canonic architecture has many of the qualities, both helpful and hindering, of canonic
sculpture. Pliny's stricture that Polykleitan statues were *paene ad unum
exemplum* is matched by the uninformed modern tourist's complaint that,
were it not for the perennial loveliness of the Hellenic landscape, it would
hardly repay the journey's time and effort to view "just another Doric temple."

In sculpture, then, variety evolved out of uniformity: in architecture,
uniformity evolved out of variety. Whence this polarity, this total reversal
of trend? We have only to review the material evidence to find an answer
to this question.

Because sculpture (like painting) is a mimetic art, imitatively reproducing appearances of an external physical world of extreme complexity,
its technical goal is an expanded repertory of types and themes and situa-
tions, which necessarily becomes increasingly multifarious as it attains
success in mirroring its prototypes in the physical realm. Consequently it
is the variety in the material world that is responsible for the variety of
sculptural representation. On the other hand, architecture does not imitate the visual world, but turns inward on its own invention. It might be
supposed that, with human ingenuity and love of novelty acting as stimulus, this inventive faculty would accumulate more and more variety in
planning and constructing buildings, somewhat as Piranesi indulged his
architectural imagination in creating the vast complexities of his engraved
Carceri dell' Invenzione. There is, of course, economic impediment (as
well as a popular demand for the approved and familiar) which effectually
prevents such tremendous structures from ever becoming more than graphic fantasies. Nonetheless some of the imperial Roman ruins and fragmen-
tary remains of complex buildings suggest that, in its more emancipated
phases, ancient architecture was capable of great imaginative expansion. If
classic Greek buildings fail to show any comparable proliferation, the explanation must be that architecture was still in its "Polykleitan phase" of
canonic perfection, convinced of the validity of abstract schematic norms.

We have already seen how a canonic use of integral ratios and a geometric theory of optical devices dominated mid-fifth-century sculpture. We have also seen how this abstract formal regimentation was weakened and finally destroyed by the opposing demands of mimetic fidelity. Had there been no such contrary influence to override the noetic formulas, Greek sculpture might very readily have remained stationary, stereotyped in canonic convention. (Much this fate beset Egyptian sculpture because the standard of control was not centered in the world of living beings but in the changeless magic of an imaginary afterworld). But because architecture was not exposed to any such aggressive force persistently at work to destroy its abstract harmonies and its self-imposed conventions, it remained in its noetic state as a canonic art of proportioned structure and standardized shapes. The only change to which the Doric Order could be susceptible was modification *inside* the canon: the column could become more slender, its capital less emphatically curved, the epistyle less massive, and a third triglyph and metope could be assigned to the column interval. But all such modifications were changes within the canon of the Order, whose sequence of elements remained unaltered, with each of these elements maintaining its characteristic shape and pattern; and the conception of the colonnaded Order as a planimetric projection without inherent depth was never relinquished.

Parenthetically, attention may be called to the fact that much the same attitude was evinced by the ancient potters in perpetuating standard shapes with only minor concession to current fashions or their own preference and taste. Once a ceramic type such as *kylix* or *oinochoe* or *amphora* had been established, the individual potter could only modify the proportions and temper the outlines within narrow limits. If he went further and stepped outside the canonic form, he had ceased to make a *kylix* or *oinochoe* or *amphora*. He would have been no longer practicing his inherited craft. One is reminded of Plato's dictum in the *Republic* that the carpenter who intends to make a bed must first look within himself at the ideated form and then shape his material to conform with this immaterial "idea." It may be objected that Plato intended merely to point out that no one could make a bed unless he already knew what a bed looked like, but that is hardly a sound interpretation of the text. To Plato, a visual-minded Greek, the bed was already there as an ideated form before any human artisan had fashioned its material counterpart.

Perhaps we need to be sympathetic to this Platonic prejudice before we can be persuaded that the "previous history" of the Doric and Ionic Orders is not to be found externally in Mycenaean buildings nor yet in Geometric timber-work, but must be sought for internally as an idea originating in the human brain. Only on such a theory would it have been possible for these Orders to materialize themselves (as they seem to have

done) within the confines of a single generation of master-builders and,
after having been materially actualized, thereafter to persist for hundreds
of years as though they had always been in existence. In biological metaphor, an abrupt and novel mutation had emerged, to perpetuate itself as a
distinct species.

It is often maintained that the plan of the Greek temple is directly
descended from the Mycenaean palace *"megaron."* But if the ground-plan
of a Mycenaean *megaron,* as the palace of Tiryns has preserved it or the
recent excavation of Pylos has revealed it (Fig. 50), is set side by side

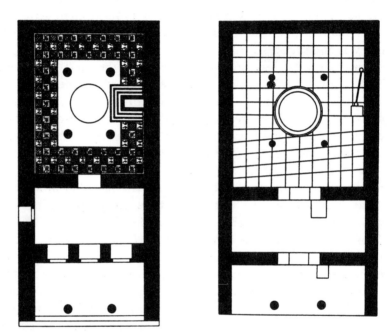

Fig. 50 Plan of Mycenean Megara at Tiryns and Pylos

with a plan of the Zeus temple at Olympia or the Poseidon temple at
Paestum or the Hephaistos Temple in Athens (Fig. 51), it is difficult to discover more than a superficial similarity. The peristyle which encloses the
Hellenic temple with a colonnaded Order is not an old Aegean but a classic
Greek device to add dignity and elegance to the blankly walled house-
plan of the normal human dwelling. Similarly, the *opisthodomos,* or rear
vestibule without communication with the interior, is not Aegean but
was added by the classic designer to produce symmetrical balance between
front and rear. With peristyle and opisthodomos stripped off, the megaron

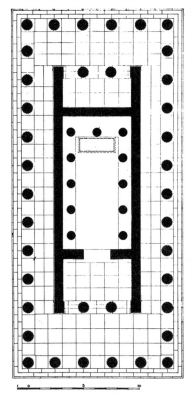

Fig. 51 Plan of the Temple of Hephaistos, Athens

proper remains as the essential kernel. But the Greek *cella,* or interior sanctuary, and this Mycenaean room differ markedly. The Aegean is nearly square, with four columns set at the corners of a smaller interior rectangle to carry the ceiling beams and (presumably) a louvred opening or clear-story for a smoke-vent above the central hearth. At Tiryns the traces of a floor pattern imply a raised throne backed against a side wall to face this hearth. The Greek temple's interior chamber shows none of these features, being rectangular in shape, divided longitudinally into nave and aisles by twin rows of columns, and setting its throne or pedestal for the divinity against or near the rear wall to face the entrance doorway. Temples of an earlier date than our fifth-century examples do not show more nearly square interior rectangles, but on the contrary more elongated ones, with ceiling and roof carried on a single line of columns down the central axis. For our comparison between the classic temple and the Mycenaean megaron, we are left with the vestibule, which is doubled at Tiryns, but single in the Greek norm. Here, both systems show a central doorway to the inner room and afford entrance from the exterior through paired columns set between the wall-ends. In both, the vestibules are narrow rectangles, but this identity of shape has a purely physical cause, being due to the use of transverse beams to support the ceiling. These beams necessarily restricted the depth of the room by their limited span, but had no effect on its lateral extension.

When the analysis has been completed, there is nothing of the Mycenaean megaron left in the classic temple except their fortuitous similarity in possessing an outer vestibule—fortuitous because this feature is standard for the East Mediterranean house in many lands and many ages as a reflection of climatic conditions. A walled living room is very generally preceded by an open covered porch where the householders may sit and eat and perhaps cook their meals in clement seasons. Since the classic temple was intended as a habitation for the local divinity, it was planned like a normal house with closed inner room and open vestibule and with its hearth permanently relegated out-of-doors as an open-air altar on which offerings could be burned.

In all this, the important innovation was the peristyle, the surrounding range of columns elaborated into a structural Order, and for this all Mycenaean evidence is lacking. At most it may be claimed that the Doric capital in its early West Colonial form of broadly cushioned *echinus* above a cavetto necking of overturned leaves may prove that classic eyes had been looking at the façades of Mycenaean beehive tombs; but this seems the only even plausible link that can be forged between Helladic and Hellenic architecture. The Ionic Order has even less to offer in token of earlier Aegean memories.

In a previous chapter a distinction was drawn between literally exact reproduction of timber-work in stone and a decorative application of characteristic timber shapes and patterns to impart structural articulation to an amorphous medium such as squared stone quarried from the mountainside. And this distinction was applied to the Doric Order, with the claim that its apparent timber form was not a direct conversion of a wooden structure into stone, but purely a visual metaphor. Just as to the sculptor a block of marble was artistically void until it had been informed with some mimetic shape, so in the builder's view limestone or marble, even when assembled to vertical walls with doors and window-openings and set to support a sheltering roof, was still artistically inactual until it had been given some sort of visible articulation of organic coherence. Most of the visible configuration of a Greek Order is mere surface appearance without mechanical function (Plate VIIII). The headband and pegged cleats on the epistyle are patterns carved on the face of the block; the grooves of the triglyphs and the pegged plates of the mutules have no structural validity; the flutings of the columns have no bearing on the shaft's utility; their capitals and abacus blocks are structurally expressive, but physically dispensable. For this reason, modern criticism has concluded that the Doric Order did not originate with the stone-masons but, because its detail resembles that which nailed planks, pegged rafters, cleated wooden strippings, and the exposed ends of beams might be presumed to show, its structural system was previously evolved in wood and thereafter integrally copied in stone.

Such a theory is in direct conflict with the evidence. If the triglyph is assumed to reproduce three upended planks held together by laying a fourth plank across their top, it must be objected that no builder would have sawed a squared tree trunk into boards only to reassemble them, when he might have used the squared beam intact. Nor would he have added a projecting strip to his epistyle beams in order to gain purchase for a horizontal cleat through which to drive a set of pegs up into the triglyph planks, when he could have nailed these fast by spiking them obliquely down to the epistyle beam before inserting the metopes. The mutules are equally illogical as literal copies of timber construction. They cannot reproduce the exposed undersides of rafters (especially as they also appear under the horizontal cornice on the façades, where no rafters run) because they are too broad and are set too close together. But if they are intended to represent some sort of transverse sheathing to weatherproof the projecting eaves from beneath, they would have had to be continuous and would never have been secured in series with an array of eighteen pegs in each. There is much else of the same sort to make it clear that no construction in wooden beams, planks, and pegs was ever put together in any sort of correspondence with the detail articulation of the Doric Order. Hence all the many efforts to explain how this Order grew out of an antecedent wooden prototype are idle, depending as they do on an erroneous initial assumption. Greek insistence on visual intelligibility and tectonic form demanded that the elements of a monumental stone structure should be appropriately distinguished so as to suggest for each a proper place and purpose within the whole, and only wooden timber-work offered a repertory of useful and intelligible patterns on which to draw for such a concept.

It is not known who first devised this ingenious synthesis of structural shapes, nor where and when his idea first found material embodiment in an actual building. But since the Doric Order was not copied from any already extant tradition and contains much which might equally logically have been formulated differently, it seems too arbitrary and too involved an invention to be anything but an individual creation. As to its universal acceptance as a prescribed architectural form throughout central and western Greek lands, and the manner of its transmission from place to place, we know nothing and can surmise little. It is, of course, possible that a single master-mason with a corps of specialized workmen traveled about, as commissions offered, like the Romanesque and Gothic master-builders of the great medieval churches—in which case the Doric Order was not only individually invented, but also personally diffused. But it is more probable that immediate and widespread approval of so extraordinarily apt a solution to the problem of endowing post-and-beam construction in stone with a coherent and striking formal pattern, sufficed to ensure its universal acceptance. On all this we have no information whatever.

That there were buildings on which the architects experimented with a lesser number of *guttae* under the triglyphs than the canonic six, with a different shape for the metopes, with variant solutions of the corner problem set by the triglyphal frieze, or a different pitch and projection of the cornice, is only to be anticipated from the Greek tendency to experiment in search of an acceptable perfection for any created form. But that in the second century there should still be erected Doric temples and shrines showing only minor modifications without mutation of the Order into novel forms is a truly remarkable instance of the tenacity of Greek adherence to an abstract conception. For the Ionic Order there is comparable proof of this firm hold of intelligible form on the Greek artistic mind, notably at Priene near the western shore of Asia Minor. There, when Alexander the Great contributed funds for a splendid new temple to the town goddess Athena, and the leading architect of the day, Pythios, fresh from his triumph in helping to build the great marble Maussoleum at Halikarnassos, was given the commission, he contented himself with erecting a completely stereotyped Ionic *peripteros* of no great size and with no unusual features (Plate IX and Fig. 49) but in such perfection of canonic proportion and such correctness of detail that he deemed it deserving of a written treatise to set forth its virtues—much as Polykleitos had accompanied his statue of the Spearman with a treatise explaining its canonic numbers and extolling it as the perfect solution of the sculptor's problem of representing the human form in bronze.

In the colonial West the material resources at the builder's disposal imposed a different procedure from that in vogue in the marble-rich Aegean lands. There is, indeed, a considerable supply of marble in Italian territory, but it was not accessible to the Greek colonists of Sicily and southern Italy. In consequence, these were forced to use whatever grade of limestone might be at hand. At times, they relied on marble stuccoing to restore a proper appearance, as at Selinos, Akragas, and Poseidonia (Paestum). But where there was plenty of timber in supply but little good stone, an alternative practice was developed in wood and baked clay, using wood for the structural framework, brick (which could be stuccoed or painted) for the rising walls above ground-water level, ornamented terracotta sheathing to protect exposed beams from the weather, and terracotta roof-tiles over all. It is an interesting confirmation of my contention that the classic Orders were not a direct petrifaction of carpentry, converting a wooden prototype without alteration into stone, that here, where timber was actually the chief material medium, neither a normal Doric nor Ionic Order automatically emerged, but a new and quite distinct architectural mode (which is sometimes called Tuscan or Latin, but more probably should be termed Central-Italian Greek, since it is fully exemplified on non-Etruscan sites such as Alatri, Segni, Satricum, and Falerii, and has intimate connection with the fictile revetment styles of Magna Graecia). At Olympia on the slight rise of ground where the dedicatory storehouses of various participant city-states were terraced, it seems to have been a matter of local pride among the colonial western Greeks to erect elaborately decorated and brilliantly colored terracotta structures in place of the carved and wax-painted marble buildings familiar to mainland Greece. This was an attractive variant for architectural form to take, but it depended on the potter's and not the sculptor's contribution to the builder's art. As such, it was destined to die out, for much the same reason that terracotta sculpture never succeeded in displacing sculpture in marble and bronze. Not because it was colonial, but because it had so little sculptural appeal, terracotta succumbed to marble as the fitting vehicle for Greek architectural form.

EVOLUTION OF THE IONIC ORDER

Under the influence of the mistaken conviction that the Doric Order is to be interpreted as a direct translation into stone of a system of construction in wood, the Ionic Order (Plate IX) has been subjected to similar scrutiny of its characteristic elements for "xylolithic" conversions—but with no more plausible result. Only the dentils, which manifestly represent the projecting ends of small beams laid athwart the epistyle to support a horizontal ceiling, appear directly copied from a timber prototype. The three-part epistyle is technically irrational if it is explained as a reproduction of horizontal planking laid in corbelled superposition to replace the mechanically simpler single beam. It was given a threefold articulation because a one-piece epistyle like the Doric would have seemed disproportionately massive in the delicate Ionic entablature. The Ionic cornice does not suggest a professional carpenter's handling of wooden eaves, though it might be taken to reproduce in solid stone some sort of terracotta sheathing. But why should it not be taken for just what it seems to be—a straightforward solution in stone of the mechanical problem of providing a bedding for rafters and carrying an upturned gutter? There remains the most distinctive element of the Order, the fluted column shaft with its base and capital, but this bears no closer resemblance to timber-work than must inevitably attend on the functional identity between a stone shaft and a wooden post. The flutings of the shaft—which may number as many as forty-four in very early examples—suggest nothing that need be done to a felled tree in order to make it serviceable as a vertical prop. It may be granted that the inserted base reflects the very usual introduction of a stone underpinning to keep a wooden post from sinking into the ground or rotting in the surface moisture of the soil. But any carved articulation of such an under-prop must be wholly decorative, and if this ornamentation takes the form of horizontal ribbing, or otherwise divides the stone pedestal into horizontal sections, we must admit a purely abstract intention in such a design, with no wooden precedent logically involved.

Finally, there is the Ionic capital (Fig. 52). The insistence that its

Fig. 52 Ionic Capital from Sardis

complex form implies some sort of wooden prototype has given occasion to endless theory and inconclusive argument. A popular suggestion has been the derivation of the peculiar profile of the Ionic capital, with its projecting bolsters on either side of the circular shaft, from a wooden saddle-block straddling a post in order to enlarge its bearing-surface. If the question is raised why a saddle-block should be shaped into scrolls which do not hug the shaft, but are merely tangent to it (compare the Byzantine dosseret for a mechanically correct device) the reply is sometimes made that these scrolls represent sections of wooden logs which have been nailed against either side of the shaft and spiked into a covering board, thus producing the characteristic configuration of the saddle. But such a ramshackle attachment, in no way increasing the carrying capacity of the column (whose greater strength in compression would have taken the load), could hardly have commended itself to any competent workman. The very early Ionic capital which topped the slender thirty-five-foot column of the Naxian votive sphinx at Delphi (to be dated on sculptural criteria as early as 575 B.C.) does indeed show exterior bolsters shaped like wooden logs, but the "cover-board" of the abacus fails to extend out over them as it should, the huge necking-band of overturned leaves is irrational, and the spiral on the bolster-faces inappropriate.

This spiral, which becomes the most striking feature of the Ionic capital in its developed form and is not mechanically necessary to the saddle-block, has been explained as a conflation with the Egyptian lily-capital, a combination of "Syrian" construction with Nilotic ornamentation presumably due to the fortuitous resemblance of the saddle-block to a spreading floral calyx. The interesting and attractive variant of the Ionic capital which enjoyed early popularity on the island of Lesbos, and for that reason is very generally called "Aeolic" in modern textbooks, much more apparently treats its volutes as a floral motive with the calyx growing vertically out of the column shaft and spiralling into curled-up petals. But here the similarity to a saddle-block is no longer evident.

All this leaves wholly unexplained the classic treatment of the Ionic capital's lateral bolsters, not as cylindrical sections such as sawed-off logs would show, but laced-in at the waist like parchment scrolls constricted by cords (Fig. 49). On early examples such as the mid-sixth-century capitals from the archaic temple of Artemis at Ephesos, the cording of the bolsters seems to be intended to present a lateral view of the ribs of the volutes which appear on the front and rear faces, but the constriction remains unexplained. In its final canonic Attic form, the Ionic capital abandons this interpretation and confines the cording to the center of the bolster as though to offer some visual explanation for the constriction of its waist.

Such speculations are extremely involved, and the more they are examined, the less satisfactory they appear and the more unreliable is their yield of acceptable results—a familiar state of affairs for a debate based on mistaken premises. Here, as in the search for a wooden origin for the Doric Order, the multiplicity of ingenious modern hypotheses, none of which have become the *communis opinio doctorum,* shows that there is something at fault in the basic assumptions.

We have badly misunderstood the mentality of ancient builders by supposing that their idiom of architectural form must be taken literally as a transference to stone of some actually existent practice. We have missed the point that, to their thinking, architecture was a representational art. However functionally conditioned in its mechanical use, its material medium was irrelevant to the appearances which it was carved to display, very much as in sculpture the marble was in and for itself irrelevant to the visual forms which the sculptors carved in it. If we do not admit this, we shall find ourselves totally at a loss to explain the intrusion of vegetal motives into the idiom of architectural articulation. These leaves and flowers, at any rate, cannot be mistaken for stone translations of any physically actual precedent.

In Egyptian architecture there are representations, carved and painted in stone, of such materially impossible constructions as column shafts made of stalks of budding lotus tied with a cord, or bundled reeds terminating in open heads of flowering papyrus. Since there are Egyptian graphic representations in which canoe-like crafts are being made out of tightly compacted bundles of reeds, we are not entitled to dispute that the roofs of mud-daubed wattle huts in the Delta could have been thus supported, but no one will argue that the floral capitals which surmount these bundled reeds in their stone reproductions as columns are to be interpreted as literal imitations of a native practice of tying together lotus plants or papyrus or setting a lily on top of reeds in order to help them carry their load. So in Greece the Corinthian capital was not intended to convey any notion that acanthus leaves had ever been tied about the heads of column shafts to support a superstructure. Or are we to imagine that the caryatids of the Erechtheion porch could have troubled the ancient spectator with any reflection that maidens with baskets on their heads do not in real life support heavy ceilings? Or, to revert to Egypt, of what are the cow-eared Hathor capitals a stone translation? In these examples we are all aware that the ancient architects were not copying actual practices in vogue in some related constructional medium, but were indulging in a sort of imaginative metaphor. But where the metaphor has been drawn from timberwork and carpentry, the reference so closely corresponds to physical possibility (being drawn from the builder's realm to be applied to a built structure) that we fail to see that it is still metaphor and not prosaic fact.

Limestone and marble, being amorphous, are in themselves inarticulate. As the sculptor could give them shape by making them appear to be human beings or animals or other objective actualities, so the builder could give them shape by making them appear to be interlocking timbers clothed in floral ornament. We accept the floral ornament as imaginary and take the timbers as though they were real. But neither one nor the other were intended to be understood as anything else than art's device for rescuing masonry from empty utilitarian mechanism. That a building must express the mechanical qualities of the material medium in which it is constructed and may include nothing else in its appearance—an axiom occasionally propounded in recent times—would have struck the ancient builders as the sheerest nonsense.

It will be granted by everyone that the sculptured Ionic frieze was not derived from any similar predecessor in timber, but the concession is irrelevant to the present issue, because no such frieze is indigenous to the Order. It will be appreciated without further argument that if the Ionic dentils are to be understood, like the Doric triglyphs, as simulated beam-ends of an interior ceiling, they should (like the triglyphs) rest directly

upon the epistyle. There is therefore no structural excuse for introducing
an additional element (whether this be construed as a second epistyle or
as the sheathing to cover some invisible timbers), and actually no such intermediary element occurs in early Ionic buildings. In fifth century Attic
practice one or the other—either a dentil course or a figured frieze—is employed; but with entire logic both do not appear together. Later, this
discrimination ceases to be observed, (though the Asia Minor architects
of the Ionian homeland show a tendency to favor the dentils at the expense
of the frieze). There can be no question therefore but that the figured
frieze is an intruder. But how did it gain entry? The question, long debated, has received a satisfactory answer.

The ultimate ancestor of the Ionic frieze now appears to be the half-
animal demon who guarded the gates of the Mesopotamian precincts and
palaces. His sculptured form was set on either side of gateway passages
and portals. And after he had taken up his guard, there were, in time,
added to him other lesser demons and, for the palaces of the Assyrian
kings, armed warriors to line the entrance passage-way, and rows of serv-
ants and other attendants, servile or dignitary, carved in relief upon either
wall to man's height above the floor. So in Sargon's palace at Khorsabad
the entrance corridors and even the inner rooms were lined with carved
attendants ministering with one service or another to the imagined needs
of the king. Such things were also to be seen later at Persepolis on the
supporting walls of the staircase to the great courtyard. The recently discovered carvings at Kara Tepe in the northern Syrian hill-country show a
similar use of sculptured slabs at ground level to line entrance walls within
a gateway.

Further west in Lycia in southwestern Asia Minor, wall reliefs were
used to decorate the tower-tombs of native princes, and Greek sculptors,
presumably Ionians, were entrusted with their execution. Perhaps to make
these carvings inaccessible to mutilation by passers-by, they were not
carried at ground-level but set higher on the exterior walls, notably at
its topmost course. Well-known instances are the Harpy Tomb from the
late sixth century and the Nereid Monument from the end of the fifth,
both erected in Lycian Xanthos, and from the mid-fourth century, elaborated into extraordinary magnificence, the Tomb of Maussolos in Carian
Halikarnassos. It is this east-Greek tradition of a sculptured frieze decorating the top of an exterior wall which was imported to Delphi for the
exquisitely ornate treasury of the Siphnians. Inevitably, such a decorative
feature was not restricted to the three blank walls of the flanks and rear
of the building, but was also carried across the front, where the interest
in sculptural adornment was greatest. Because the wall-crown was located
immediately under the projecting eaves on the flanks, its return across the

façade automatically brought it over the epistyle and made it a frieze of the Order. Since there were caryatid statues in lieu of columns in this façade and no dentils were introduced beneath the cornice, one can hardly class this treasury as an instance of the Ionic Order. But the return of a wall-crown frieze above the entrance columns—whether or not it was first established by the Siphnian treasury at Delphi (as may of course be quite reasonably doubted)—was markedly appropriate for buildings in the Ionic style. It could form an effective counterpart to the sculptured metopes of the Doric way of building which the proper frieze of the Ionic Order, being merely an undecorated series of notched teeth, could not hope to rival.

A century after the Siphnian treasury, the builders of the Parthenon repeated this device of extending an exterior wallcrown frieze in complete circuit along the flanking walls and across the vestibules. But the effect was obscured by the outer peristyle of Doric columns, and where the frieze crossed over the vestibules there resulted the anomaly that because the architect adhered to the Doric mode, the carved frieze perforce replaced the triglyphs and metopes proper to the Order. It is not entirely correct to criticize this singularity as a confusion of the two Orders, since the returning wall-crown frieze was not strictly an Ionic feature. It would be more pertinent to assert that the wall-crown frieze which had already invaded the Ionic was here proceeding to invade the Doric Order. On the slightly later and very diminutive Ionic temple of Athena Nike, built on the bastion beside the Propylaea, a wall-crown frieze on the flanks by being returned across the façades automatically assumed the role of frieze to the Order. In recognition of this condition, the Ionic epistyle of the façade was prolonged into the flanks and carried, like the frieze, around all four sides of the building. The Erechtheion adopted this solution. It established the further interesting distinction that where the figured frieze is employed, no dentils accompany it (thus attesting its recognition as the frieze of the Order), whereas in the porch of the caryatids, where dentils are present, the figured frieze has been omitted.

The carved Ionic frieze of the architectural handbooks is thus historically an intruder, so that it should be no surprise if Pythios omitted it in his canonic rendering of Athena's temple at Priene and preserved the dentils as the correct member for cresting the epistyle (Plate IX). That he (or his colleague Satyros) nevertheless included both figured frieze and dentils in the equally masterly peripteral Order of the Maussoleum has been attributed to the architect's desire to take all possible advantage of the presence of the four leading Attic sculptors of the day, who had been imported to add their skill to the sumptuous monument. The new temple of Ephesian Artemis, being built during this period, is generally restored with only dentils (a treatment whch may be explained as part of the thorough-going conformity of the new structure to its burned predecessor from the sixth century), but in general the temptation to include the ornamental brilliance of a frieze of carved and colored figures overrode any scruples of purist tradition and led to the inclusion of both figured frieze and dentiled cornice in the final standard norm of the Order. In middle Hellenistic times Hermogenes, who greatly favored the Ionic over the Doric style and is reputed to have been the source of the academic tradition promulgated by Roman Vitruvius, may have been the final authority who tied the sculptured frieze inextricably to the Ionic tradition.

By one of those peculiar reversions to the past which often confront us in human history, the frieze which had left the floor-level of the Asiatic palace corridors to climb the walls of Hellenic buildings and perch, proportionately diminished, in the entablature of Ionic columns, descended to the ground once more to resume its role of a dado carved with human figures in full size. The vastly ambitious altar of Zeus at Pergamon, from the early decades of the second century, was enclosed by an Ionic peristyle with dentils but no frieze, carried on a high podium; and on this podium the frieze reappeared in its ancestral form as a dado carved with lifesize figures in relief. Slightly more than a century and a half later, in Augustan Rome, the exterior wall of the *Ara Pacis* was adorned with a procession of nearly lifesize figures in relief, to constitute a wall-crown frieze of major proportions which was in no sense a frieze of the perfunctorily attached Order.

This long historical survey of a single element of architectural style will serve to show how little the changes in the Greek builder's art were influenced by any reference to the exterior objective world of sight, which had so tyrannously determined the technical evolution of sculptural and pictorial form. On the other hand, it may serve to suggest that the evolution of architectural style is not as extensively determined by the physical laws of gravitational support and the needs of providing shelter from the destructive inconveniences of heat and cold, sun, wind, and rain, as is sometimes pretended. There is, of course, no possibility of contraverting the restrictive demands of the material requirements which architectural construction must meet, but it would be entirely reasonable to dismiss most of these from our study of Greek art on the plea that, in architecture, the art begins where mechanical engineering leaves off. Purely structural problems in building require a mechanically practicable solution, but with so simple an engineering system as post-and-beam construction, there would be little left of a Greek Order if it were stripped of everything except the purely mechanical necessity of erecting vertical supports to carry horizontal beams of stone for transverse ceilings and supply a secure bedding for the sloping timbers of a rain-shedding cover. Beyond these purely mechanical needs, the visual articulation of structural form takes over, and this, we have seen, was basically mimetic in Greek architecture, in that the marble surfaces of the bonded blocks were carved to likenesses of timberwork and botanic growths (such as leaves and blossoms) and living forms of men and animals, each assigned to a position considered appropriate to its kind. Assignment to these positions and determination of relative sizes and respective shapes for all these elements ordered in a coherent whole, was a creative act of the human mind, a noetic activity in strictly visual terms, an imposition of imaginary form on amorphous physical matter.

Such a process of creative ordering and noetic formulation is well illustrated by the history of the Ionic column-base.

As pointed out a few pages earlier, the carved basis which carries the Ionic column-shaft must be a survival of the block of fieldstone which a primitive builder places beneath a wooden post to prevent it from sinking into the soil under the pressure of its load and to preserve it from groundwater rot. The Mycenaean megaron betrays the location of its vanished wooden columns by the survival of such stone slabs set to support them, and domestic dwellings of the classical age occasionally inform the excavator of their ground plan by similar traces. The realization that such an underpinning was mechanically meaningless where a solid foundation of stone on bed rock precluded all subsidence seems to have influenced the inventors of the Doric Order to omit any indication of such a member, without leading to a comparable decision in Ionic thinking. We can hardly attribute this discrepancy between the two Orders as due to any mechanical cause or exterior compulsion, since it would have been as easy and as logical to add a base to a Doric shaft as it would have been to omit one from the Ionic. But once the tradition had been accepted as canonic, the column-base was as much an element of the Ionic Order as the voluted capital or the fasciaed epistyle or the toothed cornice. The artistic problem was how to give it a suitable appearance.

The earliest solution was to flute or rib it horizontally, presumably for contrast with the vertical lines of the ribbed or fluted shaft and in harmony with the horizontal lines of the entablature and the podium, the intention (whether consciously formulated or instinctively sensed) being to visualize with level striations the stability of the column's underpinning. There was greater difficulty in determining an appropriate vertical contour for the block, which was turned like a column drum in agreement with the shaft above it but could not be left as a simple cylinder lest it seem to be merely an enlarged bottom drum to the shaft, wrongly fluted. The resulting quandary, whether to carve a convex or a concave profile for the base, led, in the Ionic homeland of the Order, to rather pointless compromises, such as rounding the upper half of the base outward and the lower half inward, counterbalancing a ringlike protrusion above with a single or double contraction beneath (in technical language, carving a *torus* above a single large *scotia* or above two smaller *scotiae* set off by astragals).

Those who are familiar only with the canonic form accepted by the Renaissance and perpetuated in modern Classic usage cannot but be surprised at the variety of the ancient Ionic bases before a canonic solution was reached. This is the same phenomenon already remarked for temple plans and their structural treatment, where initial experimentation in great complexity yielded to standardization in terms of a sharply restricted repertory of permissible variants. It may be difficult to explain wherein the peculiar rightness lies in the ingenious and subtle sequence of *torus-scotia-torus* (or hollow central stripe between two half-round rings) which some fifth century Attic architect seems first to have devised (Fig. 53). But we can at least see that it implies a criticism of the older Ionic bases as clumsily exaggerated in size, and that it presents a judgment that base and capital for a column, because they echo each other in mechanical function, should also correspond in height. In addition, because the Ionic rhythm tends to three-fold articulation (the total structure is tripartite: podium, colonnade, entablature; and these elements are in turn tripartite, there being normally three steps to the podium, three members to the column [base, shaft, capital] with corresponding threefold articulation to the walls, and three members to the entablature: epistyle [itself three-banded], frieze, cornice) the column base is properly threefold, with a base-ring corresponding to a crown-ring, and a contrasting concave element set between them. Since the base-ring communicates with the broad expanse of flooring and the crown-ring communicates with the shaft, the former should be wider spread and the latter contracted more nearly to the diameter of the shaft (much as the column's capital is wider where it communicates with the epistyle but narrows to column diameter where it meets the shaft). And finally, in additional refinement, the column shaft itself is made to swing its fluted profile very gently outward at its foot toward the slightly larger crown-ring of the base, as though to make visibly apparent that the one issues from the other. Later, an additional square plinth was introduced beneath the molded base, thereby drawing a distinction between a flat rectangular element appropriate to the paved flooring below and the main cylindrical element appropriate to the circular shaft, above. All this is extremely intricate, but I do not imagine that such an analysis will be dismissed as esthetic gossamer, though it may well have been formulated here in terms such as no ancient architect would have

Fig. 53 The Attic-Ionic Column Base

used for explaining why the "Attic-Ionic" column base was designed as he knew it. But if the analysis comes near the mark of truth, we have before us a cogent demonstration of the formative action of noetic control in Greek architecture.

It may be pertinent to add that, although the Ionian builders at first refused to accept the Attic pattern for the column base, all rival tradition succumbed with time in a losing struggle against the higher esthetic logic of Attic invention. In the second century, Hermogenes, having championed the intrusion of the Attic figured frieze beneath the original dentils, also prescribed the Attic type of column base for the Order, to be raised on a plinth but otherwise to be most scrupulously fifth-century Attic. Thereafter there are few traces of any revolt against this abstractly ideated form. Vitruvius recommended (or rather, tried to impose) it for Roman followers of the Greek modes; the Italian Renaissance revived it; the modern world still uses it.

The Ionic column base was referred to as an "abstractly ideated" form because of its nonmimetic character and entirely unimitative visual content. Nothing pertaining to such a base is a reproduced version of any natural object or sensed experience (unless it be argued that the base-ring had been suggested by the potter's use of a clay base-ring at the bottom of a vase to ensure stability). The formal development of the Ionic column base in shape, size, and decorative carving, as previously described, must be termed a noetic process, since the considerations which determined it were of a purely logical nature. And the logic there involved was of a very special kind, being concentrated on mechanical and structural suggestions attendant on geometric shape and other visual properties. This exercise of reason in visual terms was, in fact, a scrutiny of tectonic form in its application to architectural needs.

In the development of the Ionic capital a similar noetic trend may be detected, but here the noetic process acted to convert a mimetic motive into a nonmimetic geometric abstraction, if we may credit the very plausible claim that the Ionic volutes are stylizations of the Egyptian "lily" capital. In any case, however much or however little the earliest Ionic capitals may have resembled their Aeolic contemporaries' more obvious adoption of a calyx of curled petals, no one can detect the least likeness to a floral prototype in the finally established canonic form. Only the burst of tiny leaves at the point where the unrolling volute cuts into the necking band may remotely suggest that the ingenious falsification of a logarithmic spiral which the Ionic capital presents was a geometric perversion of an original botanical representation.

There are other more convincing examples than this uncertain and too much disputed episode in Greek architectural origins. Whatever may be thought about saddle-blocks and lily-capitals, few will question the derivation by noetic conversion of floral themes for the wonderful decorative devices of the Greek carved moldings, a feature of Greek architecture that may be little noticed by the casual layman, yet ranks supreme as its most exquisitely perfected achievement. Stripped of its superbly carved and brilliantly colored moldings, a classic building would have resembled a jewelry setting despoiled of its precious stones. The fact that the scale to which this ornamentation was restricted bespeaks a need for close inspection and assumes keen eyesight for its adequate contemplation, does not signify that it was ever considered unimportant: Greek art at its best always asks to be closely observed and never evades minute inspection.

Greek architectural moldings were conceived in more than one esthetic dimension, inasmuch as they possessed both a sculptured profile which gave them solid actuality and a carved, painted surface-design which gave them pictorial status. The surface-design was composed of some brief thematic unit indefinitely repeated in unvaried exactness and uninterrupted sequence wherever the profiled shape might lead. Considered in isolation, the various themes from which the running patterns are made were seldom purely abstract geometric schemes (like the various types of meander attached to flat fillets and headbands). Far more frequently they are seen to be geometric patternizations of some form of leaf or flower, originally put to decorative use elsewhere than in Greece, which had already lost most of its realistic likeness to any botanic prototype before the Greek builders adopted it for their use. But there is much more to Greek moldings than this simple statement conveys.

With very few exceptions the Greek decorated moldings travel horizontally. Where they are carried vertically, as on door and window frames, this is due to diversion from other use, as when the magnificent north doorway of the Erechtheion borrows a fascia-lined and -crowned Ionic epistyle for its jambs. The normal course for moldings is horizontal because they have been introduced in order to separate and distinguish from one another the various component units of the Orders. Thus in the Ionic mode the abacus atop the column shaft is set off by a decorated molding from the epistyle which it supports, the epistyle is similarly set off by a molding from the frieze, and the frieze from the cornice, which in turn is margined with a molding where it meets the roof gutter (itself a molded member with a special profile and an appropriate painted or carved decoration). Thanks to the broken light-and-shadow of the delicate carving and the brightly variegated color of the ornamental designs, the judiciously located moldings make impossible any optical fusion or confusion of the structural members which the logic of tectonic form demands should be kept distinct.

With such a simple function to perform, one might imagine that any of the various moldings would do equally well in one place as in another, but Greek architectural practice drew some precise (and to our modern way of thinking extremely arbitrary) distinctions in assigning the various moldings to what it considered appropriate positions. Thus, a hawksbeak molding, which has a heavily undercut throat at the top, was used where its well-defined shadow imparted a desirable abruptness to a vertical rise of surface, as when a wall-end functioned as a pier and required emphasis for its flattened capital, or along a wall-top to underscore the termination of the smooth stretch of panel surface, or for the water-drip of an overhanging cornice. The harsh angularity of the patterns of the Doric Order was felt to be better matched with the uncompromising rectangularity of meander-covered fillets and headbands. Some of the moldings were specifically Ionic in allegiance, others Doric, still others available to either party.

For all this there is more historical explanation than is overtly apparent. The use of moldings is not an axiomatic need of architectural construction. Mesopotamian building seems to have prospered well enough

without them. Egypt, however, was familiar with their use, though only
(it would seem) in two shapes—the half-round roll molding and the
undercut cavetto. These two were imported into Greece, for which reason
we can hardly expect to find them on Greek soil before the latter part of
the seventh century, the very time (as far as our present evidence goes)
when the two Orders were being invented and codified. For some reason
which escapes our knowledge, the cavetto was adopted by Doric, the
half-round by Ionic builders. For what ensued I can do no better than
quote the succinct summary which Dr. Shoe prefaced to her extraordinarily competent compilation and chronological ordering of the *Profiles of
Greek Mouldings* in her treatise under this title:

"In Egypt, where the post-and-lintel construction had existed from early
times, two types of moldings were used: the cavetto, as a crowning member,
and the half round, as a base or intermediate molding. These two, the simplest
possible forms to express their function, are the only moldings known to have
existed until Greek architecture of the early 6th century. Of possible prehistoric
Greek moldings we have no knowledge. The Minoan and Helladic civilizations
have left us no trace of any if they existed. Out of these two original types, then
—the cavetto and the half rounds ... the Greeks developed a variety of types
which have been the basis of nearly all architectural moldings ever since."

Once again, therefore, the independence and the novelty of Greek classical art, without inheritance or continuity from its Mycenaean past, becomes apparent. As in monumental sculpture, we are privileged to watch
the Greek genius draw its inspiration from the millennial culture of the
Nile and without further assistance evolve from it the perfection of classic
form.

The half-round roll molding, accordingly, was imported into Ionia and
with it a decorative pattern of down-turned flower petals, clumsy elongated squares rounded at their lower ends and heavily outlined with a
marginal frame. This pattern was carved like a wreath of leaves upon the
rounded surface of the molding. One has only to consult Greek ceramic
art to see what a Greek designer would have done to a sprawling static
profile like the coarse Egyptian roundel. There are pot-bellied perfume
flasks from early Greek workshops, but in general the potter's instinct was
to pull out the spherical body to a rising parabolic curve by drawing the
circle's arc more sharply out at the base and less sharply in at the top, to
shift the point of greatest projection above the midway level of the curve.
The profile which the sixth-century Attic potters gave to the amphoras
which we for our own convenience call "Nolan" is an exact echo of the
profile which the Ionian builders at much the same time were giving to
the half-round. The most surprising (yet most typically Hellenic) outcome was the accompanying change which overtook the shape of the
heavy leaves carved on the molding's surface, which it will be recalled

were straight-sided with circular ends at the bottom. As the profile of the molding was altered from a circular to a parabolic arc, the outline of the leaves became parabolic also. It is easy to misunderstand the situation. The new profile of the molding, which a cross-section through its modeled form would reveal, now reappears in the frontal plane in the design carved on its face, although there is no compulsion other than that of artistic sensibility to account for the event. As the half-round became an ovolo, the round-bottomed leaves became eggs. (Another way to formulate this curious phenomenon would be to say that if two cross-sections through the molding were confronted, they would join their curves to make the egg-shaped shield of the decorative design on the molding's face).

Greek potters of the black-figure and red-figure periods, shaping vases on the wheel, were much inclined to draw the bodies out on a parabolic curve and to narrow them again with an answering curve for shoulder and neck, thus joining a concave to a convex contour in an overall ogival swing. Late fifth-century sculptors, having discovered that ogival lines imparted movement to their draped figures, became inordinately devoted to this same sweeping rhythm. Accordingly, it cannot cause surprise if the architects, at much the same period as the potters, were moved by a similar feeling for profile shapes to give greater life and new movement to their moldings by elaborating the ovolo and the cavetto into ogival outline. A slight reversing curve added to the base of the ovolo transformed it into the redoubtable *"cyma reversa,"* the master-profile of the Ionic style. But to our modern obtuseness to such subtleties of formal harmony it remains surprising that with the conversion from a parabolic to an ogival contour in the molding the new profile promptly invaded the decorative design on its surface, replacing the parabolic egg with the pointed ogival leaf of the "Lesbian" *cymation*, a supremely remarkable design whose visual opulence belies the simplicity of its geometric formula (Fig. 54).

In similar transformation, the addition of a slight reverse curve at the base of the cavetto produced the ogival *"cyma recta"* in Doric usage. But here the Doric preference for painting the decoration without carving it into effective relief left the blunt Doric leaf unconverted to a new harmonic form, an observation from which it seems to follow that the extraordinary principle which dictated that the projecting profile of a molding shall serve as basic constituent of the design on its face was inspired by the sculptor's rather than the painter's sensibility for formal harmony. Here, presumably, lies the explanation for the failure of the lotus-and-palmette pattern to exert any effect on the shape of the member on which it appears or to be in turn modified by the solid shape of the ground on which it is displayed. Being stenciled surface-ornament (apparently imported from eastern floor designs and wall-tiling without sculptural con-

Fig. 54 Characteristic Shapes of Greek Architectural Moldings

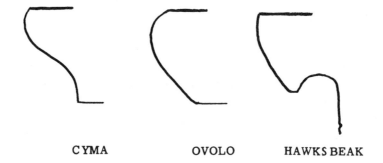

CYMA   OVOLO   HAWKS BEAK

nection), the lotus-and-palmette belongs to the flatland of purely graphic design, from which even the sculptor's etching of its delicate tracery did not free it.

Our survey has shown that Greek architectural detail originated in imitative representation of exterior objects, whether these were natural growths such as leaves and flowers or artificial creations such as timber structures. When applied to architectural purposes, an organic floral theme underwent a geometric transformation of the type universally recognized (though not very intelligibly differentiated) as "stylization." How such stylization was accomplished has become apparent from an examination of the Greek moldings and their decorative patterns. Its action may also be studied in the formal development of those other botanically inspired motives which the Greeks introduced for themselves and did not derive from others. Not having been previously stylized elsewhere (unlike the highly geometricized decorative devices on early Corinthian pottery, which were imported from the Eastern world), these novel motives at first appear in great natural fidelity. Such are the wild cucumber tendrils and blossoms in the carved detail of the mid-fourth century temple of Athena Alea at Tegea in Arcadia or, in even more exemplary manner, the acanthus leaves and sheathed tendrils of the Corinthian capitals from this same temple or the slightly earlier and even more realistic *acanthus mollis* of the capitals from the tholos at Epidauros. Thereafter, from generation to generation, the freshness of direct imitation from the living plant gives place to ever more pronounced abstract manipulation until, as on the temple of Olympian Zeus at Athens in the Hadrianic completion of the mid-Hellenistic project, progressive "stylization" has destroyed all suggestion of botanic growth. By Justinian's day, the "sprocket" and the "windblown" capitals of Early Byzantine tradition are end-terms to this long career of the noetic distraction of a mimetic shape.

Many centuries may therefore elapse before such a stylizing process ends in a stereotyped norm insusceptible to further change. But there is no recognizable temporal rate or rule. As Dr. Shoe pointed out in the concluding summary of her work on the profiles of Greek moldings:

"By the middle of the 6th century B.C. Greek architects had developed from the two original pre-Greek moldings, the cavetto and the half round, all the seven types of molding profiles which were to be used throughout Greek architecture and the many styles of architecture which have been based on the Greek ever since. Each of the seven types continued to develop the form of its profile through the 6th, 5th, and 4th centuries, following the principle of gradually increasing projection at the top of the molding. Practically no further development is to be found after about the end of the 4th century. The same forms continue into the 3rd century. The 2nd century forms are eclectic, archaistic, and degenerate."

On the other hand, the imitated timber forms adapted to articulate the two Orders seem to have acquired their canonic shapes with great rapidity during the opening phase of Greek monumental building in stone and thereafter to have suffered little change in any other respect than that of proportionate size. This lack of formative development may be construed as an objection to the claim that all the visible structure of the Orders was created from mimetic transferences from some external source, strictly comparable to the mimetic origin of the floral decorative ornaments. The criticism is usually reinforced by the observation that these floral motives are purely decorative additions, whereas the motives of the constituent members of the Order are structural fundamentals. The objection is not sound. In the first place, the florally ornamented moldings are completely misunderstood if it is supposed that they serve no structural purpose and are not functionally involved in the articulation of the Orders. They are not like colored ribbons that make gift packages attractive, and no one who has not studied them sufficiently to see how carefully they were discriminated by the Greek builders and how indissolubly they were attached to their place, form, and function, has grasped why they existed or how they were used. And secondly, the metaphoric timberwork of the Orders exhibits no comparable evolution of its patternized shapes because these shapes were not natural organic growths like leaves, fruits, and flowers, but had already been geometricized by human intervention and made appropriate to architectural articulation. Being already stylized, they neither required nor underwent any further noetic transformation.

To recapitulate:

Greek architecture was a representational art, taking its themes from various sources in the exterior world of Greek visual experience and applying them in pertinently stylized form to make visually intelligible a fully organized scheme of assembly-and-support in coherently fitted blocks of stone. If it thereby destroyed the living appearance of its representations, reducing the complex variability of the natural shapes of flower and foliage to stereotyped repetitious patterns, it may be that, in so doing, its builders were guided by a deeper sense that buildings are not living organisms and must not pretend to be other than accumulations of inert physical matter. Everything that takes part in an architectural structure must relinquish all vital natural appearance and assume rigid shapes of unchanging durability.

But if this is so, what place in such an art of abstract formal appearances has illusionistic sculpture with its mimetic reproduction of living things in action? The ancient architects (no doubt, with regret) came to see that it has no place. After the fourth century, statues disappear from temple pediments and Doric metopes are increasingly left blank. This was not because the Doric Order itself had fallen into disrepute or because everyone necessarily agreed with Hermogenes that the Doric style was unfit for temple structures "because faults and incongruities are created by its rules of symmetry" (as Vitruvius reported). There was abundant use of the Doric Order in Hellenistic and Roman times. But it was recognized that architecture must abjure the organic vitality of living forms which (as we have seen) Greek sculpture most signally set itself to capture. Sculpture in its archaic phase is as superficial in its spatial presentation as any architectural ornament, so that it created no formal contradiction when it was added to a Greek building. In its succeeding highly formal phase, sculpture possessed enough abstractly geometrical appeal to keep company with architecture's abstract geometry of structural form. But fully naturalistic sculpture creates its own spatial environment of aerial depth and disturbingly intrudes its suggestion of free movement in space into the archaic "depthlessness" beyond which Greek architectural form never progressed. It therefore failed to harmonize any longer with Greek buildings. With its more rapid evolutionary pace, sculpture had fatally outstepped architecture by early Hellenistic times. The intimate harmony between the two arts, which had previously made architecture a by-form of sculpture and encouraged sculptural presentation in architectural tectonic form, was irremediably dissolved. By the mid-third century the two arts were far apart, and each had thereafter to go its own way. This separation between the arts (concurrently observable also in the loss of contact between sculpture and painting) was, I think, one of the major sources of insecurity in Hellenistic art and an effective cause of its lapse into decadence.

PLATES

Pl. I Late-Geometric Vase in Munich

Pl. II Athens National Museum: Kouros from Anavysos

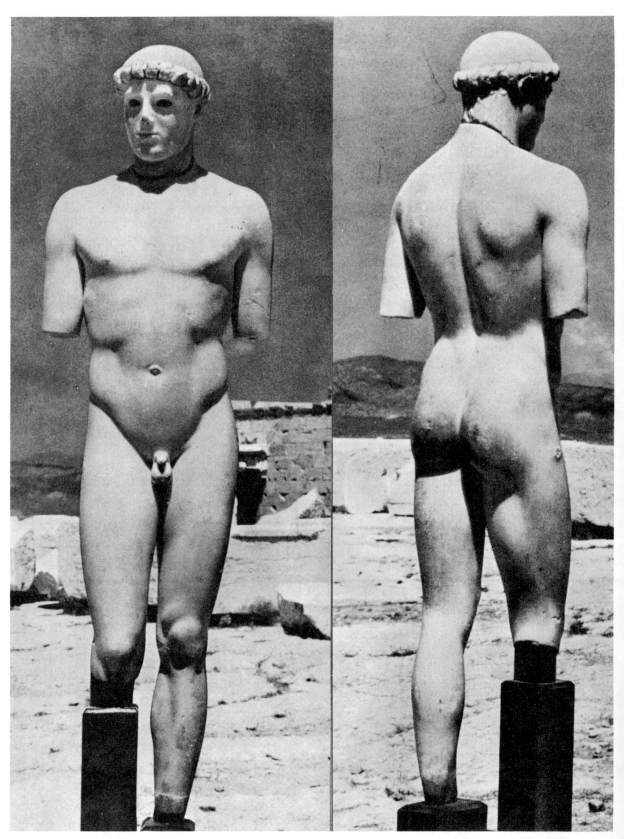

Pl. III "Kritios Boy" from the Acropolis of Athens

Pl. IV Rome, Terme National Museum: Seated Goddess

Pl. VI Pentheus and Maenads

V The Alexander Mosaic

Pl. VII Athens National Museum: the "Ball-Player"

Pl. VIII Athens, Temple of Hephaistos

Pl. IX The Ionic Order: Priene, Temple of Athena

SOURCES FOR THE ILLUSTRATIONS

I am indebted:

> to Alison Frantz for the photographs reproduced in Figures 20, 44, 45, 54, and Plates VII, VIII;

> to Bernard Ashmole for Figure 43;

> to Oscar Broneer for Figure 52;

> to the Boston Museum of Fine Arts for Figure 19, with permission to reproduce;

> to the German Archaeological Institute in Athens for Figures 1, 4, 23, and Plate II, with permission to reproduce;

> to the Rhode Island School of Design for Figure 17, with permission to reproduce;

> to the Director of the Staatliche Antiken Sammlungen in Munich for Plate I, with permission;

> to the University Museum, Philadelphia, for the photographs reproduced in Figures 46 and 47;

> to the firm of Fratelli Alinari, Florence, for five photographs, Figures 39, 40, 48, and Plates V, VI.

Figures 2B, 6, 26 are from photographs courteously supplied by the Metropolitan Museum of Art, New York.

Figures 10, 11, 12, 32 are from Roland Hampe, *Griechische Sagenbilder in Böotien*

Figure 16 is from Franz Boas, *Primitive Art*, by consent of Dover Publications, Inc., New York

Figure 18 has been adapted from Mary H. Swindler, *Ancient Painting*

Figure 49 and Plate IX are from M. Schede, *Die Ruinen von Priene*

Figure 53 is from Lucy T. Shoe, *Profiles of Greek Mouldings*

The remaining illustrations are from negatives in the photographic files of the department of Classical and Near Eastern Archaeology at Bryn Mawr College

INDEX

(Unless otherwise indicated, references are to page numbers)